Learning English

Orange Line 4

Erweiterungskurs

Unterrichtswerk für Gesamtschulen
und andere differenzierende Schulformen

Von
Ruth Arendt, Werner Beile,
Alice Beile-Bowes, Wolfgang Biederstädt,
Rosemary Hellyer-Jones, Edgar Hilgers,
Marion Horner, Wulf-Michael Kuntze,
Peter Lampater, Alan Posener
und Rolf W. Roth

unter Mitwirkung und Leitung der
Verlagsredaktion Neue Sprachen

Ernst Klett Schulbuchverlag

Learning English – Orange Line 4 Erweiterungskurs
für Klasse 8 an Gesamtschulen und anderen differenzierenden Schulformen

von
Ruth Arendt, Sigmaringen; Prof. Dr. Werner Beile und Alice Beile-Bowes M.A., Wuppertal und Iserlohn;
Wolfgang Biederstädt, Köln; Rosemary Hellyer-Jones M.A., Ehingen (Donau); Edgar Hilgers, Wuppertal;
Marion Horner, Cambridge; Wulf-Michael Kuntze M.A., Pfullingen; Peter Lampater, Ehingen (Donau);
Alan Posener, Berlin und Rolf W. Roth M.A., Idar-Oberstein

unter Mitwirkung und Leitung
der Verlagsredaktion Neue Sprachen; Mitarbeit an diesem Werk:
Bernd Binkle; Peter Cole M.A., Dr. Gregory Fuller, Heinz-Peter Gerlinger, Bärbel Huber, Verlagsredakteure

Beratende Mitarbeit:
Walter Düringer, Ketsch; Monika Lappe, Menden; Raimund A. Mader, Eschenbach i. d. Oberpf.;
Dr. Helmut Reisener, Lüneburg; Reinhard Schulz, Bochum; Elmar Tegethoff, Hannover;
Rolf-G. Wiele, Rinteln

Weitere Mitarbeit:
Noreen O'Donovan, Pforzheim;
Amelia Esten, Washington, D.C.;
Edgar Hilgers, Wuppertal (History Pages);
Gerlind Schmidt, Stuttgart (Grammatik)

Visuelle Gestaltung:
Christian Dekelver, Stuttgart (Zeichnungen, Layout)
Joachim Krüger, Korntal (Karten)
Wolfgang Metzger, Mühlacker (Layout)

Arbeitsheft zur Differenzierung

Das *Schülerbuch Orange Line 4 Erweiterungskurs* ist inhaltlich gleich mit dem *Schülerbuch Red Line 4*. Ergänzend zu diesem Lehrwerk gibt es ein *Arbeitsheft zur Differenzierung*, das Texte und Übungen für die Binnendifferenzierung nach oben und nach unten enthält. Klettnummer 58746

Sprachcassetten

Zur Verbesserung der Aussprache empfiehlt es sich, die Begleitcassetten zu diesem Lehrwerk zu verwenden.
- *1 Compact-Cassette* für Schüler und Lehrer mit Lektionstexten und Liedern. Beide Seiten besprochen. Klettnummer 58749
  Lieferung durch jede Buchhandlung oder, wo dies auf Schwierigkeiten stößt, zuzüglich Portokosten per Nachnahme vom Ernst Klett Schulbuchverlag, Postfach 11 70, 7054 Korb.
- *1 Compact-Cassette* für Lehrer mit Hörverstehenstexten, den Ausspracheübungen, den Rollenspielen und Versprachlichung der Bildgeschichten. Beide Seiten besprochen. Klettnummer 58748
  Lieferung direkt an Lehrer, Schulstempel erforderlich.

Hinweis

Die auf den Erweiterungskurs abgestimmte Grundkursausgabe von Orange Line 4 trägt die Klettnummer 58741.

---

1. Auflage   1 5 4 3 2 1 | 1994 93 92 91 90

Alle Drucke dieser Auflage können im Unterricht nebeneinander benutzt werden, sie sind untereinander unverändert. Die letzte Zahl bezeichnet das Jahr dieses Druckes.
© Ernst Klett Schulbuchverlag GmbH, Stuttgart 1990. Alle Rechte vorbehalten.
Satz: Setzerei Lihs, Ludwigsburg.
Umschlag: D. Gebhardt, Korntal (Stuttgart).
Druck: Appl, Wemding.
ISBN 3-12-587420-3

Inhaltsverzeichnis

Unit/Steps	*Sprechabsichten/Themen	Strukturen	Seite

Stopover A:
Voices of America

	– Sich vorstellen, Angaben zur Person machen – Über Pläne und Vorhaben sprechen – Handlungsabläufe beschreiben	– Revision: various tenses	8
The USA – facts and figures	– Zahlenangaben versprachlichen, Länder vergleichen		10
⟨Song: This land is your land⟩			11
		Grammar §1	

1

A What New York means to me	– Vorlieben äußern und Sachverhalte beurteilen/bewerten – Eine amerikanische Großstadt kennenlernen	– gerund as subject/object	14
⟨The Big Apple⟩	– Vielfalt und Probleme New Yorks kennenlernen – Einen Stadtplan auswerten		16
⟨Song: A heart in New York⟩			17
B Almost the best	– Das Leben einer New Yorker Familie kennenlernen – Über Hobbys und Interessen sprechen	– gerund after prepositions	18
C Up on 119th Street	– Die Lebensweise und Probleme von Jugendlichen in New York kennenlernen	– gerunds – Revision: *going to* and *will*-future	20
		Grammar §2	

2

A Should they or shouldn't they?	– Für und Wider eines geplanten Umzugs abwägen – Sich verabschieden – Bedingungen nennen	– conditional I	23
B A telex from Harry	– Aufnahme in einer amerikanischen Kleinstadt finden – Ratschläge geben	– conditional I – verbs with two objects	25
C Magic – real magic	– Jugendliche in einer amerikanischen Kleinstadt – Bedingungen und Möglichkeiten nennen	– conditional I – verbs with two objects – Revision: questions with *to do*	27
⟨Song: Small town⟩			31
		Grammar §§ 3, 4	

* Es werden bei jeder Lektion nur die wichtigsten kommunikativen Ziele der Texte und Übungen aufgeführt. Eine vollständige Übersicht über die Lernziele und ihre Wiederholung gibt das Lehrerbuch (Klettnummer 58443).

| Unit/Steps | Sprechabsichten/Themen | Strukturen | Seite |

Stopover B:
Christmas in the USA
– Weihnachtsbräuche in den USA kennenlernen
– Glückwünsche aussprechen; jdn. einladen; über das Essen sprechen
32

⟨Christmas carol: Joy to the world⟩
34

⟨Unwanted guests⟩ – Eine moderne Weihnachtsgeschichte lesen
35

3

A At the truck stop
– Reisen mit dem Auto
– Ein Hotelzimmer suchen
– Bedingungen und ihre Konsequenzen nennen
– conditional II
38

B My crazy dad
– Über berufliche und räumliche Mobilität sprechen
– Sich beklagen, Vorwürfe machen
– Sagen, seit wann und wie lange man etwas getan hat
– present perfect with *for* and *since*
– *so that, as if, as*
41

C On the road with Tessie
– Die Arbeitsbedingungen einer Lastwagenfahrerin kennenlernen
– Sagen, was man hätte besser machen können
– Die räumliche Weite der USA kennenlernen
– conditional II
– Revision: auxiliaries
44

⟨Song: Truck driving man⟩
45

⟨Getting around in the USA⟩
47

Grammar §§ 5–7

4

A This is California
– Einen wichtigen Staat der USA kennenlernen
– Einen Sachtext intensiv auswerten
49

B A letter to a pen pal
– Brieffreundschaften schließen
– Personen beschreiben, Ansichten und Meinungen darlegen
– definite article with abstract nouns and names
– Revision: relative clauses
52

⟨California⟩
55

C Death Valley
– Einen Erlebnisbericht aus der Pionierzeit lesen
– use of the indefinite article
56

Grammar §§ 8, 9

Unit/Steps	Sprechabsichten/Themen	Strukturen	Seite
opover C: America: Land of the Indians?	– Information über die Lebensweise und das Schicksal von Indianern	– Revision: adjective or adverb, position of adverbs, auxiliaries, conditional I and II	59
⟨Alone against Apaches⟩	– Eine Indianergeschichte lesen – Sich beschweren – Einen Beschwerdebrief schreiben		60
A How is it done?	– Über Trickfilmeffekte sprechen – Technische Abläufe beschreiben – Überraschung und Verwunderung ausdrücken	– the passive, simple present forms	65
B A helicopter crash	– Den Hergang eines Unfalls darstellen – Vermutungen über den Unfallhergang anstellen und Meinungen dazu äußern	– the passive, simple past forms – the passive + by-agent	68
C The fun they had	– Über Möglichkeiten und Gefahren der Technisierung sprechen – Die Bedeutung der Technik im Alltag kennenlernen	– the passive – Revision: if + past perfect	70
⟨Song: In the year 2525⟩			75
		Grammar §§ 10–12	
A The exchange	– Über Schüleraustausch sprechen – Wünsche und Pläne ausdrücken	– verb + preposition – verb + adverb	76
B He's here!	– Über Pläne sprechen – Informationen geben	– sentence structures	78
⟨Song: Ebony and Ivory⟩			78
C Ramona's Radio Show	– Über Musik und Unterhaltung sprechen – Pläne realisieren		80
⟨San Antonio⟩			83
		Grammar § 13	
[Working with your dictionary]	– Erste Einführung in den Umgang mit dem Wörterbuch		84
opover D:			
[New frontiers]	– Information über die Erschließung des amerikanischen Westens		86
[When the white man came]	– Geschehnisse, die zum Untergang der Indianer führten		88
A quiz about the USA			89

	Seite
Grammar	91
Register des Grammatikanhangs	104
Vocabulary	105
Alphabetical word list	137
List of names	151
⟨ **Useful phrases in class** ⟩	153
List of irregular verbs	155

Die Texte, auf die sich die Hörverstehensaufgaben beziehen, sind auf der Lehrercassette (Klettnummer 58448) und im Lehrerbuch (Klettnummer 58443) verfügbar.

Zeichenerklärung

Übungen, die den Schülern erlauben, über sich und ihre eigene Situation innerhalb und außerhalb des Klassenzimmers zu sprechen.

Rollenspiele

Wiederholungsübung

Wortschatzübung

⟨ ⟩ Stücke in Winkelklammern sind fakultativ.

[ ] Die in rechteckigen Klammern stehenden Pensen können in Bundesländern, in denen ihre Behandlung in Klasse 8 nicht vorgesehen ist, als fakultativ angesehen werden.

•S• Das Stück ist auf der Cassette für Schüler und Lehrer (Klettnummer 58447) verfügbar.

•L• Das Stück ist auf der Cassette für Lehrer (Klettnummer 58448) verfügbar.

Bildquellen
Peter Arnold, Inc. S. 9 re.mi.; S. 32 li.o.; S.. 35; S. 37 re.o., mi.u.; S. 46 li.u., li.u., mi.u. re.u., re.u., mi.o., re.o.; S. 47 re.o.; S. 49 li.u., mi.u.; S. 50 u.;
The Bettmann Archive, Inc.: S. 60; S. 88;
Courtesy of Brass Door Galleries, Houston, Texas: S. 83 mi.u.;
J. Allan Cash Ltd.: S. 19 li.o., li.u., re.u.;
Erwin Deckert, Stuttgart: S. 8–9 (Personen); S. 12; S. 26; S. 41 li.; S. 43 (3 Abbildungen); S. 83 li.o., S. 96 o.re., o.li.;
Deutsche Presse-Agentur GmbH (dpa): S. 47 mi.re.;
Robert Harding Picture Library: S. 16 re.o.; S. 44;
IFA-Bilderteam, München: S. 11; S. 140;
Laenderpress, Düsseldorf: S. 7; S. 8 re.u.; S. 49 mi.re., S. 55 mi.;
Bildagentur Mauritius: S. 55 re.o., li.o., li.u.; S. 77 o.; S. 83 li.o., re.o., mi.re.;
Wolfgang Metzger, Mühlacker: S. 58 mi.;
Museum of the City of New York: S. 86 re.o.;
National Geographic World: S. 67 (Sept. 1984, p. 8 top left) - National Geographic Society;
Courtesy of the Office of Customer Relations, National Railroad Passenger Corporation, Washington, D.C.: S. 47 re.u.;
Peter Newark's Western Americana: S. 59; S. 62 li.o.; S. 86 mi.li., re.u., S. 87 mi.;
Omnipress: S. 79 o.;
Oshkosh Association of Manufacturers and Commerce – The Chamber (Oshkosh, Wisconsin): S. 24 li.o. und li.mi.;
Photri: S. 8 re.o.; S. 9 li.u.; S. 37 li.o.; S. 56 o.;
Picturepoint: S. 8 mi.; S. 19 mi.u., re.o.; S. 32 li.u.; S. 38 re.o., mi.;
Alan Posener, Berlin: S. 41 re.;
David Redfern: S. 79 li.o.; S. 80 (7 Photos);
Günther Schölzel, Stuttgart: S. 83 u.;
Shostal Associates: S. 9 re.o.; S. 32 re.o., re.u.; S. 34; S. 37 mi.o., re.u.; S. 50 mi.; S. 56 mi.;
Achim Sperber: S. 16 u.; S. 20 o.; S. 37 li.u.;
Heinz Steenmans: S. 14 re.u.; S. 16 mi.re.u.; S. 43 li.; S. 49 li.o., mi.li.; S. 50 re.o.; S. 54 mi.;
Tony Stone Worldwide: S. 16 mi.mi., li.mi., mi.u.; S. 19 mi.o.;

Lonn Taylor and Ingrid Maar, *The American Cowboy*, Library of Congress, Washington 1983, Prints and Photographs Division, Music Division, American Folklife Center – Library of Congress, Recorded Sound Division: S. 62 re.u., mi.o., re.o., mi., li., mi.u., mi.re. (Aus Seiten respektive: 141, 143, 134, 91 (Buffalo Bill Historical Center, Cody, Wyoming), 151, 196, 174 (William Wilhelmi-Kaffie Gallery, Corpus Christi, Texas));
Andreas Thiemann: S. 45; S. 52;
Transglobe Agency: S. 9 li.o.; S. 40 li., u.; S. 47 mi.li.; S. 55 mi.o., mi.u., re.u.; S. 77 mi.;
Zentrale Farbbild Agentur GmbH, Düsseldorf: Umschlagphoto; S. 14 li.; S. 16 o.; S. 32 mi.u.; S. 41 mi.;

Cartoons: S. 22: PUNCH;
S. 32: *Peanuts*, Charles M. Schulz, © 1960, 1961, 1962 United Feature Syndicate, Inc.;
S. 69 li.u. und re.u.: PUNCH, Oct. 10, 1984 and March 28, 1984;
S. 82: PUNCH, Aug. 13, 1986.

Textquellen
S. 11: *This land is your land* by Woody Guthrie, © Ludlow Music, Inc. Für Deutschland, Österreich und die Schweiz: Essex Musikvertrieb GmbH, Köln. S. 17: *A Heart in New York*, © Rondor Musikverlag GmbH, Hamburg. S. 31: *Small town* by John Cougar Mellencamp, Phonogramm Hamburg, Mercury, Riva Music. S. 40: *OK Gimme* by Martin Wiley, © 1985 Martyn Wiley, Poems for Children from *Circus of Poets*, Darfield, Barnsley. S. 45: *Truck driving man* by Terry Fell, song by Dave Dudley, © Cross Music Ltd. S. 60: *Alone against Apaches*, by Louis L'Amour, from: Louis L'Amour, The Gift of Cochise, © 1952 Crowell-Collier Publishing Co. S. 70: *The fun they had* by Isaac Asimov, Liepmann AG, Zürich. S. 74: *Teevee* by Eve Merriam. From JAMBOREE Rhymes For All Times by Eve Merriam. Copyright © 1962, 1964, 1966, 1973 by Eve Merriam. All Rights Reserved. Reprinted by permission of Marian Reiner for the author. S. 75: *In the year 2525* © 1986 by Zerlad Music Enterprises Ltd. c/o Management Three, Edition Meridian Ralph Siegel, München, für Deutschl., Österr. u. Schweiz. S. 78: *Ebony and Ivory*, Text und Musik: McCartney. © 1982 by MPL COMMUNICATIONS INC. MPL MUSIK VERLAGS-GMBH, Frankfurt/Main, für Deutschland, Österreich, Schweiz, CSSR, Polen, Ungarn, Rumänien, Bulgarien, UdSSR, Jugoslawien, Albanien. Abdruck erfolgt mit freundlicher Genehmigung von MPL MUSIK VERLAGS-GMBH, Frankfurt/Main.

The Grand Canyon

Stopover A

VOICES OF AMERICA

Every day we hear voices from America: pop singers, movie stars, politicians. But what about the average American teenager? Birgit Lehmann works for a German magazine. She spent four months in the USA and talked to a lot of American teenagers. Here is what some of them told her, and these are some of the photos which she took while she was interviewing them.

Hi, I'm Paul Christiansen. My family has a farm not far from Seattle. I should be in school today, but I have to help my mom to get the hay in. My teacher understands.

Hello there! I'm Sarah Rosenbaum. We moved to Denver, Colorado, because Dad got a job with a big computer company here. Before that we lived in Baltimore. My hobby is music. I play the cello. I also play the guitar in a country group. I haven't got a very good guitar, but I'm going to get a better one soon. (Mom has promised me a new one for my birthday!)

I'm Jolene Clarke, and this is my boyfriend Bryan Schulz. My parents are divorced. I live with my mom in San Francisco. My dad lives in Arizona. A lot of us out here in California go surfing. It's great.

My name's Tracey Donahue. I live in New York City. We've got an apartment in Brooklyn. I do a lot of babysitting in my free time. My dad's a policeman.

Hi! I'm Garth Robinson, from New York City. I live on 119th Street, in Harlem. I'm the best basketball player on our block. At least, that's what *I* think. But some people don't agree. This is my sister Sheena.

Buenos días! Welcome to Texas. Down here in San Antonio, lots of people speak Spanish. I've got a Spanish name – Carmen García. My parents came to the USA from Mexico, but I've lived here all my life. I'm fifteen this year, so I'm learning to drive at school. I hope I can get my driver's license when I'm sixteen.

My name's Marco Ferranti, but everybody calls me Marc. My dad is a steelworker here in Pittsburgh, Pennsylvania. My sister Tessie drives a truck. She might take me down to Florida with her this summer. If I want to go, I'll need some money – so I'm doing a paper route now. I have to get up very early, but you know what? It's fun. And I'm earning my own money.

Hi, friends. It's me – Harry Hopper from Enid, Oklahoma. Remember? Well, we won't be in Enid much longer – but more about that later!

THE USA - FACTS AND FIGURES

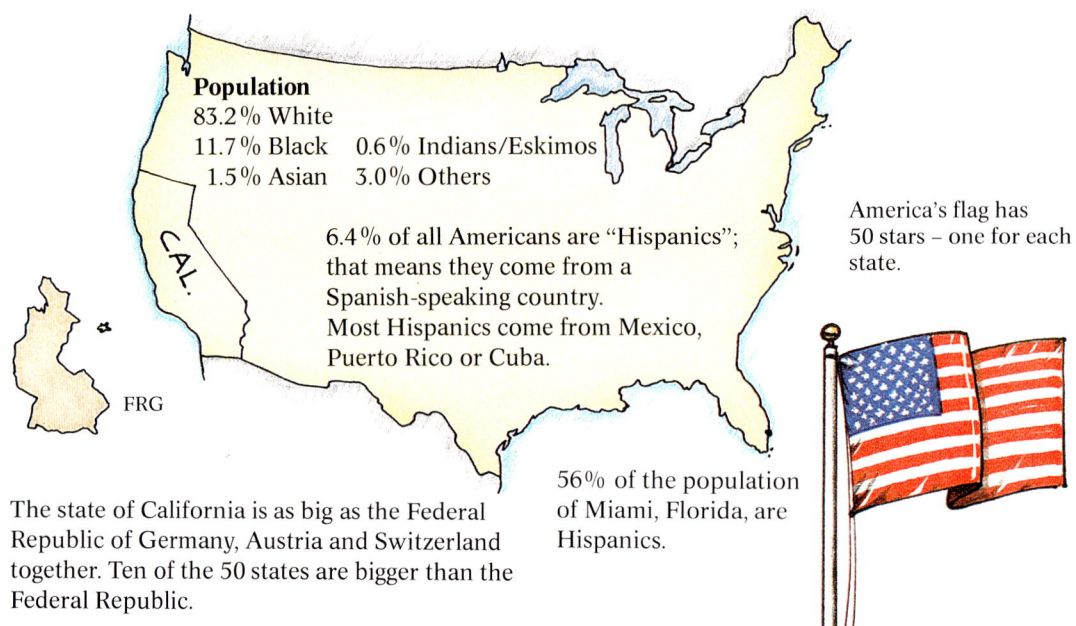

Population
83.2% White
11.7% Black   0.6% Indians/Eskimos
1.5% Asian   3.0% Others

6.4% of all Americans are "Hispanics"; that means they come from a Spanish-speaking country. Most Hispanics come from Mexico, Puerto Rico or Cuba.

FRG

America's flag has 50 stars – one for each state.

The state of California is as big as the Federal Republic of Germany, Austria and Switzerland together. Ten of the 50 states are bigger than the Federal Republic.

56% of the population of Miami, Florida, are Hispanics.

What language do the Americans speak at home? Well, 90% (that's 210 million people) speak English at home. 11.5 million speak Spanish, 1.6 million Italian, 1.6 million German, 1.5 million French, and 649,000 speak Chinese at home. At most schools everybody speaks English. But there are schools which teach some of the subjects in other languages, for example Spanish.

The average American:
- has lived in 30 homes by the time he or she dies.
- drives 13,500 miles each year.
- eats 92 hot dogs a year.
- laughs 15 times a day.
- is **twice** as happy as the average West German.

Compare:	 United States of America	 Federal Republic of Germany	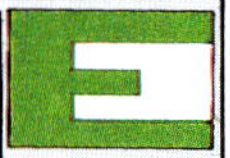 European Community (12)
area (km^2)	9.3 million	0.25 million	2 million
population	236 million	61 million	321 million
cities with over 1 million people	6	3	13

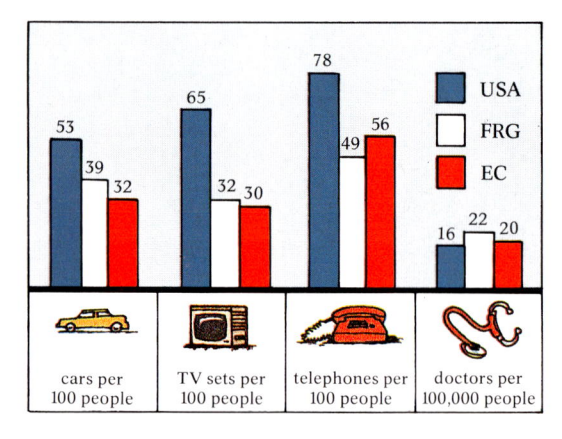

Bar chart (USA / FRG / EC):
- cars per 100 people: 53 / 39 / 32
- TV sets per 100 people: 65 / 32 / 30
- telephones per 100 people: 78 / 49 / 56
- doctors per 100,000 people: 16 / 22 / 20

Talking points
1. Compare the size of the EC and America – and their populations. What do the statistics tell you? What did you expect?
2. Do all Americans speak English at home? In which parts of the USA do you think most Hispanics live?
3. Look at the statistics on cars, TV sets, etc. What do they tell you about life in America?

I think ...
I can't believe that ...
I'm surprised to hear that ...
I didn't know that ...
It's hard to believe that ...

⟨This land is your land⟩

Chorus: This land is your land, this land is my land, from Ca-li-for-nia to the New York Island, from the Redwood forest to the Gulf Stream waters, this land was made for you and me.

This land is your land, this land is my land,
From California to the New York Island,
From the redwood forest to the Gulf Stream waters,
This land was made for you and me.

As I went walking that ribbon of highway,
I saw above me that endless skyway,
I saw below me that golden valley,
This land was made for you and me.

I roamed and rambled, and I followed my footsteps,
To the sparkling sands of her diamond deserts,
All around me a voice was sounding,
This land was made for you and me.

When the sun came shining, then I was strolling,
And the wheat fields waving, and the dust clouds rolling,
A voice was chanting as the fog was lifting,
This land was made for you and me.

Woody Guthrie

Woody Guthrie

Woody Guthrie was born in Oklahoma in 1912. At the age of 16 he left home and roamed through Texas and Louisiana. During that time he had a lot of different jobs. He worked as a newsboy, a painter, and a farm worker. After 1929 a lot of people were unemployed, and Woody rode the trains as a hobo.

Woody Guthrie wrote more than 1,000 folksongs. *This land is your land* is the most famous of all. For great folksingers such as Pete Seeger, Bob Dylan and many others, Woody was a hero. When he died in New York on October 3rd, 1967, the black singer Odetta said, "I think that *This land is your land* should be our national anthem."

Work out these questions

1. Look at the map of the United States at the front of the book. Find the places that Woody Guthrie sings about. Where is the redwood forest? Where are the Gulf Stream waters? Where can you find large wheat fields? What do you know about the highways? Have you ever heard anything about the deserts in the USA?
2. What does Woody Guthrie love about America?
3. "This land was made for you and me." – Explain this in your own words.
4. Do you like this song? Say why or why not. The phrases on page 153 may help you.
5. *Activity:* Work in groups. Collect pictures and interesting information about the different places in this song. Make a collage.

Stopover A

1 Who's who

What do you know about the teenagers Birgit interviewed? *Talk about them all. Use this plan to help you.*

from?	from?	interests?	from?	family?	from?	from?
interests?	family?	from?	family?	free time?	family?	age?
family?	friends?	family?	duties?	plans?	free time?	plans?

Example: What do you remember about Garth Robinson? Where's he from?
– He's from New York City. Yes, he lives on 119th Street – that's in Harlem.
– And what about his interests? (What is he interested in?)
– He likes basketball. In fact, he thinks he's the best player on his block.
– I know he's got a sister. I don't know whether he's got a brother or not.

2 Dialogues

Put in the right form of the verb – simple present or present progressive.

1. "… you … basketball every day, Garth?" – "Not every day. I … always … the time. But I … hard at it at the moment." – "I can see that!"
2. "Hey Carmen, where … you …?" – "Didn't you know? I … to drive now! I … to get my driver's license next year." – "Good luck then!"
3. "How often … you and Bryan … to the beach, Jolene?" – "Oh, every day. At the moment we … ready for a big surfing competition." – "Surfing … easy." – "You're right. But it's safe, if you … well."
4. "Where … you … now, Marc?" – "To the bowling center. I … my friends there every Friday evening. They … for me right now." – "Then have fun – 'Bye!"

play
not find
work
go
learn
want
come
get
not look
swim
go
meet
wait

3 What were they doing? What happened?

Paul …   *Garth …*   *Jolene and Bryan …*   *Sarah …*

Carmen …   *Tracey …*   *Marc …*   *Tessie …*

Example: 1. While Paul was helping his mother, the mailman arrived. *Or:* Paul and his mother were getting the hay in when the mailman brought some letters.
Go on, and make different sentences.

4 What had happened?

Complete the sentences.

1. *Paul:* I had to walk home yesterday because the school bus had already … (leave)
2. *Garth:* Last week I asked Sheena for some money. But she … (spend)
3. *Carmen:* I wanted to get into the car. But I … (lose)
4. *Sarah:* I wanted to wear my blue dress for the concert. But Mom … (wash)
5. *Marc:* At the end of my paper route I had one newspaper left. Then I remembered: Mr Cooper! I … (forget)
6. *Tracey:* I wanted to go to a concert on the weekend. But they … (sell)
7. *Harry:* Last week I lost a magazine which a friend … (lend)
8. *Jolene:* At last Bryan and I found a parking-space; but the film … (start)

5 A terrible crossing

Birgit is looking at an old letter that belongs to Jolene's family.
Put in the right tense of all the verbs.

New York, April 2nd 1883

My dear mother and father,
I … now in America. I … this letter in New York, where I … just … after a terrible crossing from England. My brother Daniel and I … Liverpool more than nine weeks ago. Together with hundreds of other passengers we … live on a dark, dirty deck of the ship, with no fresh air, and never enough food or water. And when we … only a short way, the most awful storms … . They … for many days, and during all this time we … very frightened. One man … mad. While I … only a few feet away from him, he … himself with a long knife.
But I … you everything yet. Four weeks after we … the crossing, cholera … on board. More than ninety passengers … their lives. My parents: In this letter I … give you the sad news that on March 12th the cholera also … my dear brother's life.
Now I … some weeks in New York before I … west with some new friends. I often … of you. Your son,
John Clarke

be
write
arrive
leave
have to
sail
begin
not stop
be
go
stand
kill
not tell
start
break out
lose
have to
take
spend
travel
think

6 Role Play: What are your plans?

Hi, Sheena/…!/Hello there!

What are your plans for Saturday?
What are you going to do tomorrow?
Have you planned anything special for tonight/this afternoon/…?

I'm going to wash my hair.
I think I'll play tennis if the weather's good.
…
I don't know yet./Not really.
I'll probably have to go to bed early.
I might go and see Stan/…
…

Really?/Are you sure?
I thought maybe we could both …
Why not do that another time? Let's …

OK, then. Great!
Sorry. I really can't manage it this time.
Well, perhaps we could do that next weekend/…

A What New York means to me

While Birgit was in New York, Tracey had to write an article for the school magazine. She decided to interview Birgit.

Tracey: Birgit, you come from a small town in Germany. How do you like New York City?
Birgit: It's funny – before I came, I was a little afraid of New York. You know, you read about how big it is, and how much crime there is. But I really enjoy walking around Manhattan. Maybe because there are so many interesting people of all races and colors here. You can wear what you want and do what you like.
Tracey: Not if your dad's a policeman like mine! – How much of New York have you seen?
Birgit: Well, getting around is part of my job, of course. But I probably haven't seen half of Manhattan yet! I still find the skyscrapers fantastic. When you look up from the street, you can hardly see the sky. I just love walking around Little Italy and Chinatown. All the smells from those different restaurants!

Tracey: Don't make me hungry, Birgit. – Tell me: Is there anything that you don't like?
Birgit: Yes, the poverty. On my first night here I went out to get a hot dog and I almost stepped on a man who was asleep on the sidewalk. And only a few blocks from Macy's, the world's biggest department store ... in the richest country in the world!
Tracey: But there are poor people in Europe, too.
Birgit: Yes, of course. But seeing a man like that was still a shock.

Tracey: You see even worse things in Spanish Harlem. But let's talk about something else. What's your favorite place in New York City?
Birgit: Oh dear, that's a difficult one. I love the view from the Statue of Liberty. I like sitting in the little cafés and music clubs in Greenwich Village ... But I suppose my favorite place is Central Park.
Tracey: Why Central Park?
Birgit: Well, people are so ... so free there. All those families out with their dogs, and kids with skateboards and rollerskates. You can take a boat out on the lake, listen to music, read –
Tracey: Or just lie on the grass and watch the world go by!
Birgit: Yes! That's what New York means to me. Watching the whole world go by – black, white, brown, yellow, red people. All in one city, with all its problems and all its wonders.

Unit 1 A

1 Talking about New York

1. Look at the dialogue again and make a list of some of the things that you can see or hear in New York.
2. Why was Birgit a little afraid before she first visited New York? Was everything as she had expected?
3. What does Birgit like about New York? What does she think is not so good?
4. Now think about a big German city that you know. What is the same as in New York, and what is different?
Here are some ideas to help you:
… people of all races? skyscrapers? parks? …

2 Who are they?

How well do you remember all the boys and girls that Birgit interviewed?
Can you say who these people are?

1. I love playing the cello and the guitar.
2. I like learning to drive.
3. I like helping on the farm.
4. I enjoy doing my paper route.
5. I enjoy playing basketball.
6. I love surfing with my friends.
7. I like babysitting.

Start like this: I think number one is … because … loves playing the cello and the guitar. Number two must be … because … likes … I'm sure number … *Go on.*

3 Keeping fit in New York

Sports are an important part of life in America. But Americans don't only enjoy watching sports. They like keeping fit themselves. Almost half of all Americans take part in keep fit activity at least once a day. In New York, Central Park is always full of people who enjoy keeping fit – and having fun.

– is good for you
– is fun
– keeps you fit
– is a great way to start the day
– … (any ideas?)

a) *What might these people say?*
Example: Jogging is good for you./Jogging is a great way to start the day.
Go on and make more sentences.

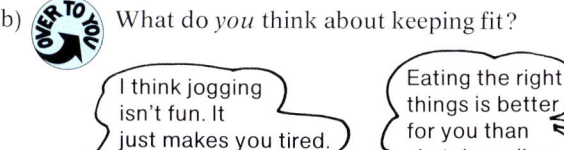

b) **OVER TO YOU** What do *you* think about keeping fit?

I think jogging isn't fun. It just makes you tired.

Eating the right things is better for you than skateboarding.

THE BIG APPLE

New York isn't the capital of the USA – that's Washington, D.C. – but it's the biggest city in the USA. About 8 million people live in its five boroughs. 1.5 million live on the island of Manhattan, the most famous part of New York. Another 1.5 million travel to work there every day.

New York's streets are always full of traffic, so most New Yorkers who want to get from one part of the city to another take the subway. The subway runs twenty-four hours a day. It is 210 miles long and has 461 stations.

The Statue of Liberty stands in New York harbor. 27 million immigrants have passed it on their way to a new life in America. Many of these immigrants never left New York. N.Y.C. has more Irish than Dublin and more Jews than Tel Aviv.

- New York's most famous newspaper, "The New York Times", weighs six pounds at the weekend – and sometimes ten pounds.
- Every year, thieves steal 80,000 cars in N.Y.C.
- There are 25,000 restaurants in N.Y.C. Statistics tell us that New Yorkers like cheesecake most of all. They eat 10,000 cheesecakes a day.

- In 1626, Peter Minuit, a Dutchman, bought Manhattan Island from the Indians for $24. Today a square meter in Manhattan costs $7,000.
- There are thousands of homeless people in N.Y.C. This is one of the city's greatest problems.

Unit 1A ⟨The Big Apple⟩

1 Streets in Manhattan

If you look at a street map of Manhattan, you will find:

- Most streets have numbers, not names.
- The *avenues* go from north to south, the *streets* run from east to west.
- Fifth Avenue is the line between the east and west sides of Manhattan.
- This means that East 23rd Street is the part of 23rd Street that lies to the east of Fifth Avenue. And West 23rd Street is the same street to the west of Fifth Avenue.

a) Find these places on the map and say where they are:
Central Park, Harlem, the Empire State Building, Grand Central Station, the World Trade Center, Chinatown, Broadway, Times Square, Madison Square Garden, Greenwich Village, Wall Street, Rockefeller Center.

b) *Activity:* Work in pairs. Plan a bus tour of Manhattan which would include all these places. What would be the best route?

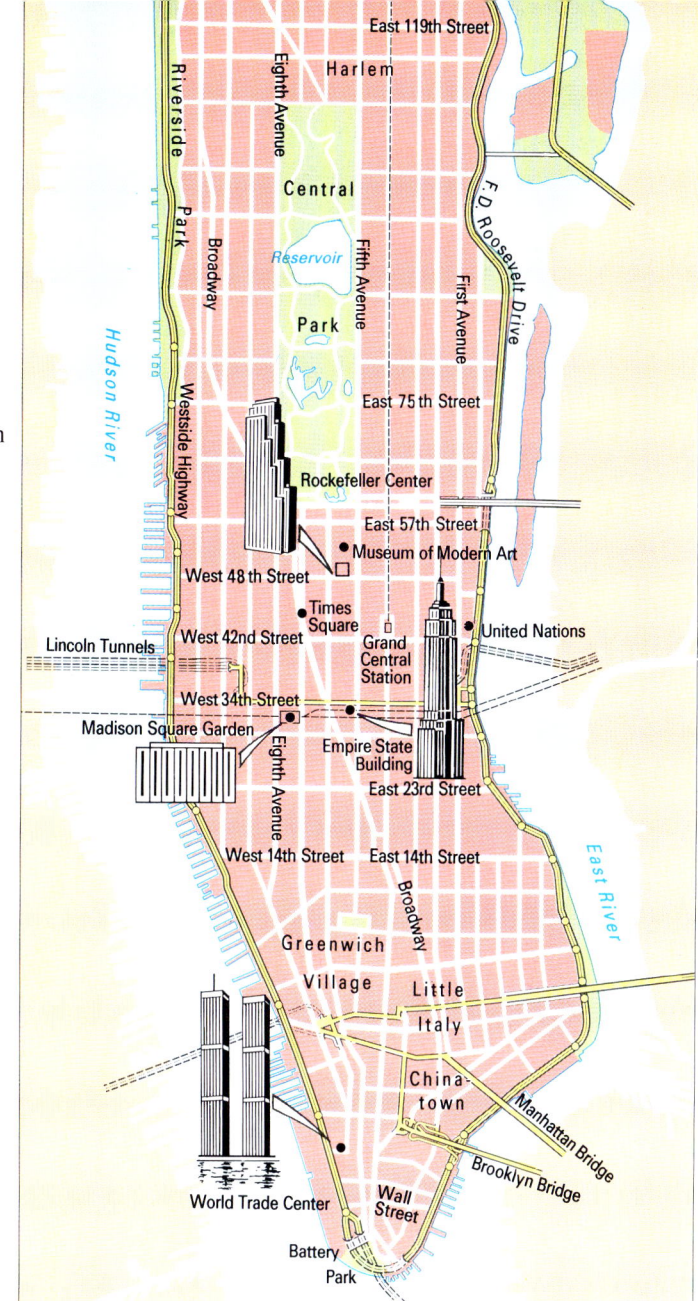

2 Song: A heart in New York

New York – to that tall skyline I come
Flying in from London to your door.
New York – looking down on Central Park
Where they say you should not wander after dark.
New York – like a scene from all those movies
That are real enough to me.

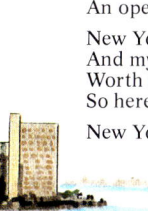

There's a heart,
A heart that lives in New York,
A heart in New York,
A rose on the street,
I write my song to that city heart beat.
A heart in New York,
A love in her eye,
An open door and a friend for tonight.

New York – you got money on your mind
And my words won't make a dime's
Worth of difference,
So here's to you New York.

New York – now my plane is touching down.

Unit 1B

B Almost the best

It was after seven o'clock – much later than he had planned – when Ted Donahue left the police-station on Friday evening. He was used to working long hours, that was part of a policeman's job. But now he had cleared his desk and it was the weekend. Ted smiled as he rode the subway home. He was looking forward to doing lots of nice things – to coaching his football team, to spending time
5 with his family, and, yes, he might do some cooking this weekend, too. He was very good at making chili con carne – the best chili con carne in New York, that's what everybody said! Suddenly Ted stopped smiling. He remembered what he had promised to do when he got home that evening. And now it was too late! Mary and Tracey would be home soon.
  While Ted was on his way home, his wife Mary finished work at the twenty-four hour supermarket.
10 She didn't like working there. She wanted to find another job nearer home because she hated driving in the New York traffic. And tonight she had to collect Tracey from the YMCA. Tracey enjoyed meeting her friends there after school on Fridays, but she was worried about walking home alone when it was dark. So it was almost eight o'clock when Mary and Tracey arrived back in the old Buick outside the Brooklyn apartment block where they lived. They were both tired and hungry.
15 They were looking forward to having the chili con carne which Ted had promised to have ready for them when they got home…
  When they walked into the apartment, Ted had already set the table. As soon as they sat down, he put a video in the video recorder and brought the chili con carne from the kitchen. "Mmm! The best chili con carne in New York City!" said Tracey when she saw it. Ted thought of the brown paper bag
20 in the garbage can. "Well, almost the best," he said modestly.

1 The Donahues

What does the text tell you about the Donahues?
Put the sentence parts together.

Ted Tracey Mary	enjoyed was used to didn't like hated was good at was worried about	working at the supermarket. walking home alone. working long hours. meeting friends at the YMCA. driving in the New York traffic. making chili con carne.

2 Doing things

Visiting other countries is great. I'm interested in finding out about other people. I'm lucky because my job is my hobby, too.

I love music. Dancing? No, I'm not crazy about dancing. I just like listening to music.

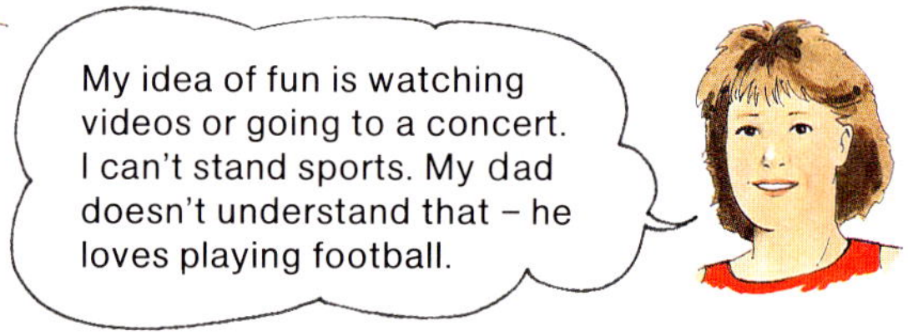

My idea of fun is watching videos or going to a concert. I can't stand sports. My dad doesn't understand that – he loves playing football.

Now talk about your activities.
– What things do you like doing?
– What can't you stand doing?
– What do your parents say about what you do in your free time?

3 Making suggestions

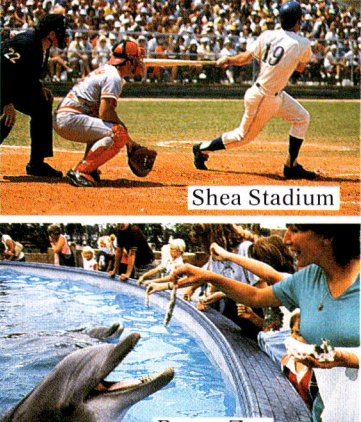

Unit 1B

Central Park
Shea Stadium
Museum of Modern Art
Bronx Zoo
Coney Island

The Donahues are making plans for a day out at the weekend.

a) *What might they say? How many suggestions and answers can you make?*
Example: What do you think of going ice-skating at Rockefeller Center?
– Oh yes, that's always fun!
How about that big game at Shea Stadium on Saturday?
– Not again! I can't stand watching baseball.

b) *Now think about what you can do where you live.*
Talk to a friend about going out together.

4 Role Play: What was your weekend like?

It's Monday morning. A friend is asking about your weekend.

- What was your weekend like?
  You look as if you had a good/bad weekend!
  Did you do anything special yesterday/on …?

- It was OK/fantastic/terrible …
  Yes, I did./No, I didn't.

- What did you do?
  Where did you go?
  Why? What happened?
  Oh, really? Why don't you tell me about it?

- Nothing much. I stayed at home.
  I went to …, and …
  I was ill, so I couldn't …
  Well, I wanted to … but …

- I'm sure you enjoyed/didn't enjoy that.
  That was fun/bad luck/…, wasn't it?

- Yes/No, I …
  Yes, it certainly was.
  You bet!

5 Look, listen and say: American pronunciation

Have you noticed that American speakers sound "different" from British speakers? Look out especially for these differences between British and American pronunciation:

Vowels: BE [ɑː] – AE [æ] bath, half, laugh, aunt, after.
BE [ɒ] – AE [ɑ] job, robber, sock, possible, top.
Consonants: Americans often pronounce 't' in the middle of a word as [d]:
beautiful ['bjuːdɪfl], butter ['bʌdər]
Americans nearly always pronounce 'r' when it is silent in BE:
after ['æːftər], understand [ˌʌndərˈstænd], sure [ʃuːr]

Now listen to the recording, and decide which speakers are American and which are British.

Unit 1 C

C Up on 119th Street

A lot of people don't like cops. I'm a cop. So a lot of people don't like me. But someone has to do the job. And sometimes something happens which reminds me why I became a cop.

Last night we were driving north of Central Park. I'm Ted
5 Donahue, and my partner's Wayne Ellis. Wayne's black, I'm Irish. The boys call our car 'Irish coffee'. Suddenly, up on 119th Street, a black girl ran in front of the car. Quick, the brakes! "Are you crazy?" I called out of the window. Then I saw that the girl was crying. "Hey, what's the matter, honey?" She didn't say a word. "Here, Wayne, you talk to
10 her." "Not here," she whispered. I could see she was afraid. People were already looking at us. Wayne got out of the car and pushed the girl into the back. As we drove off, she started to talk.

Her name was Sheena. She told us about her brother Garth. He was going around with a gang of older boys. Most of them were out of school, and out of work – but not out of money. They had started as shop-lifters, but then they had gone on to stealing car radios. Tonight they wanted to
15 break into a warehouse. And this time Garth was going to go with them. The warehouse was in East Harlem. "I know it," Wayne said. "There's a night watchman there with a gun. Step on the gas, Ted. We have to be there first!"

Outside the warehouse everything was quiet. I turned to Sheena. "Listen, honey, if you're playing a game with us …" Then Wayne saw the hole in the fence. We climbed through and started to look
20 around. Suddenly an alarm bell rang somewhere. Four or five dark figures were running away from the warehouse. "Stop! Police!" I called and started to run after one of the figures. Although I'm a good runner – I play football every Saturday – that boy was too fast for me. And was he fast!

He got to the hole in the fence before I did. Then I
25 heard a voice. "Out of the way, cop – I'll get him!" The watchman had come up behind me, and he had his gun in his hand. The
30 boy didn't have a chance. He was running past our car when the door suddenly opened. The boy slammed into the door and
35 fell down. The watchman put his gun down. "Nice work," he said. The girl was getting out of the car. She didn't look at us. "I'm sorry, Garth," she cried. "I had to."

Wayne got into the back of the car with Garth and his sister, and we drove off. "Hey, Ted, this isn't the way to the station," Wayne said. "I'm taking this big boy home," I said. "He can think better
40 at home than in jail. Now listen." I was talking to Garth now. "This was your first job. If you're smart, it'll be your last. Give yourself a chance." "What chance? I don't see any chances up on 119th Street. My last big chance went yesterday when they dropped me from the basketball team." "I don't know much about basketball, Garth," I said. "But I know something about football. And you're a born football player. You're really big, and you're the fastest runner that I've ever seen.

Tomorrow I want you down at the station – you know where it is. I'm coaching a football team and I need a runner like you." "But ...," began Garth. "No buts, boy," said Wayne. "When Ted Donahue says that you're going to play football, you just say 'Yes, sir'. Understand?" "Yes, sir." "Right." We had reached 119th Street. I stopped the car. "Remember, Garth. Two o'clock tomorrow. 'Bye, Sheena. You have a very brave sister, Garth." "Brave? What do you mean?" "Well, think about it." We drove off.

1 Comprehension

a) *Answer the questions.*
1. How did Ted's and Wayne's car get the name 'Irish coffee'? 2. How did Ted and Wayne meet Sheena? 3. Why was Sheena crying? 4. Why was Wayne worried when he heard about the warehouse? 5. How was Ted able to catch Garth? 6. Where did Ted take Garth, and why? 7. Why had Garth decided to break into the warehouse? 8. Why did Ted think of putting Garth in his football team?

b) *Things to think about.*
1. Why did Ted think Wayne should talk to Sheena? 2. Think about how Ted and Wayne did their job. Compare them with the watchman. 3. Do you think putting Garth in the football team was a good idea? Give reasons. 4. Do you think Sheena was right to tell the policemen about her brother? 5. What did Ted mean when he called Sheena "brave"? ⟨6. "A lot of people don't like cops," says Ted Donahue. Can you think why the police are often unpopular? 7. Why is sport important for a boy like Garth?⟩

c) *What did Garth think? Put the sentence parts together, and then try to add your own ideas.*

1. If I play on the team,	she'll tell them where I am.
2. Anyway, if I don't go to the station,	I'll never be out of money.
3. If they ask my sister,	maybe I'll become a famous football player.
4. But if the others in the gang see me on the team,	the cops will come and get me.
5. If I stay with the gang,	they'll laugh at me.

Garth: But if Sheena sees me with the gang, ... If I'm smart ...
If I play on the team, maybe I'll ... *Go on.*

⟨d) *What did Garth decide to do? Write an ending to the story.*⟩

2 Looking to the future

What did these girls and boys in New York City tell Birgit about themselves? *Complete the sentences.*
1. *Lincoln:* I dream of ...
2. *Donna:* I'm looking forward to ...
3. *Sheena:* I'm thinking of working with ...
4. *Joel and Julie:* We're afraid of ...
5. *Ruth:* I'm worried about ...
6. *Al and Leroy:* We often talk about ...
7. *Garth:* I'm looking forward to ...
What can you say about your future?

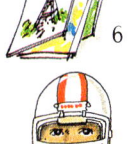

⟨3 Listening comprehension: Coney Island Blues⟩

1. Why was Sam so blue?
2. What did Sally's parents say?
3. How did Garth try to help Sam?
4. Who was Zara? What did she say?
5. Was she right? What happened in the subway?
6. What do you think Sam said to Donna?

Unit 1 C

4 What are they going to do? What will happen then?

There are always lots of tourists in New York City. They are all talking about tomorrow.
Put in the correct forms of 'going to' and 'will'.

Example: "Tomorrow morning we are **going to** take the boat around Manhattan." – "Great! Then **we'll** have a different view of New York City."

1. "You … Chinatown tomorrow, aren't you?" – "I certainly am. Then I … eat in a Chinese restaurant." (visit, be able to)
2. "… you … postcards to all your friends?" – "Of course. Then they … very pleased." (send, be)
3. "What time … we … for the airport?" – "At 8 o'clock. Then we … on time." (leave, arrive)
4. "I … tickets for a Broadway show tomorrow evening." – "OK, but then you … stand in line, you know." (buy, have to)
5. "We … some souvenirs at Macy's in the afternoon." – "Good idea. Then you … always … your trip to New York City." (look for, remember)
6. "What … you … tomorrow evening? Watch the outdoor shows in Washington Square?" – "That's right. Then I … pay." (do, not have to)

5 Roberto, the bike messenger

There are more than 5,000 bike messengers in New York. Roberto Fernandez from Puerto Rico works for the First Service messenger agency.
It was Friday afternoon. Roberto was cycling away from the UN building. He had just delivered a message there. Suddenly he heard his beeper … *Go on with the story.*

1. hear – beeper – go – call box 2. phone – agency – ask for – instructions 3. collect – packet
4. streets – full – not able to move – cycle past 5. traffic lights – red – go through 6. deliver – girl – ask 7. open – show – surprised – himself

⟨6 **Just for fun**⟩

"No, I could never never live
in the city, I commute every day."

UNIT 2

A Should they or shouldn't they?

You remember Harry Hopper of Enid, Oklahoma, don't you? Yes, Harry, the magician. Well, his parents have always dreamed of having their own business. And now at last they have the chance. They can take over a stained glass business from Mrs Hopper's
5 Uncle Bernie in Oshkosh. Oshkosh is a small town in Wisconsin, more than 700 miles away from Enid. So if they went there, it would mean a lot of changes – and perhaps problems – for everybody. Should they go? Should they take the chance? The Hoppers – Mom, Dad, Harry (14) and Herbie (16) – are talking about it:

I'm not sure. What would we do if nobody bought our windows?

Oh, no! What about Linda and me? If I left now, it would be the end.

Great! This is our big chance. If we didn't take it, we would always be sorry.

Well, if we moved, I wouldn't have Big Boggles for Geography, and …

1 Pros and cons

a) *Can you put these sentences together correctly?*
1. If we took this chance,   I wouldn't be too unhappy.
2. If I didn't see some of my teachers again,   we would lose all our money.
3. If I had to leave Linda,   we would have our own business at last.
4. If my new friends were interested in magic,   the business would go well.
5. If the business didn't go well,   I would show them some of my tricks.
6. If we worked hard,   it would be the end of our love.

b) *Look at your sentences again. Who do you think said what? Why do you think so?*
   Start like this: I think … said the first sentence because … .
                     … said the second sentence because … .

c) *If your parents wanted to move, what would you think of the idea?*
   Would you be pleased or not?

Think about:
- saying goodbye to different people
  e.g. friends, teachers
- having to make new friends
- going to a different school
- living in a new house/flat
- moving to a different part of the country
- moving to a small town/big city
  …

Now talk about moving:

If I had to move, I wouldn't be pleased at all. I've got lots of good friends here.

If I had to start at a new school, …

Living in a new place can be very exciting.

Unit 2A

2 If the Hoppers moved to Oshkosh, …

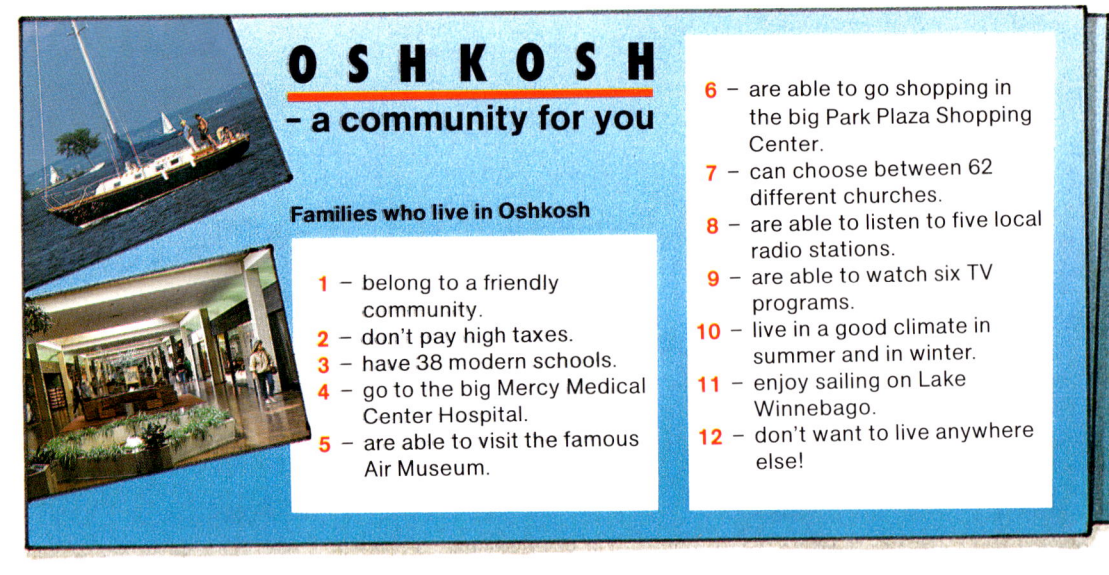

OSHKOSH
– a community for you

Families who live in Oshkosh

1 – belong to a friendly community.
2 – don't pay high taxes.
3 – have 38 modern schools.
4 – go to the big Mercy Medical Center Hospital.
5 – are able to visit the famous Air Museum.
6 – are able to go shopping in the big Park Plaza Shopping Center.
7 – can choose between 62 different churches.
8 – are able to listen to five local radio stations.
9 – are able to watch six TV programs.
10 – live in a good climate in summer and in winter.
11 – enjoy sailing on Lake Winnebago.
12 – don't want to live anywhere else!

Uncle **Bernie** has sent the Hoppers this leaflet about Oshkosh.

a) *Start like this:* 1. If Harry's family moved to Oshkosh, they would belong to a friendly community. 2. If they **took** over the business there, they wouldn't … . 3. If they lived there, … . 4. If they became very ill, … . 5. If they didn't know what to do on Sunday afternoon, … . 6. If they needed some new clothes, … . 7. If they wanted to go to church, … . 8. If they turned on the radio, … . 9. If they turned on their TV, … . 10. If they moved to Oshkosh, … . 11. If they bought a sailboat, … . 12. If they lived in Oshkosh for a year, … .

Somebody is thinking of moving to *your* town.
b) *What would you tell her or him?*
c) *Activity: Write a leaflet for him or her. Use the ideas in the Oshkosh leaflet.*

3 Role Play Saying goodbye

The Hoppers have decided to move to Oshkosh. And today's the big day.

Linda: Oh dear – Goodbye, Herbie!
Herbie: Oh, Linda – I'll miss you.
Linda: I'll miss you, too. Don't forget me.
Herbie: Of course I won't. I'll write every day.

Harry: So long then, Ben.
Ben: Bye, Harry. And good luck.
Harry: Thanks. Let me know what you're doing.
Ben: OK. Perhaps we'll visit each other soon.

Imagine one of your friends is moving to another town/is going to spend two weeks in America/must go into hospital for a few days/…
Make short dialogues.

Bye./Goodbye.
So long.
See you (later/next …).

I'll miss you/never forget you.
Have a good time/trip.
Take care.
Good luck.

Write to me./Phone me./Visit me.
Don't forget me.
Think of me.
Let me know what you're doing.

Of course I will/won't.
I'll phone/write (every week/…).
I promise.

B A telex from Harry

```
0230245357+
trt 0355 05/11
macgroup wi

247350 rtrey ok
                                                            tuesday

to   mr angus macdonald
     please give this telex to ben. thank you. harry hopper.

hi ben,

yes, it's me - harry. dad has got a telex here. great, isn't it?
i have to keep this short. i'll write you a long letter soon.

everything is ok here. oshkosh is nice, but it's different from
enid - with lots of trees. and the lake, of course. but it's also
the same. if you were here, you'd see what i mean - the people,
and school, and everything. everybody is friendly here.
here's dad. i have to stop now.

oh, i almost forgot. have you still got the magic book that i lent
you? if you airmailed it to me, i would have it by the weekend.
very important. oh, and could you please send me some leaflets
about enid? i want to show them to everybody here. and another
thing. do you remember poor old broken-hearted herbie? well, he's
got a new girlfriend already. crazy, isn't it?
when will you visit me, ben? if you came in the summer, it might
not be so cold here. but if i were you, i'd bring my hockey stick
anyway. everybody is crazy about winter sports here - ice-hockey
and cross-country skiing and ...

i really have to stop now. dad has just broken another piece of
glass.
i hope everything is fine with you.
see you,
harry

p.s. what mark did big boggles give you in geography?
     and please say 'hi' to everybody from me.

nnnn
macgroup wi
247350 rtrey ok
```

1 What was in the telex?

The day after Harry sent Ben the telex, Ben saw Linda at school.
Can you answer Linda's questions and complete the dialogue?

Linda:
Hi, Ben. Er – have you heard from Harry yet?
Oh. – Is everything OK in Oshkosh?
That's good. Um – is Oshkosh very different from Enid?
What's the weather like there?
Yes, of course. Er – And what about the people in Oshkosh?
I see. Well, I – Oh, Ben, I can't understand why I haven't heard from Herbie. What can I do?

Ben:
– Yes, I got …
– Yes, everything …
– Yes, …
– The weather …
– The people …

– … *(What would you say?)*

Unit 2 B

2 Classmate talk

What are Harry's new classmates saying?

Example: 1. You'll soon know your way around the school, Harry. But today I'll show **you the classrooms**.

2. Harry hasn't got all the textbooks. Sue, why don't you lend … 3. We'd like to know what Enid is like, Harry. Perhaps you can bring … 4. I'm thirsty. Harry, please pass … 5. We'll phone you on Saturday, Harry. Don't forget to tell … 6. You've never tried winter sports, Harry? That's OK – we can soon teach … 7. Can't you finish your lunch? Marvin and Wes will help you. Just give … 8. So Herbie has a girlfriend in Enid. I hope he has sent …

```
me          some leaflets
you         your phone number
him         a letter
her         the classrooms
us          your sandwiches
them        your French book
            ice-hockey
            the water
```

3 Neighborhood activities

- have a good time.
- sing in the choir.
- help in the hospital.
- come to the PTA meeting.
- meet all the neighbors.
- sell some windows.
- earn some money.
- make some friends.
- come to the Christmas show. …

What might/could happen if the Hoppers did these things?
Examples: If the Hoppers went to the party, they could meet all the neighbors.
If Harry did any babysitting, the baby might cry a lot.
Go on, and make more sentences.

4 Role Play: If I were you

A new pupil at your school wants to make some friends.

If I were you, I'd join some clubs. But I wouldn't worry. You'll make friends soon. …

Hey! Good idea! Thanks/ Thanks, …/ Yes, …/ No, …/ Thanks, but …/ …

1. Your friend wants to earn some money in his free time, but he isn't sure what he can do. 2. A girl in your class wants to meet a boy who travels to school on the same bus. 3. Your friend asks you what he should give his mother for her birthday. 4. Some classmates are planning to go to a disco. You went there last week and didn't like it. 5. Your friend has lost an expensive watch. He has seen another pupil with the same watch, but he isn't sure if the watch is his. 6. One of the girls in your class can't decide what food she should have at her party next week. 7. Your friend wants to go ice-skating on the lake, but you think the ice is too thin.

C Magic – real magic

When Harry walked into the school cafeteria, he saw them at once – the three girls. They were sitting together. Sandy – the one with the short, dark hair – smiled and waved to him. Harry smiled back, but not really at Sandy. His eyes were on Victoria – Victoria Cabot with her long blond hair and those big green eyes. The third girl, Anne-Marie, looked up, too, and smiled as Harry went past their table. Victoria did not seem to notice him.

"That was Harry. Harry Hooper," Victoria laughed quietly. "He's in the Photo Club. He joined just because of me. What a loser! But what can you expect? He's from the South."

"From Oklahoma. That's not really the South," Anne-Marie said, and looked at Sandy.

"Bad enough," Victoria answered.

"His name is Hopper, not Hooper." Sandy spoke angrily. "I think he's very nice. *And* he can do great magic tricks."

"Magic tricks? Really?" Anne-Marie said.

"Magic tricks. How wonderful," Victoria said very sweetly. "Don't be stupid, Sandy. I'll show you just what a loser this Harry What's-his-name is. You know I'm going to give a party this weekend – well, I'll invite him, too. He can do some of his great magic tricks and then we'll make fun of him. I know just how we can do it. He'll look like a fool, you'll see. It'll be a lot of fun."

Anne-Marie only stared at Victoria, but Sandy shouted "Victoria! I don't believe –" She stopped because Harry was coming back past their table with his food.

"Yoohoo! *Haaarry!*" Victoria called in her sweet voice, and invited him to her party. "Oh, and *Haaarry*," she went on, "it would be so wonderful if you did some of your great magic tricks for us. *Please.*"

As soon as Harry had said yes, Victoria got up and left. Harry, too, walked away. He sat down at a table near the window, pushed his food to one side and stared out at the grey winter sky. What a beautiful day …

"What are you going to do?" Anne-Marie asked Sandy when they were leaving the cafeteria.

"What do you mean?"

"You know what I mean. You like Harry and –"

"I don't know what you're talking about," Sandy said as she took the long way to the door, the way past Harry's table. But Harry did not see her – or anything else. He seemed to be in another world.

"We'll see," Sandy said to herself.

On Saturday evening Harry and Sandy were sitting in the back seat of Sandy's brother's car. It was icy cold outside.

"It's nice of you to take me to Victoria's party," Harry said to Sandy. "And nice of your brother, too, of course."

"Oh, seventeen-year-old brothers can be OK," Sandy smiled. "Bret's glad to help. And I am, too."

"You know, if you wanted, you could be my partner," Harry said a little later. "In the magic show tonight, I mean."

"Really, Harry? That would be great."

And then it happened.

The car stopped.

"Oh, damn! Not again!" Bret said.

"What's the matter?" Sandy was worried.

"It's this stupid car. It's broken down again." Bret seemed to be very unhappy.

"Can I do anything?" Harry asked.

"If you were a real magician, Harry, it might help," Bret said. "Real magic is what we need now, isn't it, Sandy?"

Sandy didn't answer that. "But Victoria's party!" she said.

"I'm sorry," Bret tried to look and sound sorry. "But I don't think we'll get there."

"Oh, no! Now Harry won't be able to do his magic tricks," Sandy said, and took Harry's hand. Harry smiled a little. Sandy was a very nice girl – and pretty, too.

Unit 2C

On Monday morning Victoria was standing on the front steps of the school when Harry and Sandy arrived together.
"I'm sorry we didn't get to your party, Victoria," Harry said.
"It was because of Bret's car. I told you on the phone," Sandy said.
"How was the party?" Harry asked.
"It was OK," Victoria answered, but Anne-Marie, who had just joined them, said, "No, it wasn't. Everybody was looking forward to seeing Harry's tricks."

"Oh?" Sandy looked at her, and Anne-Marie nodded.
"Sorry," Harry said. "I –"
"Don't worry, Harry. It wasn't your fault," Anne-Marie smiled. "We'll have a special magic show soon – at my house. We'll invite everybody again."
"Great!" Harry said. He was looking at Sandy and did not even notice that Victoria had walked away.

1 The facts

a) *Complete these sentences so that you have the most important facts about the story.*

1. When Harry walked into the cafeteria … 2. Sandy smiled at Harry because … 3. Victoria called Harry a loser because … 4. She invited Harry to her party so that … 5. Sandy asked Bret for his help so that … 6. While Bret was driving Harry and Sandy to the party … 7. When Anne-Marie heard what Victoria told Harry and Sandy about the party … 8. Harry didn't notice that Victoria had walked away because …

b) *Divide the story into four main parts. Explain in one or two sentences what each part is about. Then give each part a heading.*

2 How did they feel?

Can you say how these people felt? Why do you think they felt like this?

1. Harry – when he saw the girls in the cafeteria.
2. Sandy – when Victoria called Harry a loser.
3. Victoria – when she invited Harry to her party.
4. Harry – when Victoria invited him to her party.
5. Sandy – when Bret's car suddenly stopped.
6. Harry – when Sandy took his hand.
7. Sandy – when she heard what the party had been like.
8. Victoria – when Anne-Marie talked about a magic show.

These words might help you:

angry, happy, great, bad, excited, lonely, pleased, fantastic, unhappy, sorry, clever, surprised, sad, worried

Example: 1. "I think Harry was happy. Perhaps he was a little excited when he saw the girls in the cafeteria. He liked Victoria very much."   *Go on.*

3 What were they thinking?

Sometimes, while people are saying one thing, they are really thinking something different.
Can you imagine what these girls were really thinking?

1. *Victoria:* "It would be so wonderful if you did some of your great magic tricks for us." (line 37)
2. *Sandy:* "I don't know what you're talking about." (line 49) 3. *Sandy:* "Bret's glad to help. And I am, too." (line 62) 4. *Sandy:* "Oh, no! Now Harry won't be able to do his magic tricks." (line 82)
5. *Victoria:* "It was OK." (line 94)

Unit 2C

4 Day dreams

Example: If I were a bird, I'd fly away to another country.
If I had an elephant, I'd take it everywhere with me.

5 Brother talk

Complete the sentences.
Example: "Are you going to give your new girlfriend that record, Herbie?"
"Yes. I hope she'll be pleased when I **give it to her**."

1. "You must show your new friends your best magic trick, Harry."
   "Don't worry. I will. They won't believe it when I show … to …"
2. "Can you lend me your yellow socks, Herbie?"
   "All right. But you must promise to look after them if I lend …"
3. "Are you going to tell Sandy those jokes that I told you, Harry?"
   "Yes. I bet she'll laugh when I …"
4. "Shall I read you my article for the neighborhood newsletter, Herbie?"
   "Yes, OK. I'll tell you what I think of it if you …"
5. "When are you going to send Ben that book, Harry?"
   "Soon. But if you want, you can look at it before I …"
6. "Oh, Herbie, let's not forget. We have to take Anne-Marie some cassettes for the party tomorrow."
   "Come on then. Let's …"

⟨6 Just for fun: People Greeters⟩

Have you ever seen someone on the bus or in a café and thought, "If only I could meet that boy (or girl)!"? Saying hello to somebody that you don't know isn't easy. But in the USA some teenagers give People Greeters – little cards with a funny message on one side and the name and telephone number of the greeter on the other side. Here are some People Greeters:

You don't have to kiss a FROG if you want a prince. Try me!

I don't look too good, but
☐ I'm really a princess.
☐ I've got a heart of gold.
☐ I can dance well.
☐ who cares?
Call me!
Name……………… Tel. …………

I'd like to be your SCHOOL-BAG. Then you'd carry me home.

I'd like to talk to you, but
☐ I can't find the words.
☐ I'm in a hurry.
☐ My mom's with me.

Activity: What do you think of the idea? How about making your own People Greeters?

Unit 2C

7 A friend to everybody

Mary Burgess is 80 years old, but every day she makes wonderful meals for many different people in her small home. When Harry's class had to write about somebody interesting for homework, Harry went to interview Miss Burgess. *Look at the notes that he made during the interview. Can you imagine what he asked?*

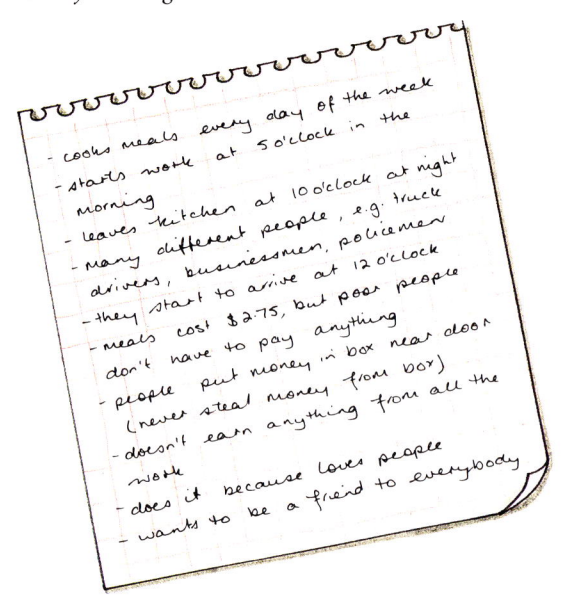

- cooks meals every day of the week
- starts work at 5 o'clock in the morning
- leaves kitchen at 10 o'clock at night
- many different people, e.g. truck drivers, businessmen, policemen
- they start to arrive at 12 o'clock
- meals cost $2.75, but poor people don't have to pay anything
- people put money in box near door (never steal money from box)
- doesn't earn anything from all the work
- does it because loves people
- wants to be a friend to everybody

When? Where? Why? Who? How much? Do/Don't... What? How often?

You can start like this:
Harry: Miss Burgess, how often do you cook for other people?
Mary: Oh, I cook meals every day of the week.
Harry: Really? When do you …?
Go on with the dialogue.

⟨8 A phone-in⟩

Monika is an exchange student from Tübingen. This morning she is at one of the local radio stations in Oshkosh. People can phone her on Phil's Phone-In show. Monika answers in English – but she still has to think in German first! *Can you take her part?*

Phil: And now, friends, it's Phil's Phone-In again. Here I am, Phil Philpott, and this morning I have a very special young student with me. Monika comes from Germany. Just dial 375-1284 and she will answer your questions. – Ah, here's our first caller.
Caller: Well, Monika, I would like to ask you what the weather is like in winter where you come from.
Monika: Januar und Februar sind die kältesten Monate. Dann schneit es normalerweise recht oft.
Phil: Thanks for calling. – And our next caller is already waiting.
Caller: Do you have lots of activities at your school in Germany?
Monika: Es gibt nicht viele Aktivitäten in der Schule. Ich gehöre einem Schwimmverein an, würde gern auch Tennis spielen, aber dazu habe ich nicht genug Geld.
Caller: How old do you have to be in Germany before you can get your driver's license?
Monika: Man muß mindestens 18 sein, wenn man einen Führerschein machen will.
Caller: Do Germans all speak with the same accent?
Monika: Es gibt verschiedene Akzente, man kann einander aber überall verstehen.
Caller: Do you have as many different TV programs as we have in the States?
Monika: Es gibt drei Fernsehprogramme und auch mehr und mehr private Fernsehstationen.
Caller: Where do you spend your holidays?
Monika: Ich war letztes Jahr mit meinen Eltern in Spanien, das Jahr davor zu Hause, und vor drei Jahren war ich an der Nordsee.
Phil: Well, thank you all for your calls. And a special thank you to you, Monika, for talking to us this morning.

9 Working with words: Prefixes

a) If you use a prefix, you can make new words out of many of the words that you already know.

Look at these examples of opposites.

un-	in-	dis-
friendly	(im- before p,	honest
comfortable	ir- before r)	pleased
employed	correct	to like
happy	expensive	to qualify
to tie	perfect	to believe
to lock	probable	
	regular	

Now complete these sentences.
Use opposites that you have made with the prefixes.

1. He's a … boy. He never tells the truth. 2. This chair is … . It's too hard. 3. Can you help me? Is 'to speak' an … verb? 4. Just a minute. I'll get out my key and … the door. 5. Some people think New York City is the capital of the USA. That's …, of course. 6. Please don't cook Irish stew again. You know how we … it!

b) It's important to know about prefixes if you want to use a dictionary. For example, not all words with the prefix *un-* are in every dictionary. So if you want to look up a word like 'uninteresting', you can take away the prefix and look up 'interesting'. You know that the meaning which you want is the opposite.

Look at these sentences, find the words with prefixes and check the meanings. Then try to make your own sentences with the words.

1. If she was nicer to everybody, she wouldn't be so unpopular.
2. I think this town is boring. – Well, I disagree. I think it's a great place!
3. The shock was so great that he was unable to speak.
4. Watch this trick. I'm going to pull a rabbit out of a hat. – That's impossible!
5. I'm always unlucky in competitions. I never win anything.

⟨10 Song: Small town⟩

1. Well I was born in a small town
   And I live in a small town
   Prob'ly die in a small town
   Oh, those small communities

2. All my friends are so small town
   My parents live in the same small town
   My job is so small town
   Provides little opportunity

3. Educated in a small town
   Taught the fear of Jesus in a small town
   Used to daydream in that small town
   Another boring romantic that's me

4. But I've seen it all in a small town
   Had myself a ball in a small town
   Married an L.A. doll and brought her to this small town
   Now she's small town just like me

5. No, I cannot forget where it is that I come from
   I cannot forget the people who love me
   Yeah, I can be myself here in this small town
   And people let me be just what I want to be

6. Got nothing against a big town
   Still hayseed enough to say
   Look who's in the big town
   But my bed is in a small town
   Oh, and that's good enough for me

7. Well I was born in a small town
   And I can breathe in a small town
   Gonna die in this small town
   And that's prob'ly where they'll bury me

John Cougar Mellencamp

Stopover B

CHRISTMAS IN THE USA

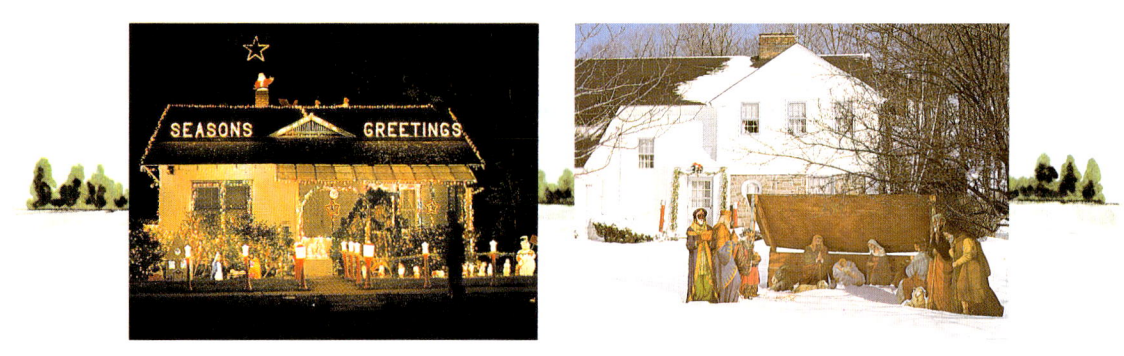

Christmas in the USA is a very merry time. It is merry in Britain, too. In fact, most of the American Christmas traditions come from the British Isles: the holly, the brightly-colored decorations, the carol-singing … One tradition comes from Germany – the Christmas tree. But in the USA, people like to put colored lights on it. It is merrier that way. Americans make sure that everything else looks merry, too – their doors, their windows, their cars …

On Christmas Eve the shops stay open late for last-minute shopping. Some people go to church at midnight. But the big day is the 25th – Christmas Day. On the morning of the 25th, children get up very early and look for what Santa Claus has brought them – very often in the stockings that they have hung up at the fireplace. (Santa Claus, of course, comes down the chimney, while his reindeer wait on the roof.) They can find other presents under the tree.

Christmas has come at last. It's time to put the turkey in the oven!

Stopover B

1 What do you say?

The things that the Donahues and Aunt Mabel say to each other can be useful at other times, too. *What can you say…*

1. … if you meet someone on Christmas Day?
2. … to your friends on January 1st?
3. … if you want to invite someone to a party?
4. … if you want to say "yes" to an invitation?
5. … to someone who has won a prize?
6. … if someone has cooked a very good meal?
7. … when someone offers you something to eat?
8. … to someone who is going on a holiday?
9. … if you have not been very nice to someone?
10. … if someone has given you something nice?

2 At the table

You are having your Christmas dinner. *Find the answer and complete the sentence.*

1. What about some more turkey?
2. Could you pass the salt, please?
3. Any more potatoes?
4. Do you need some salt?
5. Who'd like some more coffee?
6. Did you enjoy your dinner?
7. Well – who'd like to wash the dishes?

a) Oh, yes, please. With milk and …
b) No thanks. Everything's …
c) Sure. Here you …
d) Oh, yes! It was …
e) No thank you. They're … but …
f) Yes, please. It …
g) …

Stopover B

3 Role Play — Christmas time is party time

I'm going to have a Christmas party.	(Yes) I'd love to come.
▼	Great! I love parties.
Would you like to come?	Oh, thanks for inviting me.
I hope you'll be able to come.	Well, I'm not sure.
I'd like to invite you.	▼
	When is it/the party?
It's on … at … o'clock.	When should I come?
I'm going to have it on …	
Be here at …	Oh, that's fine.
	Right. I'm looking forward to it.
Good. See you on …	Well, I might be a bit late.
Don't forget now.	I'd love to come – but …
That's OK/too bad.	Oh dear, I can't manage it then
Oh – well, never mind.	because …
Perhaps another time, then.	I'm sorry, but …
Oh, come on now. Forget about/…	The problem is …

⟨4 A Christmas carol: Joy to the world⟩

Joy to the world! the Lord is come;
Let earth receive her King; Let ev-'ry
heart prepare Him room,
And heav'n and nature sing,
And heav'n and nature sing,
And heav'n and heav'n and nature sing.

2. Joy to the world! the Savior reigns;
   Let men their songs employ;
   While fields and floods,
   Rocks, hills, and plains

   Repeat the sounding joy,
   Repeat the sounding joy,
   Repeat, repeat the sounding joy.

---

1. joy – Freude   Lord – *hier:* der Herr   to receive – *hier:* empfangen   to prepare – (vor)bereiten
heav'n = heaven – Himmel   2. Savior – Erlöser   to reign – herrschen   their songs employ – *hier:* ihre
Lieder singen   floods – *hier:* Flüsse   plains – Ebenen   to repeat – wiederholen   sounding – schallend

⟨Unwanted guests⟩

1. It was four o'clock on Christmas Eve when the phone rang. "It's probably your dad – late again at the office party," said Bernadette's mom. But it wasn't Dad.
"Hello? – Oh, it's you, Father O'Reilly … Thank you, and the same to you … What? … But – but Father, it's Christmas Eve! … Yes, I know, but where can I put them? My sister's coming with her family all the way from Philadelphia, and … Vietnam? … Oh … I see … Yes … Goodbye, Father." Mom put down the phone. "What's the matter, Mom?" called Bernadette, but Mom was already dialing a new number.
"Hello? Can I have Mr Fitzgerald, please? … This is *Mrs* Fitzgerald … Thank you … Oh, Jack, it's me. Father O'Reilly has just called. He says we have to take two refugees for Christmas … no, not Christmas trees, dear, *refugees*, … Remember … Father O'Reilly asked us last summer … It seems there's no room for them anywhere else … Anyway, they're coming, and I need some help with the kids and the tree and everything … good … OK, Jack."
"What are refugees, Mom?" Bernadette asked because Mom wasn't very happy. "They're – they're people who have lost their homes, dear. Now – you know your aunt and uncle are going to have the big guest room and Cousin Linda the small one, so will you be Mom's big girl and let the refugees have your room? You can sleep with Gary." Gary was Bernadette's younger brother. Seven years old and really terrible.
"Mom!" This was awful. "Mom! You can't do that! It's Christmas! First you say I'm a big girl and then you say I have to sleep with my baby brother! It's my room and I'm keeping it! If you like your – your refugees so much, let them have *your* room!"
"Who's a baby?" Gary called. "But dear …" Mom said.
Bernadette wasn't listening. She ran up the stairs to her room. Inside, she turned the key. Nobody, *nobody* was going to get her room. It wasn't fair! Refugees – huh!
Half an hour later, Bernadette heard the doorbell, and then strange voices in the house. They were coming – coming to take her room. "Bernadette! Bernadette! Open the door!" her mom called. But Bernadette didn't move. Then everything was quiet. Soon she heard footsteps on the stairs. The voices and the footsteps went past her door and upstairs to the attic.

2. At about six o'clock, Bernadette heard Dad's car. She went downstairs to meet him. Dad came in with a red face and a big smile. "Well?" he said loudly. "Where are they?"
"Shhh, Jack! They're in the attic."
"In the attic? Isn't it a little cold up there?"

"Well, what could I do? Your daughter won't give them her room. And the worst thing is …" Mom whispered something into Dad's ear. Bernadette and Gary were never allowed to whisper. Typical!
"Pregnant?!" shouted Dad.
"Shhh! Not in front of the children!" said Mom. "Don't worry. They're looking for friends in California. They won't be here long: two or three days."
"Well, it's not right. She should be in the hospital. Christmas is for the family, and now we've got the house full of strangers from …"
Bernadette wasn't listening. She was thinking about her cousin Linda Conti. Linda was very pretty, and she knew it. When Linda and Bernadette went out together, all the boys wanted to talk to Linda. But this year would be different. Bernadette had spent all her pocket money on some "Teen-Glam" make-up (she hadn't told her parents). And Mom was going to give her that gold necklace – the necklace she had dreamed about for so long. She had seen a little packet from the shop in Mom's room! Mom always hid their presents under the bed. Bernadette looked around at the beautiful blue plastic Christmas tree. She thought of the colored lights on the trees in their garden and the electric sign over the door which said, "The Fitzgerald Family Wishes Everybody A Merry Christmas And A Happy New Year". Why wasn't she happy?

3. It was late. Bernadette's parents had gone to Midnight Mass. Bernadette had stayed at home to look after Gary. He was watching a late-night Western on TV. Suddenly, Bernadette heard something from upstairs. Was somebody crying? There – again. She went slowly up the stairs to the attic. Someone cried again. She knocked on the door. "Come in!" called a man's voice.
It was colder in the attic than in the rest of the house, although Mom had given the refugees an electric heater. There was one small light in the attic, an old table, two chairs, and some mattresses in the corner – that was all. This is awful! Bernadette thought. The woman was lying on the mattresses. She had cried out, and Bernadette, who liked watching hospital films on TV, could see why. She was having a baby!
"A baby – yes. We are so sorry. We didn't think – it is too early, you see. But the long trip … We are so sorry … Your family is very nice. But we didn't know …"
Bernadette's face was burning. Nice family! But there was no time to think about that now.
"I'll call the doctor," she said. "Your wife needs a doctor." "Yes …" said the man. "And please … perhaps some hot water." Bernadette ran to the telephone. She found the number of the family doctor, Dr. Wagner. She dialed and listened: "Good evening! This is a recorded message. Dr. Wagner is not in at this moment, but he will be back soon. Please leave your message, and the doctor will call you back." Peep! "Oh, Dr. Wagner, it's me, Bernadette Fitzgerald, you've got to come, she's having a baby, our refugee I mean. Please hurry!" There – the woman cried again. Hot water! Bernadette ran upstairs.
Just after midnight the child was there. "A girl," said Bernadette. "An American girl," said the new father. The mother smiled.
Not much later, Dr. Wagner arrived. He looked at the mother and the baby. "They're fine," he told the father. "But your wife and the baby will be more –" he looked around the attic "– more comfortable in the hospital. We'll find room for all three."
He looked at Bernadette. "You did a good job, Bernadette. I guess you need some sleep now."

4. Bernadette woke up. It was Christmas morning. It was time to open her presents – *the* present! And then she remembered what she had done with the necklace. What would Mom say? And Dad? The necklace had been expensive, she knew that. It was something special. It was beautiful and she had wanted it more than anything else. And now she had given it away. Her cousin Linda would laugh at her. She wouldn't understand. And Mom and Dad? Maybe they would be angry. So why did she feel so happy?

Stopover B

⟨5 Thinking about the story⟩

Can you read "between the lines"?

1. You only hear Mrs Fitzgerald's voice on the phone (lines 5–11). What do you think Father O'Reilly said?
2. Why does Mrs Fitzgerald say "Your daughter …" (and not "My daughter") in line 47?
3. How does Bernadette feel when she hears about the baby (line 70–71)? How do you know?
4. Why does the new father say the baby is "an American girl"? (line 82)
5. What exactly had Bernadette done with the necklace?
6. Bernadette's cousin Linda "wouldn't understand" (line 92) why she had done it. Do you?

6 What do you think of Christmas?

Here's what some American people think about Christmas.

1. I love getting ready for Christmas. I enjoy decorating the tree.
2. Spend, spend, spend! That's what Christmas means to most people.
3. Carol singing is great fun!
4. Christmas? Just boring.
5. We think it's fun to get lots of presents.
6. When Christmas comes at last, I'm too tired to enjoy it.

OVER TO YOU
a) *Do you agree with any of these people? Explain why.*
b) *What do you like best about Christmas? What don't you like?*

⟨7 Egg nog⟩

Egg nog – you can't have an American Christmas without it!

Here's what you need:

4 eggs
4 tablespoons of sugar
1 cup (= 25 cl) of
  whipping cream
liquid vanilla extract
nutmeg

– serves four –

Here's what you do:

1. Separate all egg whites from egg yolks.
2. Beat sugar into egg yolks.
3. Whip the cream and mix it into the egg and sugar mixture.
4. Whip egg whites separately.
5. Slowly put into egg yolk mixture.
6. Add vanilla.
7. Pour into glasses, put nutmeg on top.

Christmas Menu

Egg nog

* * *

Turkey with cranberry sauce
Roast potatoes and beans

* * *

Plum pudding with
brandy butter sauce

A At the truck stop

Speech bubbles (from the image):

- Dad! This hamburger is awful!
- You see, Steve! It would have been better if we had gone to McDuck's.
- So I say, "C'mon, be a friend, cop. I was only doing 60. I'm late." And he says, "If you had driven 55, I wouldn't have stopped you. You could have been half way to Texas by now."
- What are you so happy about?
- I'm looking forward to seeing Marc next week – that's my brother, you know.
- Oh dear, Jolene, it's very expensive here. But we don't have enough gas to get to the next station.
- I told you, Dad. If we had turned off the highway, we could have found a cheaper place.
- Gee, I'm still hungry …
- Well, if you had ordered the 'trucker's special', you would have had more to eat, Sal.

Sign: PETER SIMON PRESENTS / POP'S OASIS / CASINO – BAR – CAFE / TRUCKERS ½ PRICE ON FOOD / COORS DRAFT 35¢ / GLIDER RIDES DIESEL $1.04⁹ / CASH ONLY WITH PERMIT

1 What would have happened …

a) *Look at the text and put the sentences together.*

1. If Steve had gone to McDuck's,
2. If Sal had ordered the trucker's special,
3. If Mr Clarke had listened to Jolene,
4. If Jolene and her dad had had enough gas,
5. If the trucker hadn't been late,
6. If the policeman hadn't stopped him,

they would have found a cheaper gas station.
he wouldn't have driven so fast.
he could have been half way to Texas.
he would have had a better hamburger.
they could have gone on to the next station.
she wouldn't have been hungry after the meal.

⟨b⟩ What would Steve's dad/… have told them?⟩

    Example: Steve's dad: Well – put some ketchup on your hamburger.
                    or: Just add some salt!
              Jolene: …

"You should…"
"Don't buy so much…"
"Order some more…"
"Well, in future…"

2 Travel problems

a) "I'm not sure which road we should take."
"This stupid car – it's broken down."
"I don't feel well."
"This motel is full, too."
"Oh dear, I've lost my purse."
"I think we're out of gas."

If only

… we had stopped at the last gas station.
… you had not eaten so much.
… you had checked the engine.
… we had bought a map!
… we had booked a room.
… you had put it in a safe place.

Which sentences belong together?

Example: "I'm not sure which road we should take." – "If only we had bought a map!"

b) *Imagine you're on a cycling tour with a friend. What problems might there be? What would you say? Here are a few ideas:*

pump   food   nice beach   feeling comfortable at home

3 A bad night

Mr Clarke was taking Jolene back to San Francisco where she lives with her mother. It was a two-day trip. So they decided to spend a night at a motel. But all the motel rooms were full.

Jolene: If only we hadn't stopped on the way yesterday!
Mr Clarke: Yes – if we hadn't stopped on the way, we wouldn't have lost so much time! And if we hadn't …
Jolene: Yes. If we had …

Can you go on? arrive at the motel earlier → get a room → not spend the night in the car → be more comfortable → sleep better → not feel so tired in the morning

4 Look, listen and say

In English, the meaning of a sentence often depends on the emphasis that you give to the words. This example shows how the same sentence can have different meanings:

a) **I** didn't want to buy gas at that truck stop. (= it wasn't my idea, but someone else's.)
b) I didn't **want** to buy gas at that truck stop. (= but I had to; there was nothing else that I could do.)
c) I didn't want to buy **gas** at that truck stop. (= I wanted to buy something else there.)
d) I didn't want to buy gas at **that** truck stop. (= I wanted to get it somewhere else.)

Now read these sentences, and put the emphasis on different words in each sentence. Explain the different meanings.
1. We can't lend you our hockey stick. (emphasis on a) **we**; b) **lend**; c) **you**; d) **our**; e) **hockey stick**)
2. You'll never manage to start a business in Oshkosh. (a) **you**; b) **never**; c) **business**; d) **Oshkosh**)
3. Do you want to give me all those books? (a) **you**; b) **give**; c) **me**; d) **all**; e) **those**.)

5 At a motel

When you arrive at an American motel, you just ask for a room. The rooms all have bathrooms, and all cost the same, whether they are for one or two people. But you might want to know:

- how much the room costs.
- if the room has air-conditioning/color TV/ a telephone/a bath or a shower.

You might have to say:

- how long you want to stay.
- how you're going to pay: in cash/by credit card/by (traveler's) check.

If there aren't any vacancies you can ask:

- where else you might find a room.
- how far it is to the next motel.

a) *Complete these dialogues and act them with your partner.*
b) *Can you make more dialogues?*

Receptionist: Hello, can I help you?
You: Yes, I'd like …
Receptionist: Certainly. For how long?
You: Just for … – How much does …?
Receptionist: $21 a night.
You: That's okay. Do all the rooms have …?
Receptionist: Yes, they do. – How would you like to pay?
You: …
Receptionist: That's fine. Your room is number 23. It's in the second block on the left. Good night.

* * *

Receptionist: Sorry, we're full up.
You: Oh, dear. How far …?
Receptionist: Which way are you traveling?
You: Towards …
Receptionist: Well, there's a big motel 5 miles down the road.
You: …
Receptionist: Have a nice evening.

6 Just for fun

OK Gimme

OK Gimme
OK Gimme
2 Quarter Pounders
2 Cheeseburgers
4 Side orders of
French Fries
2 Coca-colas
2 Doc Peppers
All to go?
Yeah all to go
we got to go

Over 35 million sold
Over 35 million sold
Okay that will be
9 dollars and 50
Have a nice day
Have a nice day
Have a nice day

(Martyn Wiley)

OK Gimme is the rhythm of the whole poem. *Snap your fingers in time and read the poem all together. Then make three groups – blue, red and green – and read the poem as a dialogue.*

B My crazy dad

When Birgit Lehmann talked to the young people she met in America, she asked some of them about their families, and where they came from. Here is what Jolene Clarke told Birgit about her dad:

"My dad's 37, and he's been crazy for the last 37 years. I mean, that's what **he** says, and I believe him. He was born in Boston, but he's lived out West for a long time now. At first he wanted to be a cowboy in Texas, but he wasn't too good at that as he couldn't ride. Then he became a dog-catcher in San Francisco. The job looked as if it might be fun – until a dog bit him one day. After that he *almost* became a rock star. He's had his guitar for 20 years now, and he can still only play one song. Oh well. Then my dad had another idea. People who live in the desert need electricians who can repair their freezers and air-conditioning. So Dad bought a book "How to be an electrician", and a mobile home, and moved to Bluff City, Utah – which is so small that you can't find it on most maps. He often tells people about his first job there. "Can you fix this freezer?" a young woman asked him. "No problem. I've been an electrician for as long as I can remember," Dad said. He took it to pieces and then he couldn't put the pieces together again. That would have worried most people, but not my dad. Very soon he married the young woman – that's my mom, of course – and they got a new freezer. And me. I mean, I was born there, in the middle of the desert. I remember Bluff well, although I haven't been back there since the day that we left. It was OK in some ways. We could go rock-climbing in the canyons, and we had a raft on the San Juan river. We had made it ourselves. There was a café, a small motel, a gas station, and not much else. The nearest supermarket or movie theater or disco was 25 miles away. And the high school. Can you imagine driving 50 miles every day, just so that you can get to – ugh! – school and back? I'm glad we left, although I miss my dad. He became a good electrician later. But as a husband he was a little too crazy. I don't know. Anyway, my parents got divorced five years ago, and since then I've lived in San Francisco with my mom. Dad's in Arizona now, but he might move to Alaska next. You never know with my dad."

1 Looking at the text

a) 1. What jobs has Jolene's father tried?
2. Make a list of the places that Jolene talks about. Look them up on a map. Find out something about them.
3. Why do people call Jolene's father "crazy"?

⟨b⟩ 4. Do you think the things that Jolene tells Birgit could have happened in Germany?
5. Compare the life of Jolene's father to the life of "average" people.
Which of the two would *you* prefer?

2 It's been a long time!

What might Jolene's father tell you about his life?   *Make sentences with 'since' and 'for'.*
Example: I've had a crazy life for 37 years./... for as long as I can remember./... since the day that I was born.

I've	had a crazy life lived in the West been a good electrician had a guitar lived alone	since for	37 years. the day that I was born. a long time. 1970. I left Boston. many years. then. 20 years. I was seventeen. we got divorced. as long as I can remember.

How long?
– *since* Tuesday/1986/then/...
– *for* a week/years/a long time/...

3 Jolene – and you

a) *Put in 'since' or 'for'.*
  1. Jolene has lived in San Francisco ... five years now. 2. She hasn't been back to Bluff City ... the day they left. 3. Jolene goes to Redwood High. She has gone to school there ... she was twelve.
  4. She loves music, and has had a cassette-recorder ... last Christmas – a present from her dad.
  5. She doesn't like school at all. She hasn't liked it ... she went to high school in Utah. 6. Jolene and her dad haven't lived together ... her parents got divorced. 7. Jolene loves to go surfing. She has been able to surf really well ... last summer. 8. She spends a lot of time on the beach with Bryan – that's her boyfriend. She has known him ... two years now.

b) *Where do you live? How long have you lived there?*
   What school do you go to? And what about your free time and your friends?

   I live in ... . I've lived there ... .
   I go to ... . I've been a student there ... .
   In my free time/... . I can ... . I've been able to ... .
   My best friend(s) is/are ... . I've known her/him/them ... .

4 Role Play You could have done it by now!

Do you ever get angry when you have to wait too long for something or somebody?

> Hurry up! You've been in the bathroom for hours.
>
> I won't be long.
>
> Come on – you could have had **two** baths by now!

> Where are my records? You've had them for weeks.
>
> Oh, sorry, I forgot.
>
> You could have given them back by now!

Make more dialogues like this.

1. in the shop – choose ten T-shirts
2. on the telephone – talk to all the neighbors on the block
3. in the kitchen – make twenty sandwiches

1. magazine – read it
2. cassette-recorder – record your interview
3. maths book – do your homework

Unit 3 B

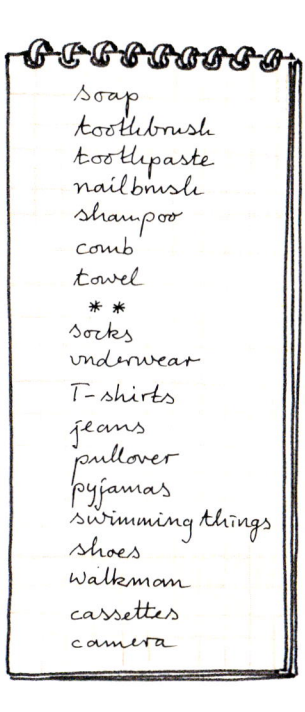

5 Things to take on a trip

soap
toothbrush
toothpaste
nailbrush
shampoo
comb
towel
* *
socks
underwear
T-shirts
jeans
pullover
pyjamas
swimming things
shoes
walkman
cassettes
camera

Remember Marc Ferranti from Pittsburgh? He is getting ready for his trip down to Florida with his sister Tessie. He has made a list of things that he wants to pack.

a) *Complete these sentences with words from the list.*
  1. I want to wash my hair. Have you got any …? 2. Oh, what can I wear in bed? I've forgotten to pack my …. 3. I can't dry myself with this …. It's too small. 4. I'm cold. If only I'd brought a …. 5. My hair looks so untidy, but I can't find my…. 6. Should I take a pair of good trousers with me? – No, your … will be all right.

b) *Make a list of the things that you would pack for a special trip.* (a trip to the mountains/a week at a big hotel in New York/a beach holiday/a cycling trip/…)

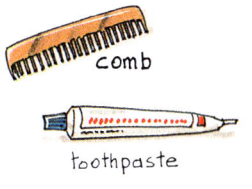

shampoo   pyjamas   towel   comb   toothbrush   toothpaste

6 Have you ever…?

Have you ever been in the desert?
Yes, I have. But it was too hot for me!

Have you ever traveled in a big truck?
No, I haven't. But I'd love to.

a) *Talk to your friends about some interesting things that they did. Ask questions with "Have you ever…?" Think about:* traveling, visiting places, moving, meeting people, earning money, taking part in interesting/crazy activities.

Here are some ideas to help you. Remember – your answers don't have to be true!

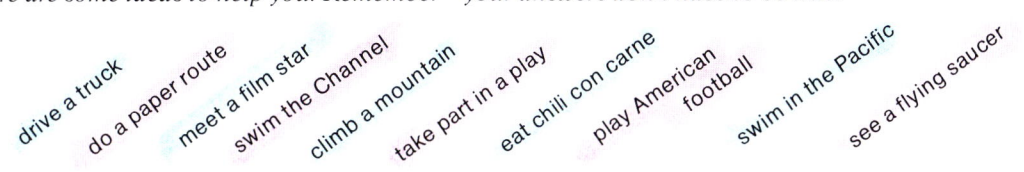

drive a truck   do a paper route   meet a film star   swim the Channel   climb a mountain   take part in a play   eat chili con carne   play American football   swim in the Pacific   see a flying saucer

⟨b⟩ *Activity:* Choose one topic (traveling, hobbies, meeting people …) and write a questionnaire for your classmates. Report the results to the class. How many of your classmates have been to a foreign country/at the seaside/…?

7 Jolene's dad

Put the sentences together.

1. Jolene's dad wasn't a good cowboy		he really knew all about freezers.
2. And a dog-catcher's job looked	so that	he couldn't ride.
3. After that he bought a guitar	as if	he can get a job in Alaska.
4. In Bluff City he talked	as	it might be too dangerous.
5. But he couldn't finish his first job		he could become a rock star.
6. Now he's learning about oil		an electrician.

C On the road with Tessie

"OK" Tessie Ferranti called. "Come on up!" It wasn't easy. Marc had to pull himself up, then hold on with one hand and open the door with the other – while his bag with all his things in it was in his mouth. But soon he was sitting next to his sister, high up in the big truck, and they were rolling out of the depot in Pittsburgh. At last! He was on his way to Florida!

As there was a lot of traffic, Tessie had to drive carefully through the city. But when they were driving south on Highway 79 she turned to Marc. "Feeling OK?" she asked. "You bet! I'm king of the road now," Marc answered. "Well, Marc, it's going to be a long ride down to Nashville, that's 500 miles away, in Tennessee. Why don't you try to sleep?" Sleep! Marc was much too excited, although it was four o'clock in the morning and he was tired. "I've looked forward to this trip since Christmas," he said.

Marc imagined he was driving the 35-ton truck: 18 wheels, 13 forward gears, 3 sets of brakes, on its way down to Nashville with heavy machine parts on board. Outside, the highway signs flashed by as if they were moving, too: "Gas-Oil: 75 miles"; "Don't drink and drive – the life that you save could be your own"; "Speed limit 55 mph". Inside, Tessie turned on the radio. "Hi, truckers, all you cowboys and cowgirls, this is Big John Trimble with your favorite country music from Jarell's truck plaza in Doswell, Virginia – and this is a real oldie: 'Truck Driving Man' by Dave Dudley."

The music started: "I wheeled into a truck stop in Texas …" Marc woke up. How long had he been asleep? Tessie was driving into a service station. "Fill her up!" she said to the girl there. The girl smiled at Marc. "You got a new partner, Tessie? He looks nice." "I don't know if he's nice. He's been asleep ever since Pittsburgh." "Aw, Tessie, you should have woken me up," Marc said. "Well, as you're awake now, let's have a cup of coffee. Come on, we've just got time if we hurry. You know I'm not allowed to drive for more than ten hours – then I have to take a rest. We've got to reach Nashville today. 29 cents a mile – time is money in this job."

Tessie pulled into the depot in Nashville just after two o'clock in the afternoon. Her company had booked a room for her at the truck stop next to the depot. She lay down on the bed and was asleep at once. Marc turned on the TV. A man in gray was saying, "It's all in here in this easy-to-read Bible, believe me. Now if you want to read the word of God, and I know you do, just send $ 5.99 to …" Click. Next station. Country music. Click. Sesame Street. Click. "Yesterday the President said …" Click. "It's the BIGGEST, BEST …" Click. Ah – an old Frankenstein movie.

The telephone next to Tessie's bed rang at seven. She was awake at once. "Yeah, Ferranti here … sure … OK." She put the phone down. "They've got her ready, Marc. It's whiskey down to Atlanta, Georgia now. But first let's have breakfast." "Breakfast? But it's seven o'clock in the evening." "Well, for me it's the start of another ten-hour day. And I like to start the day with a good breakfast."

Unit 3C

1 Getting the facts right

1. The truck was so high that …
2. When Marc was sitting next to his sister he felt as if …
3. He didn't want to sleep because …
4. Marc didn't hear the whole song 'Truck Driving Man' because …
5. They had a cup of coffee although …
6. Tessie didn't want to stay at the service station too long because …
7. As …, they didn't have to look for a room in Nashville.
8. When the phone rang Tessie was awake at once although …
9. She wanted to have 'breakfast' although …

2 Working with the text

1. Divide the text into different 'parts'. Give each 'part' a heading.
2. What does the text tell you about a trucker's way of life (the work that truckers do, the hours that they work, what they do after work)?
3. Do you think you would like to be a trucker? Say what you would (not) like about the job.

⟨3 Truck driving man⟩

This is a typical truckers' song.

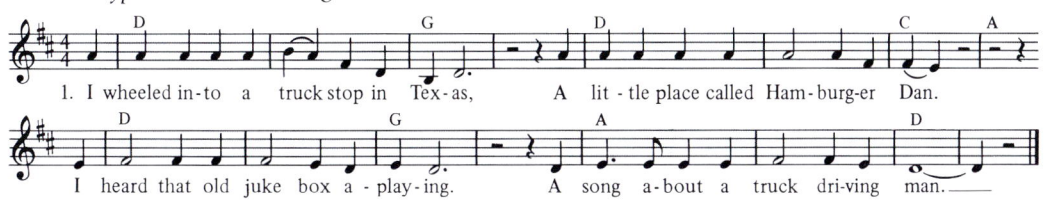

1. I wheeled in-to a truck stop in Tex-as, A lit-tle place called Ham-burg-er Dan.
   I heard that old juke box a-play-ing. A song a-bout a truck dri-ving man.

2. That waitress done brought me my coffee
   I thanked her and I called her back again
   I said you know that song sure do fit me
   I'm just a truck driving man

   Chorus:
   So pour me another cup of coffee
   For it is the best in the land
   And drop another quarter in the juke box
   For a song about a truck driving man

3. I climbed up aboard my old semi
   And like a flash I was gone
   Got all them big wheels a-rollin'
   I'm on my way to San Anton'

   Chorus

Work out these questions.

1. Where did the driver stop?
2. Why do you think he soon felt at home?
3. Why did the trucker like the juke box song?
4. Which words or expressions tell you that the trucker likes his job?
5. Where was he heading for?
6. Look at these adjectives and say what you think of the music of this song: exciting, slow, nice, fast.
7. *Activity:* Do you know any famous country singers? What kind of instruments do they play? Collect more information about country music.

Unit 3C

4 A difficult situation

At a truck stop near Atlanta, Georgia:
"I was in a difficult situation last night, Tessie. I was driving towards Macon when I saw a man on the road. He was standing next to his car. He stopped me because he had no gas, and his wife had to get to the hospital in Albany. The woman was lying in the back seat. She was very sick. – No, I don't think it was a trick. – But Albany was off my route, and anyway I was already late. If I'd taken them to Albany, I wouldn't have reached Atlanta last night. I would have had to stop somewhere. And I had fresh Florida pineapples on board. They might have gone bad. I could have lost my job …"

"So you left them there? But Frank, you could have …
　　　　　　　　　　　　　　you might have …
　　　　　　　　　　　　　　you should have …"

What do you think Tessie said? These ideas may help you:
call the cops/call other truckers on CB radio/drive faster/phone the company/take them to a different hospital/…　*What would you have done?*

Have you ever found yourself in any of these situations? Say what you did – and ask your friends what they would have done.　Example: If I had got lost in a strange town,
　　　　　　　　　　　　　　　　　　　　　　　　　　　　　　　　I would have gone …

break a neighbor's
window with a ball

get lost
in a strange town

see someone who is
doing something wrong

lose your way
in a forest

have no money
to pay for your meal

lose your keys and be
locked out of your house

5　Signs along the way

These are some of the signs that Birgit saw on her trip round the US. They told her …
– what she was/wasn't able to do.
– what she was/wasn't allowed to do.
– what she had/didn't have to do.

How many sentences can you make?

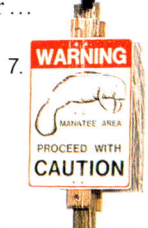

1. PANTHER CROSSING NEXT 7 MI.
2. GOOSE CROSSING
3. HANDICAPPED PARKING
4. SLOW CHILDREN
5. HORSE CROSSING
6. WARNING WILD ELEPHANT SEALS STAY BACK 20 FEET
7. WARNING MANATEE AREA PROCEED WITH CAUTION

　　　　　　　　　　　　　　　　Examples: She had to watch out for …
　　　　　　　　　　　　　　　　　　　　　　She wasn't allowed to drive very …

Unit 3C

⟨Getting around in the USA⟩

"There is very little public transport in most American cities. Young people that can't drive themselves have to ask their parents to take them where they want to go. So learning to drive and getting a driver's license is more important to the average teenager than anything else in life. To be grown-up is to be "free". And to be "free" – in the USA – you have to be able to drive.

There are drive-ins all over the USA – drive-in cinemas, drive-in banks, drive-in restaurants, drive-in stores – even drive-in churches.

Americans fly a lot, too! There's a plane from N.Y. to Washington, D.C. every hour.

Many young people who want to tour around the USA go by Greyhound bus. With a Greyhound ticket, you can get almost anywhere – and it's cheap.

Traveling by train seems old-fashioned to most Americans. But you *can* travel by train between most big cities. One of the most famous modern trains, the San Francisco Zephyr, follows the wagon train of the pioneers between Chicago and California."

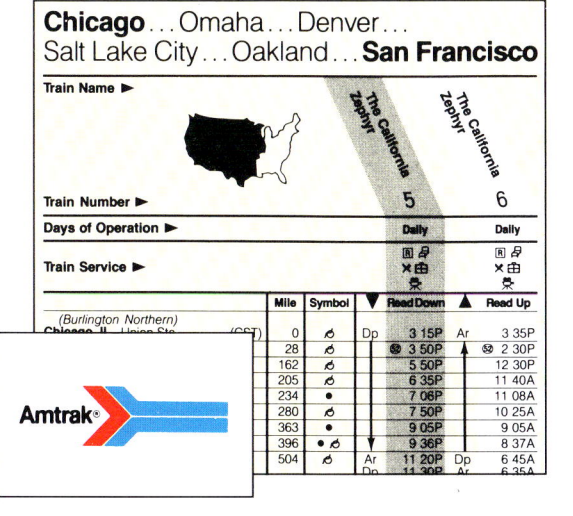

Unit 3C

6 On the road again

On her next trip, Tessie had to take California oranges all the way to Wyoming.
Put these sentences together, and you will have the full story:

1. As she had a long way to go,
2. Although there wasn't much time in the morning,
3. As she knew the roads well,
4. Although she wasn't allowed to drive fast,
5. As she had friends at Bell's Truck Stop,
6. Although she had asked for a 4.30 am call,
7. Although it was a long way to Cheyenne,
8. As she didn't have to leave again until next day,

she stopped there for the night.
she still traveled more than 500 miles that day.
she got up early.
she was already awake at 4 am.
she delivered the oranges in time.
she had a good breakfast before she left.
she was able to have a good rest.
she didn't need a map.

7 Listening comprehension: Breakfast at the Hungry Horse Truck Stop

a) *Listen to the recording first. Then answer these questions.*

1. Who do Tessie and Marc meet when they go in?
2. What do Tessie and Marc order?
3. Why do the truckers laugh when the waitress brings the things?
4. What does Tammy tell Marc when he goes to help?
5. What do the truckers think of this?
6. What do Tessie and the other truckers do before they leave? Why?

b) *Listen to the recording again. Check your answers to the questions in a). Now write a short summary of what happened at the truck stop that evening.*

8 The country star

Sarah Rosenbaum's favorite country star is Debbie Preston. Sarah herself plays in a country group with her friends Janey and Don. They call themselves The Denver Dreamers, and they play at a lot of school dances and concerts. They practice very hard. One day Janey and Don were just arriving at Sarah's house when … *Go on with the story.*

1. arrive – fall down – drop 2. take out – guitar – broken – not be able to repair 3. unhappy – no money – say 4. go – city center – start to sing 5. people – listen – throw – money 6. see – in crowd – think 7. enjoy – music – give – enough for a new guitar

48

A This is California

UNIT 4

When you think of California, you probably think of sun, sand and surfing. But that's only a small part of California. This state has every kind of landscape that you can imagine. There are snowy mountains, hot deserts and very good 5
farm land.

There are great national parks with rivers and forests, and huge cities with people of all
10 kinds and races.

The North of California can be cool. San Francisco has a pleasant climate, but did you know that sea-fog often hides the Golden Gate Bridge from view? And in the hot South the buildings have to have air-conditioning. You often have to put on a jacket when you go *inside*!   15

In places like Los Angeles the pollution from a million cars and air-conditioning units makes the blue sky
20 grey in the middle of the summer. But in the clear air of the wilderness you can see further than you ever thought possible.

Unit 4 A

It has the tallest trees in America, the giant redwoods. Many of them are over 120 meters. It also has the oldest trees on earth. Some of them are 4,600 years old.

California has the highest mountain in the USA outside Alaska (Mount Whitney, 4,418 meters above sea-level), and only 140 kilometers away the lowest place in the USA, in Death Valley, 86 meters below sea-level.

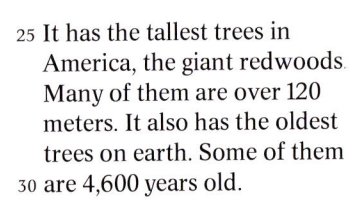

California is a very rich state. It is famous for its oil, its computers and its film industry in Hollywood. People in Europe often don't know that California is one of the most important industrial states in the USA. The agricultural production is higher than in any other state.

60% of the population live in the South of California, where they have a huge problem – water. It doesn't look like such a problem when you see all the swimming-pools in the gardens there. In fact the largest water system in the world brings an extra 9,000,000,000 (nine billion!) liters of water daily from mountain rivers nearly 600 kilometers away. That's another record for California!

50

Unit 4 A

1 Get it right

1. *Look at the text again.*
   a) Make a list of the different kinds of landscape in California.
   b) Find the information that the text gives you about the climate in different parts of California.
   c) Say which records California holds.

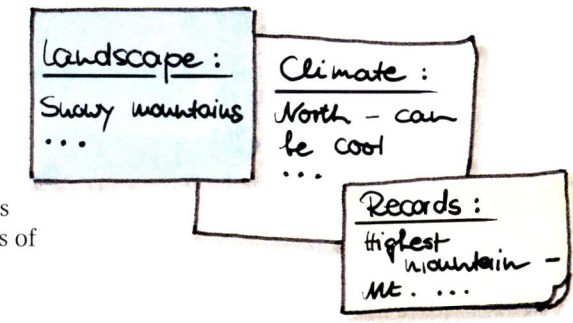

2. *Now look at the information that you have collected and see what contrasts you can find.*
   Example: California has got very good farm land, but it has also got wilderness where nothing grows.

3. *Find out from the text* – why the sky above Los Angeles is often grey.
   – what California is famous for.
   – why California is a rich state.
   – where most of the water in the South of the state comes from.

2 What did you know?

a) *What facts in the text did you know already? Where did you get the information?*

   I already knew that … I saw on TV that …
   I read about … in a book/magazine. I watched a film that showed …

b) *What was new to you in the text?*

   I didn't know that … I hadn't heard before that … It was new to me that …

⟨c⟩ *Activity: Do you know anything else about California that isn't in the text? Collect as much extra information as you can.*

3 Looking at the language

1. Find all the words in the text that mean 'big' or 'very big'.
   Now check again which of these words go with: mountain, tree, city, national park, problem.
2. Find the words in the text that mean a) in the world b) the people who live in a place c) a hot and very dry part of a country d) every day.
3. Now try to explain these words yourself: fog, farm land, air-conditioning, climate.

   Example: You have fog when warm air meets cold air. In San Francisco they even have …

⟨4 Activity⟩

Look at the pages about California again. Work with a partner and write a magazine page about the part of Germany where you live. Think of:

- the landscape
- the climate
- the people
- important industries
- other special facts and figures
- interesting photos

Unit 4B

B A letter to a pen pal

'Light' temblor felt from Santa Cruz to Pin

earthquake registering 4.5 on the Scale shook the Bay Area from Santa Cruz County to Marin and Costa counties early today. There reports of injury or serious dam—

U.S. Geological Survey's national ke center in Golden, Colo., called or "light" while the University of Seismology Station at Berkeley "moderate."

stations put the epicenter on the eas Fault at about 10 miles north of

Watsonville.
Police switchboards all over the Bay Area received hundreds of calls after the 1:44 a.m. shake, which was felt for 70 miles from Santa Cruz to Pinole.

Downtown San Francisco high-rises swayed with the jolt for about five seconds, according to night workers and apartment residents.

A San Jose police dispatcher said residents said the earthquake was a "single, sharp shock," while residents of the East Bay described it as a "rocking and gentle

gliding" motion.
San Jose police communicatio for Rich McIntosh said: "One ma woke up on the floor. A few oth said they were thrown out of be haven't heard of any injuries or age."

Residents of Cupertino and San items were "knocked from the sh their homes.

Callers to radio stations repor damage — broken glass and dish
—See back pa

15th February

Jolene Clarke
646 MacArthur Drive
San Francisco, California 94187

Dear Sandra,

I was so pleased to get your letter. Sure, I'd love to be your pen pal! Let me tell you something about myself. I'm 15 years old and I'm in 9th Grade. I don't like school very much but my favorite subjects are Biology and Art. I live with my mother here in San Francisco — my parents are divorced. That's not so nice. My hobbies are surfing, painting, and watching old Walt Disney cartoons. I'd like to work for a cartoon film company when I leave school.

You ask in your letter about our famous cable cars. Well, a lot of our streets are so steep that in the old days the horses weren't able to pull the wagons up and down the hills safely. So someone invented the cable car. There's an underground cable that pulls the cable cars up and down. It's very slow, but very safe. The steep streets are still a problem in modern San Francisco. There's a law that when you park your car you have to turn your front wheels to the sidewalk — so that the car doesn't start to roll down the hill!

You also ask if we aren't afraid of earthquakes in San Francisco. Well, the last big one was in 1906. It was a terrible day in the history of this city. Thousands of houses collapsed, and then fire broke out. The people of San Francisco weren't able to put out the fire for three days — until it rained. My mom always puts a glass on a plate next to her bed, and when we have a tremor, the glass makes a noise so that she wakes up. They say it's only a question of time until there is another big earthquake, but until now we have only had little tremors.

Now I have some questions for you. In your last letter you told me something about your hobbies. But you didn't write me anything about your family. Do you have any brothers or sisters? And I also want to know what life is like for you kids in Germany. It must be different from the life that we have over here. And can you tell me something about the school that you go to? I'm looking forward to hearing from you. Write soon.

Love from

Jolene

Unit 4B

1 Notes

a) *Here are some notes about Sandra. Have a look at them, then take down the same kind of notes about Jolene.*

⟨b⟩ *Can you answer Jolene's letter? Look again at the questions which Jolene asked, and use the notes on the left.*

> 14 years old
> favorite subjects
>   English, Art
> lives with
>   parents
>
> has 2 older brothers
> hobbies: playing
>   tennis, painting,
>   watching adventure
>   films

2 San Francisco

What can you find out about San Francisco? Complete these sentences.
1. The horses weren't able to pull the wagons safely because … 2. The cable car has that name because … 3. You have to turn the front wheels of your car to the sidewalk when … 4. They made this law so that … 5. 1906 is an important date in the history of the city because … 6. The fire burned until … 7. Jolene's mother keeps a glass on a plate next to her bed so that … 8. There have only been small tremors although …

3 Pen pals

Will you be my PEN PAL? Write your first letter to my box number	Susie Hernandez (14), Los Angeles. Hobbies: dancing, pop music, clothes. Box no. H 4836	John Cooper (16), New York. Hobbies: country music, guitar, reading. Box no. O 5318	Claire Bates (15), Laramie, Wyoming. Hobbies: computer games, collecting old teddies, riding, watching old movies. Box no. T 7229	Harry Hopper (15), Oshkosh, Wisconsin. Hobbies: magic tricks, cross-country skiing, collecting jokes. Box no. H 4837
	Paul MacArthur (17),	Mary Randall (13),		

a) Magazines can sometimes help you to find a pen pal.
  1. What information does the magazine give you about these people?
  2. Who would you like to write to? Give reasons.

b) *Write a letter to a pen pal.*
  Choose a pen pal from the people above and write a letter. You can tell your pen pal something about yourself, your family and where you live. Then think what you would like to know about him/her, and ask some questions.

4 Life in San Francisco

Complete the dialogues. Where do you need 'the'?
1. "You like …, don't you? Let's go to the Golden Gate Club." – "Oh yes, I love … that they play there!" (music)
2. "I've already spent … that Mom gave me last week." – "Never mind. We can go to the beach. You don't need … to have a good time there." (money)
3. "I hate … ." – "Yes, and I'll never finish … that I've got to do." (work)
4. "If you're interested in …, we can go and look at some pictures this weekend." – "I'd love to. I'm especially interested in … of the West Coast." (art)
5. "What's … ?" – "It's five o'clock already. … goes fast when you're surfing, doesn't it?" (time)
6. "… is great, don't you think?" – "Yes, it is, and in a place like San Francisco, you can live … of a king!" (life)

5 San Francisco's problems

What problems of city life are Jolene and her classmates talking about at school?
What do they think about these problems in San Francisco? crime poverty pollution noise

Example: Jolene is talking about **crime**. She thinks that **the crime** in San Francisco is getting worse.

1. *Jolene:* "You can't walk around safely. It's getting worse here in Frisco."
2. *Mike:* "There are so many poor people. It's terrible in parts of this city."
3. *Cliff:* "The air isn't at all clean here. But it isn't as bad here as in New York."
4. *Alison:* "You can hardly find a quiet place. It's worst near the airports."
5. *Bob:* "Building prisons isn't the answer. It's this city's biggest problem."

Now think of your town. What problems does it have?

6 Sandra's letter

Sandra is thinking about her letter to Jolene:

- Thank you for the letter. I got it last week.
- Hm – gefällt mir nicht. Irgendwie muß ich die beiden Sätze zusammenschieben.
- Thank you for the letter which I got last week.
- Aha! Das klingt jetzt viel besser!

Here are some more of Sandra's ideas.
Use relative clauses and put the sentences together.

1. I hope you like the photo.
   I am sending it with this letter.
2. I'm the tall girl.
   You can see me on the left.
3. My dad works for a big company.
   It sells all kinds of machine parts.
4. One of my brothers has a pen pal.
   He lives in Pittsburgh.
5. School's OK, but I don't like the homework.
   We get it every day.
6. I'm sending you a timetable.
   It shows all our subjects.
7. We have an English teacher.
   She makes the lessons very interesting.
8. Would you please send me some postcards?
   I can put them on my bedroom wall.

7 A nice place to live?

New York City	Oshkosh	Bluff City	San Francisco
a) Central Park The Statue of Liberty Macy's	a) Lake Winnebago Air Museum cross-country skiing	a) San Juan River desert rock-climbing	a) the Golden Gate Bridge people of all races cable cars
***	***	***	***
b) crime pollution	b) long winter small town	b) not many shops school far away	b) earthquakes sea-fog

Talk about these places. First look at the examples.

a) "I think New York is a great/… place to live." – "Yes, you can have lots of fun/… in Central Park."
b) "New York is a terrible/… place to live." – "Yes, just think of/… the crime there."

⟨California⟩

Having fun on roller-skates

San Francisco by night

Disneyland

Pioneer's 'reunion'

C Death Valley

1. The wagon train set off from Salt Lake City on the last part of the long journey across America to California. There were a hundred wagons with about four hundred men, women and children, and their horses and oxen. The year was 1849, the year of the gold rush.
It was late in the year. There was already snow on the usual trail. The wagons were trying to follow a horse-trail where wagons had never been before. It wasn't easy. When they met with a group of men on horseback who told them about a short cut to California, twenty-seven wagons decided to leave the wagon train and try to find it. Among these was the wagon with Louis Nusbaumer and his friends. Louis Nusbaumer, twenty-nine years old, had emigrated from the Black Forest in Germany to New York a year earlier, and when he heard about the gold in California, he had left his wife and baby in New York and set off west.

2. At first traveling was pleasant, and there was enough to eat and drink for the horses and oxen. But then it became hotter and drier. There was no more water and grass, only sand and rock. Some wagons began to fall behind, and soon there were only seven wagons together. The weeks that followed were terrible. The ground was so hot that the people had to tie pieces of leather not only around their own shoes but also around the hooves of the animals. And if they had not met Indians who showed them where there was good water, they would have died.

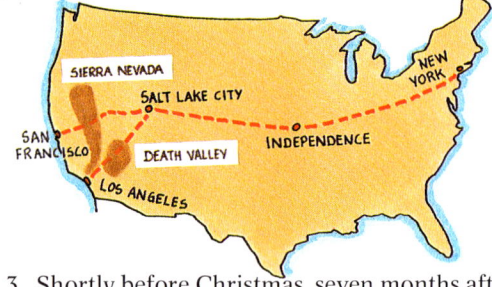

3. Shortly before Christmas, seven months after Nusbaumer had left New York, the wagons moved over a hill. In front of them they saw a huge valley, long and deep with tall mountains on every side. And in the valley was a huge lake. Water at last! They hurried on, but they found that the water was only a mirage. And on Christmas Day one of the two oxen that were pulling Nusbaumer's wagon became sick. Nusbaumer and his friends had to leave it and the wagon and go on foot with one ox, which carried as much as possible. Sometimes they found water, but often they were terribly thirsty. Nusbaumer once tried to exchange his last two shirts and his coat for a drink from a man who still had water, but the man just turned away. Later Nusbaumer and his friends killed the ox and drank its blood.

4. They could find no way out of the valley that was later called 'Death Valley'. On January 14th, 1850, the people who were still together decided that the two strongest men should try to find a way out, and the others would stay in the valley. The two men planned to come back in ten days. But when they had still not come back after twenty-three days, Nusbaumer and his two friends joined a family called Ehrhardt and set off in their wagon. And for the first time on the whole journey luck was on Nusbaumer's side. Two weeks later, on February 22nd, they at last came out of the desert and saw the Mojave River in California. On March 1st, almost a year after Nusbaumer had left New York, he had a meal at a Spanish ranch. It was the best food and drink that he had ever tasted.

Unit 4C

This story about Louis Nusbaumer is a true story. We know what happened from the diaries which Nusbaumer wrote on his journey.
The two men who had set off alone from Death Valley came back after 26 days, three days after Nusbaumer had left. They led the other men, women and children to safety.
45 Nusbaumer stayed in California and in 1851 his wife came with their son by sea to join him. He didn't find gold – he became a farmer.
Thousands of people went west in the gold rush of 1849. They were called the 'Forty-niners'. Between 1846 and 1856 more than a million Germans emigrated.

1 Nusbaumer's journey

1. Louis Nusbaumer left New York
2. He joined a wagon train
3. Twenty-seven wagons left the others
4. Although the journey was pleasant at first
5. Many of the animals died
6. The people came into a huge valley
7. They couldn't find a way out of the valley
8. They waited 23 days for the two men
9. As the men didn't come back
10. He arrived in California almost a year

a) traveling soon became very difficult.
b) Nusbaumer set off with the Ehrhardt family.
c) which later got the name 'Death Valley'.
d) because he wanted to find gold.
e) after he had left New York.
f) with about a hundred wagons.
g) because there was no grass or water for them.
h) so two men set off alone.
i) who were trying to find a way out.
j) when they heard about a short cut.

2 Talking points

1. What problems did Nusbaumer have on his journey? What other problems might he have had?
2. When people are in a really serious situation, they sometimes do things that they wouldn't usually be able to do. Can you find an example of this in the text?

OVER TO YOU Could you have done this? Say why or why not.

3 A trip to Death Valley

Bryan is telling Jolene a true story about himself. *Put in 'a' or 'an', but only where you need it.*

"It happened ? few years ago in the summer. My big brother had just bought ? old car, and he decided to take me to Death Valley. I was really excited about it. I had seen ? lots of pictures of Death Valley, but I had never been there myself. Well, we got there all right, and we were driving along at ? slow speed. There weren't ? lot of other cars around. (I didn't know that although ? lots of tourists visit Death Valley in the winter, it isn't ? good idea in the summer.) It was ? terribly hot day. I was thinking of the poor people who had had to cross Death Valley on foot more than ? hundred years ago, when suddenly the car broke down. My brother, who's ? taxi-driver, jumped out and had ? look at the engine, but he didn't know what was wrong. We had to wait until the next car came along. Well, I've never been in ? hot place like that in all my life. I was very thirsty, and soon I had ? headache, too. I looked at my watch two or three times ? minute. Each minute was like ? hour. We probably only waited about half ? hour, but it seemed ? very long time. At last another car came. What ? good luck – the driver was ? mechanic! He fixed our car for us: all we needed was ? little water. Then we drove out of Death Valley as quickly as possible!"

Unit 4C

4 What did you think of it?

I thought it was very interesting.

What did you think of Nusbaumer's story?

I've never read such a good story.
I couldn't put it down!

Who wants to read about things that happened over 100 years ago?

I didn't like it.

Now make short dialogues about:
*books that you've read *films that you've seen *TV programs that you've watched
*records/cassettes that you've heard *museums/… that you've visited
For more help look at page 153.

⟨5 Can you explain?⟩

You have a friend from the USA who knows hardly any German. So there are a lot of signs in your town which he doesn't understand. *Explain what they mean – even if you don't know the proper translation for some of the words.*

Abfahrt der Busse
↓ Ausgang Mitte
← Gleis 1 u.103 u. 104
Stadtmitte → Ausgang Ost
ANKUNFT DER ZÜGE:

P Central Parkhaus

Privataufzug! Nur für Besucher der Ladengeschäfte

Fußweg zum Krankenhaus

Motorräder und Fahrräder abstellen verboten

Für Garderobe keine Haftung

Jugendliche unter 16 Jahren erhalten keinen Alkohol

Frühstück bis 11 Uhr

Stück Pizza auch zum Mitnehmen 2.50

6 55 miles an hour

| 15¢ a pound | 29¢ a mile | 55 miles an hour | $21 a night |
| 35 miles an hour | 50 miles a day | 10 hours a day | a year |

Fill in:

1. In most American states you mustn't drive faster than … . 2. Strawberries are cheap in California. They cost … . 3. Motels are cheap, too. Some rooms cost only … . 4. Tessie Ferranti earns … . 5. She is allowed to drive … . 6. When she lived in Bluff City, Jolene's mother had to drive her … to get to school and back. 7. In San Francisco, they have a few small tremors … . 8. Bryan and his brother drove through Death Valley at a very slow speed, only … .

⟨7 Listening comprehension: Calico Ghost Town⟩

Calico Ghost Town is in the middle of the desert between Los Angeles and Las Vegas. For 50¢ visitors can listen to a recorded talk about it. *Listen carefully two or three times. You can make notes while you listen.*

a) *Complete these sentences:*
   1. People started living in Calico in 1882 when … .
   2. Walter Knott bought the town and … . 3. One day a dog arrived out of the desert and two brothers … .

b) *Tell the story of the dog in your own words.*

Stopover C

AMERICA: LAND OF THE INDIANS?

1 The trail of tears

At the beginning of the 19th century, the Cherokee Indians lived on good land in Tennessee and Georgia. They did not have any trouble with the whites who had settled there. They learned from the European settlers, and built their own roads, schools and churches. They had their own alphabet; Sequoya, a Cherokee Indian who had never been to school himself, had developed it. But in the 1830s white men found gold in the mountains that belonged to the Cherokees. The white settlers wanted to have the land for themselves, and the government agreed to move the Indians away.

still/happily
usually/already
quickly/soon
even
immediately/soon

The Cherokees were peaceful people, and they did nothing to stop the soldiers who came in the fall of 1838. A few hundred of them escaped to the Smoky Mountains. The others – over 10,000 – had to move to Indian Territory. It was a long long way, and fall changed to winter. The weather was cold and wet, and many Indians became ill. By the time they reached their new "home" in Oklahoma, nearly 2,000 of them had died of cold or hunger. They developed their land in Oklahoma and started a new life there, but they never forgot this terrible journey west. Cherokees call it "the trail of tears".

suddenly
only/secretly
slowly
quickly
terribly/soon
already
soon/bravely
sadly

a) *With the help of adverbs, you can give extra information – and make a text more interesting. When you have read the text, write it with the adverbs at the side.*
b) *Find the most important information in the text and write a short summary of it. Use your own words as much as you can.*

2 Life on Indian reservations

Complete the text. Adjective or adverb?

In the 19th century the white Americans … moved into more and more Indian country. They drove the Indians from their own … land and put them into … reservations. Often these reservations were thousands of miles away from their … home. Today, a … number of North American Indians still live on reservations. There are over 200 altogether. Some of them are very …, but there are some … reservations, too, … in South Dakota and in Arizona. The … thing is that much of the land that now belongs to the Indians is …; although most Indians on today's reservations are farmers, it is often … for them to grow … crops. Many Indians, like the Navajos, cannot live … on a reservation. For hundreds of years they moved about … from place to place, and now their only home is a reservation that is … desert.

slow
good
special
real
large
small
huge
main
sad
poor
hard
good
happy
free
main

Of course, Indians are allowed to leave their reservations, but they do not settle … in white towns, because the whites' way of life is so … from their own. Another … reason is that the education that Indians … get on their reservations is often not … enough to prepare them … for jobs in the white community. Indians who cannot find work in the cities often go back to their reservations in the end. Some become "tourist Indians" – they sit … at the side of the road and offer tourists … carpets and other Indian goods. Others … give up hope. Unemployment among Indians is a … problem and there is a lot of poverty. So it is hardly … that so many Indians become alcoholics. And although their population is growing …, the suicide rate is very …

easy
different
important
usual
good, good
quiet
pretty
slow
great
surprising
quick
high

59

Stopover C

⟨3 Alone against Apaches⟩

The Apache Indians lived in the American Southwest – the dry desert country of Arizona and New Mexico. For 250 years the Spanish settlers in Mexico had been their enemies. When the first white American settlers moved west to Arizona, the Apaches allowed the pioneers to go through their country on the way to California. They also hoped that the new settlers would help them to
5 *fight the Mexicans. But the white Americans did not trust the wild-looking Apaches, and fighting soon broke out between them. The great Apache chief, Cochise (1815–1874), who had wanted peace with the whites at first, now tried to drive them out of Apache country. He and his 300 warriors attacked settlements and wagon trains. During the 1860s not many white families in the Southwest felt safe.*

10 *There are many stories about this time of American history. Here is part of one by the famous Western writer, Louis L'Amour.*

White in the face, Angie Lowe stood in the door of her cabin with a shotgun in her hands. Beside the door was a Winchester, and on the table inside the house were two Walker Colts. 15
Outside the cabin were twelve Apaches on ponies, and one of the Indians had lifted his hand. The Apache on the white pony was Cochise.
Beside Angie were her seven-year-old son Jimmy 20 and her five-year-old daughter Jane.
Cochise sat on his pony without a word; his black eyes carefully looked at the woman, the children, the cabin, and the small garden. He looked at the two ponies in the corral and the 25 three cows.
Three times the warriors of Cochise had attacked this lonely cabin and three times the whites had turned them back. His warriors reported that there was no man in the house, 30 only a woman and two children. So Cochise had come himself to see this woman who used a shotgun so well against his fighting men.
These were some of the same fighting men who had beaten the finest American army, an army that
35 had outnumbered the Apaches by a hundred to one. Yet a woman with two small children had fought them off, and the woman was hardly more than a girl. The Apache's old eyes looked at her. He was a fighting man, and he understood fighting blood.
"Where is your man?"
"He has gone to El Paso." Angie's voice was steady, but she was frightened as she had never been
40 before. She recognized Cochise from descriptions, and she knew that if he decided to kill her, he would do it.
"He has been gone a long time. How long?"
Angie found that she could not lie. "He has been gone four months."
"Your man is dead," Cochise said.
45 Angie waited. Her heart beat heavily. She had guessed long ago that something had happened to Ed, but the way Cochise spoke did not seem to say that Apaches had killed him, only that he must be dead or he would have come back.
"You fight well," Cochise said. "Against my young men."
"Your young men attacked me. They stole my horses."
50 "Your man is gone. Why do you not leave?"

Angie looked at him with surprise. "Leave? Why, this is my home. This land is mine. This spring is mine. I won't leave."

"This was an Apache spring," Cochise reminded her.

"The Apache lives in the mountains," Angie answered. "He does not need this spring. I have two children, and I need it."

"But when the Apache comes this way, where shall he drink? His mouth is dry and you keep him from water."

The fact that Cochise was ready to talk raised her hopes. There had been a time when the Apache and the white man were friends. "If the people of Cochise come in peace," she said, "they may drink at this spring."

The Apache smiled a little. He looked at Jimmy. "The small one – does he also shoot?"

"He does," said Angie proudly. "And well, too!" She pointed to a leaf of prickly pear. "Show them, Jimmy."

The prickly pear was at least two hundred yards away, and the Winchester was long and heavy, but he lifted it as his father had taught him, held it carefully, then fired. The leaf on top of the prickly pear was gone.

The warriors looked at each other in surprise. "The little warrior shoots well," Cochise said. "It is good that you have no man. You might raise an army of little warriors to fight my people."

"I have no wish to fight your people," Angie said quietly. "Your people have your way of life, and I have mine. I live in peace when your people leave me in peace."

The Apache looked at her, then turned his pony away. "My people will worry you no longer," he said. "You are the mother of a strong son."

"What about my two ponies?" she called after him. "Your young men took them from me."

Cochise did not look back, and the other Apaches followed him away. Angie stepped back into the cabin and closed the door. Then she sat down. Her face was white, and her legs were trembling. When morning came, she went to the spring for water. Her ponies were back in the corral. The Apaches had returned them during the night.

(*From:* Louis L'Amour: *The Gift of Cochise*, adapted)

P.S. By 1875 most of the Apache Indians were on reservations – or had moved to Mexico. Cochise himself died on a reservation in 1874. But the few Apaches in Arizona still "made trouble" for the whites until 1886, when an American army of 5,000 soldiers went out to fight against the last famous Apache chief, Geronimo, and his "army" of 24 warriors. They took the Apaches and sent them to a prison camp far away in Florida. So the great days of these famous Indians ended.

⟨4 Understanding the story⟩

1. Why did Cochise want to see the woman with his own eyes?
2. How did Angie recognize Cochise?
3. Why was she very frightened?
4. Where was Angie's husband?
5. Why were the Indians surprised?
6. Cochise said: "My people will worry you no longer." How did Angie know that Cochise wasn't lying?

⟨5 Talking points⟩

1. How were Angie and her children able to turn back the warriors?
2. Would you have left the land if you had been in Angie's place? Say why you would have left or stayed.
3. Talk about the difference between the Apaches in this story and the Cherokee Indians that you read about in 'The trail of tears'.

6 Cowboys – some facts that you may not know

Put in the verbs in the correct form. Be careful. Sometimes you will need to use two verbs together.

All of us … often … (see) cowboys on TV. People who …… (enjoy/watch) Westerns usually … (think) they …… (be able to/imagine) exactly what cowboys in 19th century America … (be) like. But the picture of a cowboy's life that we … (see) in films … (be) really far from the truth.

Cowboys in Westerns … (be) always white. But really the 19th century cowboy … (be) often black or brown (Mexican). There … (be) even a few Indian cowboys, especially in Oklahoma. The cowboys that … (appear) in films … not … (work) with cattle; they usually … not …… (have to/work) at all! The Hollywood cowboy hero … (ride) after bandits and … (rescue) pretty young ladies from dangerous situations. He …… (be able to/use) his gun at fantastic speed, and he … (be) good at … (fight) with his hands, too.

Real cowboys in those days … not … (have) time for bandits. They …… (have to/work) hard; they usually … (work) 10–14 hours a day, summer and winter. They …… (have to/round up) the cattle, and then they … (drive) the animals many long miles to the train stations. From there, trains … (take) the cattle to slaughterhouses in Chicago and Kansas City. The cowboys' most difficult job was … (drive) the cattle from Texas to the nearest train stations. It usually … (take) two or three months, and during that time the cowboys always …… (have to/stay) with the cattle; they … (swim) across rivers with them and … (round up) all the animals again. It … (be) hard work, but the cowboys …… (love/look after) their cattle.

Stopover C

7 Indian problems

High suicide rate   Many reservations on poor land   High unemployment   'We can't go on like this'

If only things were better for the North American Indians …
Put suitable sentences together.

If the Indians lived on better land,	they might settle more easily in white cities.
If more Indians spoke English,	the suicide rate would go down.
If the schools on reservations were better,	they would be able to grow good crops.
If there weren't so many unemployed Indians,	more Indians would find good jobs.
If they had more help from the government,	there would be fewer alcoholics among them.
If the Indians had happier lives,	their chances in life would be greater.

8 What might have happened?

Find suitable endings to these sentences.

⟨a⟩ *Think about the story of Angie Lowe.*

Example: 1. If Angie Lowe had not been able to fight, …
              … she **wouldn't have had** a chance against the Apaches.
          or: … the Apaches **might have killed** her and her children.
2. If Angie's husband had not gone to El Paso, …
3. Jimmy would not have known how to use a gun if …
4. Angie would never have fought the Indians if …
5. If Cochise had not respected Angie so much, …

b) *Now think about the Cherokee Indians.*

1. If the whites had not found gold in the Cherokees' mountains, …
2. If the Cherokees had not been such peaceful people, …
3. Their journey west would not have been so terrible if …

9 Little words that mean so much

Read these "mini" dialogues.   "Did I step on your foot? Sorry!" – "That's all right."

"Yes please?" – "I'd like two hamburgers, please." – "Here you are." – "Thank you."

"Excuse me. Can you tell me the way to the station?" – "Certainly."

"Would you like another drink?" – "Pardon?" – "Would you like another drink?"
– "Oh, no thank you."   "How are you?" – "I'm very well, thank you."

"Can I carry your bag for you?" – "Oh, thank you – that's nice of you." – "You're welcome."

Now try to put these dialogues into good English.

1. „Bitte schön?" – „Ein Stück Erdbeerkuchen, bitte." 2. „Wie geht's deinem Vater?" – „Wie bitte?" – „Ich hab' gefragt: Wie geht's deinem Vater?" – „Danke, es geht ihm gut." 3. „Zwei Kaffee? – Bitte schön!" – „Danke." 4. „Möchten Sie noch Brot?" – „Danke, nein." 5. „Darf ich Ihnen helfen?" – „Danke schön. Sehr nett von Ihnen." – „Bitte sehr." 6. „Entschuldigung – wissen Sie, wieviel Uhr es ist?" – „Halb zwei." – „Vielen Dank." 7. „Könnte ich bitte noch Tee haben?" – „Aber selbstverständlich." 8. „Ich bin jetzt dran." – „Oh, Entschuldigung – ich habe Sie nicht gesehen." – „Bitte."

Stopover C

10 How to complain – when things go wrong

a) *There are times when it is best to complain by writing a letter. Like this:*

WESTWARD TRAIL ADVENTURE HOLIDAYS

Enjoy a completely different holiday this year – a holiday on the trail! Out in the open air day after day, moving westward by wagon train, just like in the old days! Complete with cowboys and Indians!

Write for details NOW!

Horizon Holidays
269 Elvis Presley Boulevard
Memphis
Tennessee

```
Dear Sir/Madam,
    I have just got home after 3 weeks on
one of your "Westward Trail" adventure
holidays. I am sorry to say that it was
the worst holiday I have ever booked.
    The wagons were dirty and let the rain
through, the beds were uncomfortable, and
the food at the camping-site was terrible.
Once we got no food at all because the
truck that brought it had broken down. The
Indians that we expected to "attack" us
never came, and the "cowboys" that we had
with us couldn't even shoot – or sing any
proper Western songs.
    I was very angry; this holiday was a
complete waste of money. I should be
pleased if you would refund my payment
immediately.
                        Yours faithfully,
                        Steve Casey
```

b) *You are in America! Imagine the following situations. Work in groups for this exercise.*

1. You and your friend are at a new snack bar. The food there is terrible. Complain to the girl behind the counter.
2. You have an appointment at the doctor's. You arrive on time. After two hours, it still isn't your turn. Complain to a nurse.
3. A few weeks ago you ordered two cassettes from a catalog – and sent the money for them. But they haven't arrived yet. Write a letter and complain.
4. You have taken a pair of shoes to a man to repair them. You have been to the shop to collect them three times now, and they are still not ready. Complain to the man in the shop.
5. You have bought a new bag, but you find that one of the zippers on it is broken. Take it back to the shop and ask the assistant to give you another one.

⟨**11 An Indian poem**⟩

Do you know what is wrong with the white people?
They have no roots.
They are always trying to plant themselves and yet
They will blow away in the wind because
They are born with wheels.

⟨**12 Song of Sitting Bull**⟩

A warrior
I have been.
Now
It is all over.
A hard time
I have.

A How is it done?

UNIT 5

BEHIND THE SCENES WITH FIZZ
SPECIAL EFFECTS
VIDEO TRICKS

You've seen a lot of trick photography at the cinema, haven't you? Or on TV? But have you ever thought how this photography is done? A lot of hard work goes into special effects like the ones that you've seen in films. Most of them are done with the 'Blue Screen' method. Pictures are taken separately. Then they are mixed electronically with other pictures. Here's how it works.

1 The TV news example: The newsreader sits in front of a blue screen. In the control room the blue background – or part of it – is filtered out of the TV picture, and other pictures (for example, maps or films) are put in its place. So the newsreader is seen with the other pictures in the background.

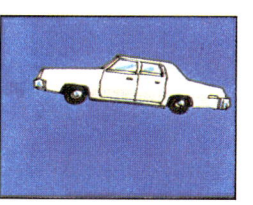

2 The flying car example: The car – or model of a car – is filmed against a blue background. The 'real' background for the film is taken with another camera. Then the blue background is filtered out of the first film, the two films are mixed – and there is the flying car!

3 The huge monster example: Have you ever seen a movie where a huge monster is chasing somebody? This is how effects like this are done. The monster (it might be a real ape, or a computer-controlled model) is filmed against – you've guessed it! – a blue background. And the girl is filmed against the real background, but from further away so that he or she looks smaller. Of course, when the two films are put together, the ape is changed into a huge monster, and the person looks much smaller.

Unit 5 A

1 Two boys on a flying carpet

Look back at the information in the text, then put the sentences together.

First the floor	is filtered out of the first film.
Then a carpet	are seen on a flying carpet.
And two boys on the carpet	is put on the floor.
Another film of the sky	is painted blue.
The blue background	are mixed electronically.
Then the two films	are filmed against a blue background.
And so the boys	is taken from a plane.

Start like this: First the floor is painted blue. Then a carpet is put …

2 Scenes from the movies

Jolene is telling her friends about *The Ghost House*, a movie that she has seen.

A ghost		seen changed	in an old castle.
Strange noises			in the night.
Two girls	is	felt pushed	through a dark forest.
A cold hand	are		on someone's face.
A car		driven	into a hole in the ground.
Some people		chased heard	out of a window.
A man			into a monster.

What does Jolene tell her friends? Start like this: The Ghost House is a very exciting movie.
In one scene a ghost is seen in an old castle. And there's a scene where strange noises … in the night.
In another scene … ." *Go on.*

3 Cartoons and computers

Fill in the correct passive forms of the verbs. Use the words from left to right.

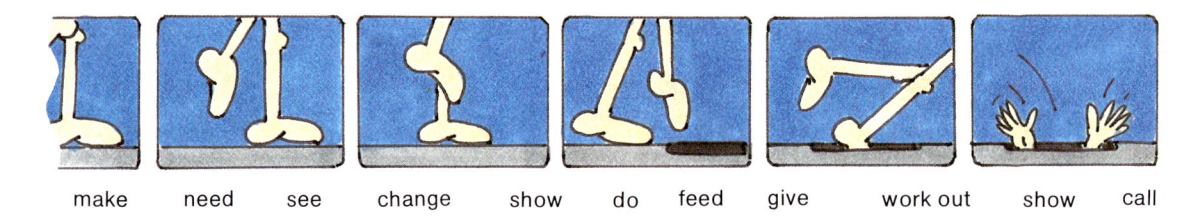

make   need   see   change   show   do   feed   give   work out   show   call

When a cartoon film …, thousands of pictures … . In these pictures the cartoon figures … in lots of different positions. In every picture the position … a little. So when the film … at the right speed, the figures look as if they are moving. In the old days people had to draw all these pictures, but now very often the work … with the help of computers. This is how computers make cartoon films. Think of a short scene where one of the figures is walking. The first position of the legs … into a computer, and the last position …, too. With this information the computer can draw all the other pictures. The correct leg positions … much more quickly on a computer than a person could work them out. The computer pictures … on a screen. This method of making cartoon films … 'inbetweening'.

66

4 The special effects people

Bryan Schulz and some of his friends are visiting a famous special effects studio just north of San Francisco. Ken Smith, who works there, is showing them around.

Ken: In the model shop here, we *build* exact models of things like cars or spaceships. And in the monster shop over there, we *make* all kinds of monsters and strange animals. Look at this one here!

Bryan: Wow! How does it move?

Ken: We *use* two different methods. With the older method we *photograph* the monster, then *move* it a little, then *photograph* it again, and so on. Then, when we *run* the film at the usual speed, the monster seems to move. With the more modern method we *use* computer-controlled models. We get a more realistic effect with them.

Jolene: What about the fantastic backgrounds for some movies? How do you *make* them?

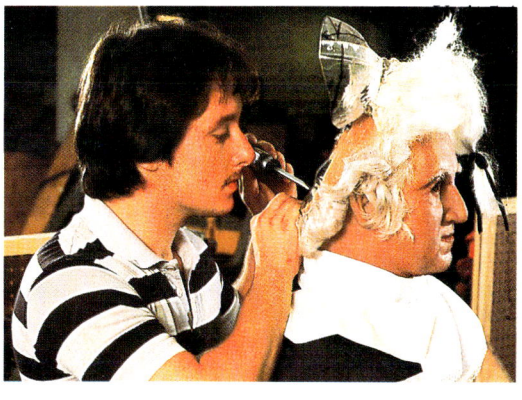

Ken: Sometimes we *paint* the backgrounds – and sometimes we *make* models. And then we *use* the blue screen method to put the pictures together.

Greg: That's easy.

Ken: Perhaps. But you'd be surprised how much work we *put* into all this. Sometimes we *spend* six to eight months on a three or four minute scene.

Bryan: Six to eight months! That sure is a long time!

When you have read the dialogue, make a report out of it. Use the passive. Start like this:
In the model shop exact models of things like cars or spaceships are built. In the monster shop all kinds of …

5 Role Play — Shocks and surprises

Make a dialogue. What could have happened to you?

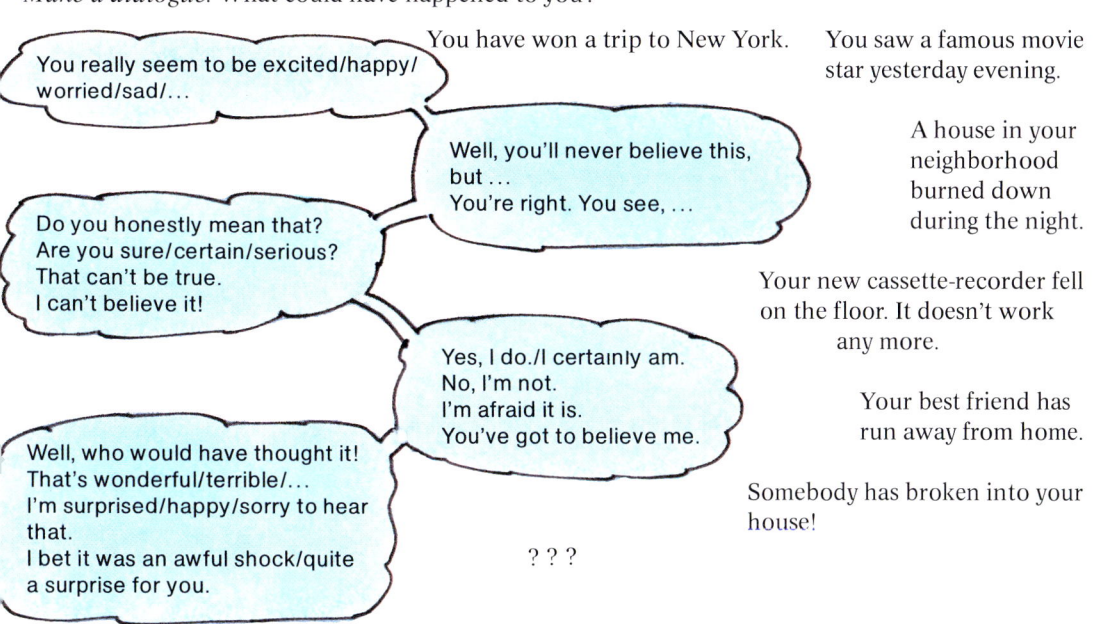

- You have won a trip to New York.
- You saw a famous movie star yesterday evening.
- A house in your neighborhood burned down during the night.
- Your new cassette-recorder fell on the floor. It doesn't work any more.
- Your best friend has run away from home.
- Somebody has broken into your house!

Speech bubbles:

- You really seem to be excited/happy/worried/sad/…
- Well, you'll never believe this, but …
  You're right. You see, …
- Do you honestly mean that?
  Are you sure/certain/serious?
  That can't be true.
  I can't believe it!
- Yes, I do./I certainly am.
  No, I'm not.
  I'm afraid it is.
  You've got to believe me.
- Well, who would have thought it!
  That's wonderful/terrible/…
  I'm surprised/happy/sorry to hear that.
  I bet it was an awful shock/quite a surprise for you.
- ? ? ?

Unit 5 B

B A helicopter crash

MOVIE STAR INJURED IN HELICOPTER CRASH

Movie star Shane West was injured in a helicopter crash early yesterday morning. The accident happened near Seattle where West was filming a special effects scene for his new movie 'So long, pilot'. The helicopter was flying low when it suddenly crashed to the ground. Luckily West and the pilot were thrown out before the helicopter started to burn. They were rushed to a hospital in Seattle. It is expected that the star will have to stay in the hospital for a few weeks. Experts are trying to find the cause of the crash. It was dark at the time, and the helicopter was flying 'blind' with the help of its avionics. It seems possible that the accident was caused by a fault in the computer-controlled equipment.

1 Whose fault was it?

Paul Christiansen and his friends are talking about the possible causes of the crash.

It's possible that Well, I think that Maybe	the helicopter the avionics the computer the computer program the flying instructions	was (not) were (not)	fed in built programed written checked made given	well. badly. correctly. wrongly. clearly. properly.

You could say: Maybe the helicopter wasn't built correctly. It's possible that …

2 Finding the cause

a) What was done by the experts after the helicopter accident?
   Start like this: 1. The film scene was watched. 2. A lot of photos were …   *Go on.*

⟨b⟩ *Imagine you are Shane West. Tell the reporter about the helicopter crash.*

| to watch | to take | to interview |
| to check | to collect | to write |

Unit 5B

3 All these things happened yesterday

Example: A boy was knocked down by a bus.

| to knock down | to injure | to take | to catch |
| to hit | to damage | to break | to frighten/mouse |

4 Working with words: nouns or verbs

If you look up words in a dictionary, you will often find that exactly the same word is used as a noun or as a verb.

a) *Nouns can explain these verbs.*
   Example: 1. Sarah *numbered* all her cassettes.
   → She put **numbers** on her cassettes.

2. The spaceship *was named* 'New World'.
3. Bryan wasn't allowed to *film* the monsters in the studio.
4. They *listed* all the possible causes of the crash.
5. Modern machines *have changed* our lives.
6. Two helicopters *crashed* into each other.

b) *Now write these sentences with verbs, not with nouns. Use the passive.*

   Example: 1. A computer fault was *the cause* of the accident. → The accident **was caused** by a computer fault.

2. A boy took *a photograph* of the flying saucer.
3. An expert fed *the program* into the computer.
4. The visitors asked the man lots of *questions*.
5. The computer kept the robot under *control*.
6. A cameraman made *a film* of the crash.

⟨5 Just for fun⟩

"A computer has replaced us."

"Oops!"

Unit 5 C

C The fun they had

Margie even wrote about it that night in her diary. On the page for May 17, 2157, she wrote, "Today Tommy found a real book!"
It was a very old book. Margie's grandfather had told her: There was once a time when all stories were printed on paper.
5 They turned the pages, and it was awfully funny to read words that didn't move in the usual way – on a screen, you know. And then, when they turned back to the page before, it had the same words on it that it had had when they read it the first time.
"Gee," said Tommy, "what a waste. When you're through with the book, you just throw it away. Our television screen must have had a million books on it, and it's good for many more. I wouldn't
10 throw *it* away."
"Same with mine," said Margie. "Where did you find it?"
"In my house. In the attic."
"What's it about?"
"School."
15 "School? What's there to write about school? I hate school."
Margie always hated school, but now she hated it more than ever. The mechanical teacher had given her test after test in Geography and she had done worse and worse until her mother had sent for the County Inspector.
He was a little man with a red face and a whole box of tools. He smiled at Margie and gave her an
20 apple, then took the teacher to pieces. Margie had hoped he wouldn't be able to put it together again, but after an hour or so, there it was again, large and black and ugly, with a big screen where all the lessons were shown and the questions were asked. That wasn't so bad. The part that Margie hated most was the slot where she had to put homework and test papers.
The inspector had said to her mother, "It's not Margie's fault, Mrs Jones. I think the Geography
25 sector was a little too quick. Her progress is quite all right." Margie was disappointed. She had hoped they would take the teacher away altogether. They had once taken Tommy's teacher away for nearly a month because the History sector was completely broken.
She said to Tommy, "Why would anyone write about school?"
Tommy looked at her. "Because it's not our kind of school, stupid. This is the old kind of school that
30 they had hundreds and hundreds of years ago."
"Well, I don't know what kind of school they had all that time ago." She read the book over his shoulder for a time. "Anyway, they had a teacher."
"Sure they had a teacher, but it wasn't a *real* teacher. It was a man."
"A man? How could a man be a teacher?"
35 "Well, he just told the boys and girls things and gave them homework and asked them questions."
"A man isn't smart enough."
"Sure he is. My father knows as much as my teacher."
"He can't. A man can't know as much as a teacher."
"He knows *almost* as much."
40 "I wouldn't want a strange man in the house."
Tommy laughed. "You don't know much, Margie. The teachers didn't live in the house. There was a special building and all the kids went there."
"And all the kids learned the same thing?"
"Sure, if they were the same age."

45 "But a teacher has to be set differently for each boy and girl. Each kid has to be taught differently."
"If you don't like it, you don't have to read the book."
"I didn't say that," Margie said quickly. She wanted to read about those funny schools.
They weren't even half-finished when Margie's mother called, "Margie! School!"
Margie said to Tommy, "Can I read the book with you after school?"
50 "Perhaps," he said.
Margie went into the schoolroom. It was next to her bedroom, and the mechanical teacher was waiting for her. It was always on at the same time every day except Saturday and Sunday. On the screen it said, "Please put yesterday's homework in the proper slot."
Margie did so with a sigh. She was thinking about the old schools that they had when her
55 grandfather was a boy. All the kids from the whole neighborhood had come, they had laughed and shouted in the schoolyard, they had sat together in the schoolroom and had gone home together at the end of the day. They had learned the same things, so they could help each other with their homework and talk about it.
And the teachers were people …
60 The mechanical teacher was flashing on the screen: "Today's Maths lesson –"
Margie was thinking about how the kids must have loved it in the old days. She was thinking about the fun they had.

Isaac Asimov (adapted)

1 Working with the text

The fun they had is a science fiction story. It gives a picture of what school might be like in the future.

a) *Collect facts about*
   1. … Margie's school.
   2. … the kind of teacher that she is taught by.
   3. … what the teacher looks like.
   4. … different teachers for different children.

b) *Compare Margie's school with your school.*

	Margie's school	your school
place	…	…
lessons	…	…
teacher	…	…
…	…	…

⟨c⟩ *Think about the future.*
Do you think the story gives a realistic picture of what school might be like one day?
What do you think people in the future will say about our time?

Unit 5C

2 Emergencies at home
What must be done? Example: 1. The fuses must/should } **be checked**.

1. All the lights have gone out. (check the fuses)
2. There is water all over the bathroom floor. (pump out the water)
3. Somebody is badly injured. (call an ambulance)
4. You have cut yourself in the kitchen. (Stop the bleeding)
5. It has started to rain heavily. (close the window)
6. There is a terrible thunderstorm outside. (Switch off the TV)
7. Someone in your family is seriously ill. (Send for a doctor)
8. Burglars have broken into your home. (tell the police)

3 Information diagrams

Sarah's father gave her a new personal computer last year. She stores what she thinks is interesting information in her computer. She uses diagrams to compare things. In some diagrams the size of the words or pictures is important, and in others different colors help to give the information.
Talk about the information that is given in these diagrams.

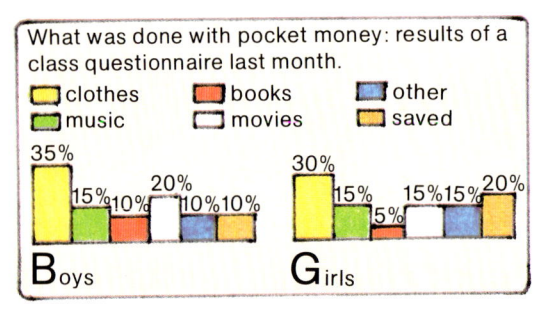

What was done with pocket money: results of a class questionnaire last month.
- clothes
- music
- books
- movies
- other
- saved

Boys: 35%, 15%, 10%, 20%, 10%, 10%
Girls: 30%, 15%, 5%, 15%, 15%, 20%

Films, Quiz shows, Children's programs, Nature programs

UniTV, AstroTV

Example: More clothes **were bought by** boys than by girls. 35% of the boys' money **was spent** on clothes.

Example: Only a few films **are shown** on UniTV, but lots of films **can be seen** on AstroTV.

4 Doing the sensible thing

Machines have made life a lot easier and more comfortable than it was. But what about all the energy that we use? And the things that we throw away? *Say what these people are doing wrong. Then write an information leaflet, with the verbs in the passive.*

Your heating should always be turned down at night. If you do this, heating costs can …

- turn heating down / cut heating costs
- switch engine off / save gas
- not throw bottles away / take to bottle bank / use again
- not throw litter around / keep countryside clean

Unit 5C

5 If only …

What do you think in these situations?

Example: 1. You are out for a day in the mountains, in short trousers and a T-shirt. It starts to rain …
If only I'd brought my waterproof jacket!
If only I hadn't put short trousers on this morning!
If only I'd worn something warmer!

2. You are late one morning and miss the bus to school …
3. A friend has invited you to a birthday party on Sunday. On Saturday afternoon you remember you haven't got a present yet – and the shops are closed …
4. You have done badly in an English test …
5. You borrow your friend's skateboard, fall off it and break your arm …
6. You order a hamburger in a snack bar. It isn't very good …

⟨6 Moon race⟩

Sarah's German pen pal Peter has sent her a new computer game – but the instructions are in German! "Very difficult German, too!" says Mr Rosenbaum when he tries to help Sarah.

Sarah: Moon race! I suppose it's about a race from the Earth to the moon …
Mr Rosenbaum: …
Sarah: Oh, I see. But what do you have to do to win?
Mr Rosenbaum: …
Sarah: Sounds easy. "Energiefelder" – that's "energy fields", I suppose. But what have they got to do with the race?
Mr Rosenbaum: …
Sarah: You press "P" to send in a new pilot, I guess. But I don't understand what happens when you press "R".
Mr Rosenbaum: …
Sarah: Brakes? You mean you can stop the spaceship in the middle of the race?
Mr Rosenbaum: …

Das Rennen der Raumschiffe findet auf dem neuen Rennkurs um den Mond statt.
Es geht darum, das eigene Raumschiff schnell und sicher durch den Rennkurs zu steuern und anschließend auf dem Mond zu landen. Links und rechts sind Energiefelder, deren Berührung das Rennen sofort beendet.
● Mit der P-Taste wird ein neuer Pilot ins Rennen geschickt.
● Mit der R-Taste wird das Raumschiff gestartet oder nach einem Bremsvorgang beschleunigt.
● Mit der B-Taste werden die Bremsen betätigt (dadurch wird die Geschwindigkeit des Raumschiffes auf die Hälfte verringert).
● Gesteuert wird durch die Links/Rechts/Oben/Unten-Pfeile.

Sarah: I see. That makes it easier to steer – but then I might lose the race. Oh, does it say how to steer?
Mr Rosenbaum: …

7 Look, listen and say

In English your voice often goes up or down.

Questions without a question word
Can I help you?
Will you be at home this evening?
Are you feeling all right?
Have you got a 50 ¢ piece?

Questions with a question word
What can I do for you?
Where did you put the purse?
When did you go to bed last night?
Who's been using my writing-paper?

Now say these sentences.
1. Where's the snack bar? 2. May I call you tomorrow? 3. Would you like to come to my party?
4. Who took my biro? 5. Can I come, too? 6. Why can't I come? 7. Could you please help me?

73

Unit 5 C

8 Sandy's birthday present

Write the story in about 120 words. Give it an ending.

9 What happened?

Look at these dialogues. In English you often use the passive when you don't want to say that something was your fault.
1. "Oh, what happened to my white socks? They're grey now!" – "Er – they **were washed** with some dark things." – "You mean *you* washed them with some dark things." – "Oh dear. Yes, I did."
2. "Water is coming out of the freezer! What happened?" – "Er – the door **wasn't closed** properly." – "You mean *you* didn't close it properly." – "I'm very sorry."

Now make more dialogues like this.
3. The best glasses are broken. You shouldn't have put them in the dish-washer.
4. The video recorder didn't record the right program. You should have checked the program times.
5. The pullovers have all shrunk. You shouldn't have set the washing-machine at the wrong temperature.
6. It's late. The alarm clock didn't switch itself on this morning. You should have set the alarm.
7. The TV dinners are black. You should have taken them out of the oven at the right time.

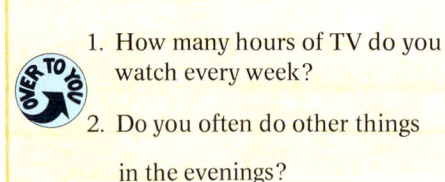

OVER TO YOU
1. How many hours of TV do you watch every week?
2. Do you often do other things in the evenings?
3. Talk about the poem. What is Eve Merriam telling us?

10 A poem: Teevee

TEEVEE

In the house
of Mr and Mrs Spouse
he and she
would watch teevee
and never a word
between them spoken
until the day
the set was broken.

Then "How do you do?"
said he to she,
"I don't believe
that we've met yet.
Spouse is my name.
What's yours?" he asked.

"Why, mine's the same!"
said she to he,
"Do you suppose that we could be –?"

But the set came suddenly right about,
and so they never did find out.

EVE MERRIAM

⟨Song: In the year 2525⟩

IN THE YEAR 2525

(Freely) In the year twenty-five, twenty-five, ___ if man is still a-live, if wo-man can sur-vive they may find ... In the year thirty-five, thirty-five, ___ Ain't gonna need to tell the truth, tell no lies, ___ Ev'ry-thing you think, do and say ___ is in the pill you took to-day.

In the year 2525
If man is still alive,
If woman can survive they may find ...

In the year 3535
Ain't gonna need to tell the truth, tell no lies,
Ev'rything you think, do and say
Is in the pill you took today.

In the year 4545
Ain't gonna need your teeth, won't need your eyes,
You won't find a thing to chew,
Nobody's gonna look at you.

In the year 5555
Your arms are hangin' limp at your side,
Your legs got nothin' to do,
Some machine's doin' that for you.

In the year 6565
Ain't gonna need no husband, won't need no wife,
You'll pick your son, pick your daughter, too
From the bottom of a long glass tube.

In the year 7510
If God's a-coming he ought to make it by then,
Maybe he'll look around himself and say:
Guess it's time for the Judgement Day.

In the year 8510
God is gonna shake his mighty head,
He'll either say I'm pleased where man has been
Or tear it down and start again.

In the year 9595
I'm kind of wond'rin' if man is gonna be alive,
He's taken everything this old earth can give
And he ain't put back nothin'.

Now it's been 10,000 years, man has cried a billion tears
For what he never knew – now man's reign is through.
But through eternal night the twinkling of starlight
So very far away – maybe it's only yesterday.

In the year 2525 if man is still alive ...
In the year 2525 ...

a) *Do you understand this song?*

1. Why can't people tell any lies in the year 3535?
2. Why won't people need their teeth or eyes any longer?
3. Who will do all the work?
4. Where will all the children come from?
5. What will God do in 7510?
6. What will God have to decide in the year 8510?
7. Why might man not be alive in the year 9595?

b) *Does this song give you something to think about?*

1. Would you like to live in a world as it is described in this song?
2. What are the dangers for people if machines do all the work for them? Give reasons.
3. How do you feel when you hear this song? The following adjectives may help you to explain your ideas.

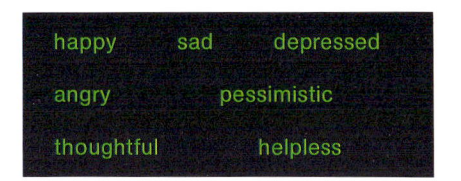

happy	sad	depressed
angry		pessimistic
thoughtful		helpless

c) *Activity:* Draw a picture and show what you believe people in the year 6565 may look like. Discuss your pictures in class.

A The exchange

UNIT 6

German-American exchange
Barnaby Stubbs
(name)
1202 West Richmond Avenue
San Antonio, Texas 78216
(address)

German-American exchange
Carmen García
(name)
2516 N. Bilbao Avenue
San Antonio, Texas 78220
(address)
15
(age)
1 brother (16)   two sisters (5,8)
(number of brothers and sisters)

Carmen García and Barney Stubbs want to take part in a German-American exchange program. They have already filled out their questionnaires, but they still have to write a few sentences about why they want to take part. Here are some of the ideas that they have already put down:

Barney:

- I think it would be great to have a German friend — especially because I don't have any brothers or sisters.
- We could do lots of things together, for example:
  - listen to my records
  - eat Mexican food (my favorite — but I like sauerkraut and schnitzels, too. So there would be no problem for me in Germany.)
- San Antonio isn't too far from Mexico...

Carmen:

- I'd really like to learn German. I've already had one year in school and I'm sure I could pick it up fast in Germany.
- My partner could learn English and Spanish because my family and most of my friends speak both languages.
- I would like to make lots of German friends. It would be nice to go out with some of those German boys in their leather shorts and little green hats. I would put on a beautiful dirndl every day...

1 Carmen and Barney

a) *Can you complete the sentences?*
1. Carmen and Barney have already filled out ... 2. Now they have to write about ... 3. They have already put down ... 4. Carmen thinks she could pick up ... 5. She would like to go out with ...
6. And she imagines that German girls always put on ... 7. Barney enjoys listening to ... 8. When he thinks of German food, he thinks of ...

b) **OVER TO YOU** *What do you think of their ideas? Do you agree with everything that they say about Germany?*
Would you like to take part in a German-American exchange? Say why or why not.

⟨c⟩ *If you wanted to go to San Antonio on an exchange, what notes would you put down first?*

Unit 6 A

2 San Antonio

Before Barney's partner, Rainer Wirth, arrived in San Antonio, Barney sent him some information.

a) *Put in the missing prepositions after the verbs:* about, around, at, for, in, of, to, up

SAN ANTONIO – Places of interest for everyone!

Tower of the Americas: Why not ride ___ the tower, 750 feet high? It was built for the World's Fair, Hemisfair in '68.
El Mercado: The old Mexican market. Walk ___ it and look ___ a souvenir of your visit to San Antonio.
La Villita: A part of the city for people who are interested ___ art or who enjoy listening ___ Spanish music.
The Institute of Texan Cultures: Learn ___ Texas through the eyes of the different national groups that have taken part ___ its proud history.
The Alamo: Stand and stare ___ it, and think ___ Davy Crockett and his friends who were killed there when they fought against more than 2,000 Mexicans in 1836.
The Hertzberg Collection: Things that belong ___ the wonderful world of the circus.

b) Here's the letter that Barney sent with the leaflet.

Put in the missing adverbs after the verbs.

off   behind
around   up
in
       out
back

```
Dear Rainer,
This will be my last letter before you come
to San Antonio next month. Here's some
information about San Antonio for you. I'm
really looking forward to showing you ? .
There are so many places that we can visit.
(Lots of the names are Spanish, I'm afraid –
but you'll soon pick them ? !) Have a look
at everything and find ? what there is to
see. If you still have time before you set ? ,
you can write ? and let me know what you'd
like to do first. See you soon, Barney

P.S. I'm putting ? a photo of me. Don't
leave it ? in Germany, or you won't know me
at the airport!
```

3 At Carmen's house

At Carmen's house everybody is talking about the exchange.
Can you complete the sentences with these verbs and adverbs?

clean up   look up   go out   find out   turn on   show around   throw away

Example: "What are the exact dates of the exchange, Carmen?" – "I'm not sure. But I can look at the notice-board at school and **find them out**."

1. "Carmen, your room isn't very clean. Your partner will have to share it, you know." – "Don't worry. Before she gets here, I'll … it …"
2. "Can I come out with you and your partner, Carmen?" – "Yes, you can help to … her …"
3. "Where's this place in Germany where she comes from?" – "I think it's in the South of Germany. Let's get the map and … it …"
4. "Do you need all these leaflets about San Antonio, Carmen?" – "Yes, I do. So don't …"
5. "That TV program about Germany is just starting." – "Oh, really? Would you please … ?"
6. "Are German boys nice, Carmen?" – "Sure! And I hope I can … with some of them!"

Unit 6 B

B He's here!

Barney's exchange partner has arrived. Rainer comes from Mainz. Rainer, Barney and his mom are talking now.

Mom: I hope you like music, Rainer, because Barney's crazy about it. You can usually hear his music all over the house.
Barney: I don't like all kinds of music. I don't like – er – well, opera.
Rainer: Oh, opera's awful!
Barney: Whew! I was worried about that. My favorite music is American rock.
Rainer: I don't know too much about that.
Barney: No problem. I've got millions of records. I guess that's why my money always goes so fast. I'll play you everything. Oh, there's a group that's going to play at the school tonight. Let's go there. I'd love to hear them.
Rainer: Good idea.
Barney: Right. And then you could see where we'll go to school in September. It's a great place – most of the time.
Mom: Boys, why don't you wait until Dad comes home? He might –
Barney: Hey, and after lunch we could go to the Mexican market. I sometimes try the Mexican specialties there. They're really fantastic! And we could go to the old part of San Antonio. It's wonderful there! Hey, and the Sunken Gardens. They're so beautiful –
Mom: Barney, not so fast! It's only the first day. You'll soon find out, Rainer. He's always like this!

1 Finding out about Barney

What has Rainer already found out about his partner Barney?
Make sentences with the adverbs in the correct position.

Example: Barney **often** plays his guitar **in his room**.

Barney	always sometimes usually never	eats Mexican food listens to his rock records tries the specialties spends his money listens to opera	anywhere! all over the house. in Mexico. very fast. at the Mexican market.

Imagine that you have an exchange partner.
What would he/she find out about you?

⟨2 Song: Ebony and Ivory⟩

1. Ebony and Ivory
   Live together
       in perfect harmony …
   side by side on my piano
       keyboard
   Oh Lord, why don't we?

2. We all know
   That people are the same
   wherever you go
   There is good and bad
   in everyone …
   We learn to give each other
   What we need to survive
   Together alive

3. Ebony and Ivory
   Live together
       in perfect harmony …
   side by side on my piano
       keyboard
   Oh Lord, why don't we?

3

a) *Complete the text with the following words:*

surprisingly	repeatedly asked	even got
sold	quickly went	
mainly		've always liked
played	became	
finally left	well known	once said

TINA TURNER

The story of Anna "Tina" Mae Bullock began on November 26th, 1939, when she was born in Nutbush, Tennessee. She sang gospel music as a young girl. At the age of 17 she moved to St. Louis and tried to join the Ike Turner Soul Revue there. Although Tina … Ike Turner if she could sing with his band, he always said "no". But one night he gave her a chance. In 1958 they … married. Ike and Tina later … when they recorded "River Deep – Mountain High", one of the finest songs of all time. It … to the top in Great Britain but not in the USA. After a lot of personal troubles with her husband she … him in the middle of a tour, with just 36 cents in her pocket.
For the next eight years Tina Turner … in clubs in Las Vegas or opened concerts for bigger names. In 1984 she had a comeback with her LP "Private Dancer" which … more than a million copies. She … about her music: "I … the way the Rolling Stones mix white and black music."

⟨b⟩ *Activity: Write a short text for the cover of a record by your favorite singer or group.*

4 Staying as a guest

Carmen's exchange partner Heike speaks English quite well, but sometimes she finds it difficult to put the words in the right order. English word order is so often different from German!

a) *Look at what Heike wants to say. Can you get it right for her?*

1. „Darf ich den Fernseher einschalten?"
2. „Du sprichst immer so schnell!"
3. „Diese Platte möchte ich gerne hören."
4. „Ich habe vergessen, meine Zahnbürste mitzubringen."
5. „Was kann ich als Andenken an San Antonio kaufen?"
6. „Du fährst gut!"
7. „Ich muß meine Bluse heute waschen."
8. „Ich weiß nicht, ob ich Chili con carne mag. Ich habe es noch nie gegessen."

b) *What do you think Carmen might answer?*
Make short dialogues between Heike and Carmen.
The words in the box will help you to start Carmen's answers.

Yes/No, …
Oh, I'll …
Well, you can …
Why not …
Sorry, but I …

Unit 6 C

C Ramona's Radio Show

James Brown *Chuck Berry* *Fats Domino* *Muddy Waters* *Aretha Franklin* *Little Richard* *Ray Charles*

DJ: Hi, out there, this is Ramona Díaz at KFAQ where things are happening. Right now the temperature in San Antonio is 93 degrees – it's hot, people, hot – like our guest this afternoon: LeRoy Jones, rock'n'roll star from New York City.

LeRoy: Hi there!

DJ: And we've got free tickets for LeRoy's show at the Top Club tonight for the winner of our Phone-in Quiz Question – so don't turn your radio off. Now, LeRoy, tell us how you got into the music business.

LeRoy: Well, it was my grandma really – yeah, it's true. She sings in the gospel choir in our church back in Harlem. The church choir – that's where I learned all about rhythm.

DJ: OK, we'll come back to you in a minute, LeRoy, after we've listened to some of that old gospel music. This is the Chapman Family with "He's My Rock, My Sword, My Shield".

* * *

Great music! Do you think gospel music is your main influence?

LeRoy: That's hard to say. It sure is one of them. Gospel is one of the roots of black music – like blues.

DJ: Take Ray Charles, Tina Turner and Aretha Franklin – they began as gospel singers, didn't they?

LeRoy: Right. Aretha's been around for some time now, and she's one of my favorites.

DJ: Do you want to hear something by Aretha? This one is from the 60s. It had an important message then. It's called "Respect".

* * *

LeRoy: The 60s were a time when things changed for us blacks. Martin Luther King did a lot for us then. And you could hear it in our soul music. Black people were singing "Say it loud – I'm black and I'm proud". People like my parents.

DJ: And James Brown, who made the record which is next on my list. Here it is.

* * *

Can you tell us something about where soul music came from?

LeRoy: Sure. I guess it grew out of the blues. The blues started down south, you know. It was the music of slaves, and later of the poor blacks. Very simple music – with feeling. Usually just one guy who sang and played a guitar. Robert Johnson, King of the Delta Blues, is a good example. Well, when the poor blacks moved to the cities, went north to Chicago, Detroit, they took the music with them. They started playing electric guitars and so on – I guess that's where rock music started.

DJ: Yeah, the blacks called it rhythm'n'blues – kind of blues with a beat. Let's hear some. This is Muddy Waters with "I'm Ready".

* * *

So rock'n'roll and soul music both grew out of the blues, LeRoy?
LeRoy: I'd say so. Rock was taken over by white singers like Elvis Presley, and later by groups like the Beatles and the Rolling Stones. But it was really black music. It was started by guys like Fats Domino and Little Richard – and of course Chuck Berry.
DJ: Was he an influence on you, LeRoy?
LeRoy: I guess so, because I still *love* his songs. Back in the 60s he was an influence on nearly every rock singer, it seems. Everybody danced to his music, white and black. Take "Roll Over, Beethoven" …
DJ: That's exactly what I'm going to do …

* * *

The sad thing about Chuck Berry is that his songs made a lot of money – for other people, especially white people who copied them.
LeRoy: Right. But you could say the same of all the early black rock'n'roll singers.
DJ: I guess so. Well, LeRoy, if we can turn from you for a moment, it's time for our Phone-in Quiz Question. Are you ready? I want to know who this singer is. Double-two, four-two's the number to call.

* * *

Here's our first caller. Hello.
Caller: Hi, this is Moose Gregson. My dad says it's Elvis Presley. Sounds to me more like a black singer.
DJ: Well, your dad's right, Moose. It's Elvis. You know back in the 50s a white record producer believed that he would be able to make a million dollars if he found a white guy who sang like a black. – Well, they found Elvis.

1 Talking about the text

a) *Make a list of the different kinds of black music, together with information about them.*

> Gospel music – one of the roots of black music. It's sung in church choirs. It has got a lot of rhythm.
> Blues – …

b) *Find out from the text*
 – why Chuck Berry was so important.
 – what Muddy Waters' influence was.
 – why a record producer wanted to make records with Elvis Presley.

c) 1. Do you like black music or do you like other kinds of music more?
 2. Which of the songs do you like best?
 3. Do you and your parents like the same kind of music?
 4. When you listen to a record, are you interested in the music or the words?

⟨d⟩ *Activity:* 1. *Collect information about what happened to black music in the 70s and 80s.*
  Find out • the names of the stars and their most famous songs.
   • which parts of the USA they came from.
   • what kind of music they sang/played.
 2. *Make your own radio show. You can use Ramona's Radio Show for ideas.*

Unit 6 C

2 Listening comprehension: Tina Turner – Queen of rock'n'roll

1. What was Tina Turner's real name?
2. What do we learn about her home and family?
3. Do you think the Bullocks were a happy family?
4. Why did Tina go to St. Louis, Missouri?
5. Who was Ike Turner?
6. Why did Ike marry Tina?
7. What was life like in Ike's band?
8. Why did Tina leave Ike?
9. What happened in 1984?
10. What can we learn from Tina Turner's story?

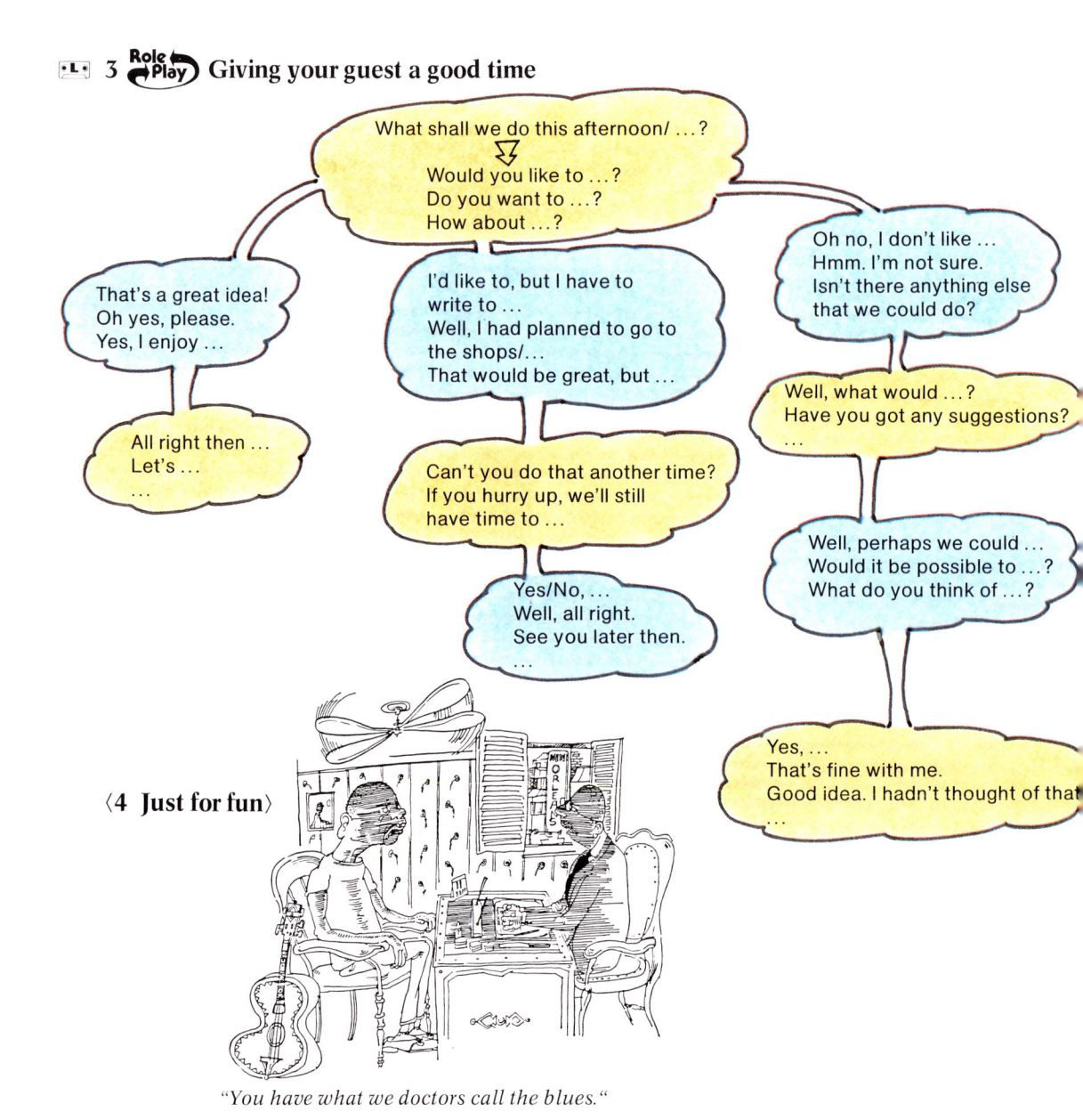

3 Role Play – Giving your guest a good time

What shall we do this afternoon/ …?
Would you like to …?
Do you want to …?
How about …?

That's a great idea!
Oh yes, please.
Yes, I enjoy …

All right then …
Let's …
…

I'd like to, but I have to write to …
Well, I had planned to go to the shops/…
That would be great, but …

Can't you do that another time?
If you hurry up, we'll still have time to …

Yes/No, …
Well, all right.
See you later then.
…

Oh no, I don't like …
Hmm. I'm not sure.
Isn't there anything else that we could do?

Well, what would …?
Have you got any suggestions?
…

Well, perhaps we could …
Would it be possible to …?
What do you think of …?

Yes, …
That's fine with me.
Good idea. I hadn't thought of that
…

4 Just for fun

"You have what we doctors call the blues."

⟨**San Antonio**⟩

I love San Antone!

A Spanish villa

The Spanish Governor's Palace

The old Mission Concepción

The battle of the Alamo, 1836

The 'Paseo del Rio'

(Working with your dictionary)

1 Finding the word that you are looking for

a) The words that are explained in your dictionary are **in alphabetical order**. When you want to look up a word, you will find that there are **headwords, derivatives** (headwords with endings), **compounds** (which are made by adding other words to headwords), and **useful phrases**.
Examples:

Headword	Some derivatives	Some compounds	Some useful phrases
watch	watcher, watchful	watchdog, watchman	to be on the watch, to keep watch
love	loveliness, lovely	lovesick, lovesong	to fall in love, to send one's love

Look up the following words in the dictionary, and make a list of the most useful **derivatives, compounds,** *and* **phrases** *that you can find.*
1. **tooth**; 2. **cook**; 3. **wonder**; 4. **break**; 5. **shop**.

b) The dictionary also tells you what **part of speech** each word is. Look out for these abbreviations:

n = *noun* (e.g. **town**); *adj* = *adjective* (e.g. **happy**); *adv* = *adverb* (e.g. **happily**); *vt* = *verb transitive* – *this verb can take an object* (e.g. **eat** something); *vi* = *verb intransitive – this verb has no object* (e.g. **sleep**); *prep* = *preposition* (e.g. **under**); *conj* = *conjunction* (e.g. **because**).

The following words can be used as more than one **part of speech**. *Make a sentence for each part of speech. Your dictionary will help you.*
Example: sail (2) – 1. The boat has two **sails**. (*n*)
                    2. Columbus **sailed** to America in 1492. (*vi*)
1. **address** (2); 2. **round** (3); 3. **guess** (2); 4. **pretty** (2); 5. **lock** (2); 6. **before** (2).

c) Sometimes you will find that one **headword** can have more than one meaning – or can be used in different ways. The dictionary gives these headwords numbers, and explains each one separately.

Example: – **call** 1. (Ruf); **call** 2. (Anruf); **call** 3. (Aufruf, Berufung); **call** 4. (Besuch), etc.

Look up the word **fall** *in your dictionary, look at the different meanings, then try to translate these sentences into good German.*

1. There was a heavy **fall** of rain last night. 2. You've hurt your leg. Have you had a **fall**? 3. We're going to visit the Hoppers next **fall**. 4. His face **fell** when he heard the news. 5. Many of the pioneers **fell** ill on their way out West. 6. When night **fell**, the birds had all flown to their nests. 7. Harry has **fallen** in love again. 8. Bret's car is **falling** to pieces.

2 Same word in German – different words in English

You will sometimes find that one word in German has two or more meanings – and for each meaning you will find a different word in English. **Example: Tor** can be **gate** (of a garden); **door** (of a garage); **goal** (in sports).

a) *Look up the word* **Platz** *in your German-English dictionary, then try to translate these sentences into correct English.*

1. In diesem Schrank ist viel **Platz** für Bücher. 2. Bitte nehmen Sie **Platz**! 3. Ich stellte den Mülleimer wieder an seinen **Platz**. 4. In der Stadtmitte ist ein großer **Platz**. 5. Der Fußball**platz** ist hinter dem Schulgebäude, neben den Tennis**plätzen**.

b) *Now complete these sentences with the correct English words.*
1. **vorstellen:** a) Let me … you to my neighbor, Mr Hartung.
   b) I can't … why he hasn't arrived yet.
   c) He's … his car … the garage, so we can't drive out!
2. **Satz:** a) He wrote the … on the blackboard.
   b) I like the last … of the symphony best.
   c) John lost the match in the third …
3. **Weg:** a) Let's take this … through the trees.
   b) Please don't stand in my …!
   c) The long … has made us all tired. Let's go to bed early.

3 What's the word?

Sometimes you will need a dictionary to look up everyday words that you don't yet know in English.
Example: Jürgen and his brother have got a lovely new room – up in the attic. When Jürgen writes to his American cousin, he wants to tell him all about it. But he soon realizes that he doesn't know the English words for these things:

Look up the words in your German/English dictionary. ⟨*Then imagine that* **you** *are Jürgen. Write the letter and describe the new room.*⟩

4 Getting the meaning

The article on the right is from an American teenagers' magazine. You will not find it hard to understand – but there are a number of words in it that you don't know yet.
Look them up carefully in your dictionary until you find the right meaning.

ski-jump [ˈskiːdʒʌmp] *n* (*action*) Skisprung *m*; (*place*) Sprungschanze *f*; **ski-jumping** *n* Skispringen *nt*.
skilful, (*US*) **skillful** [ˈskɪlfʊl] *adj* geschickt; *piano-playing etc also* gewandt; *sculpture, painting etc* kunstvoll.
skilfully, (*US*) **skillfully** [ˈskɪlfəlɪ] *adv see adj.*
skilfulness, (*US*) **skillfulness** [ˈskɪlfʊlnɪs] *n see* **skill 1**.
ski-lift [ˈskiːlɪft] *n* Skilift *m*.
skill [skɪl] *n* **1.** *no pl* (*skilfulness*) Geschick *nt*, Geschicklichkeit *f*; (*of sculptor etc*) Kunst(fertigkeit) *f*. **his ~ at billiards/in persuading people** sein Geschick beim Billard/sein Geschick *or* seine Fähigkeit, andere zu überreden.
2. (*acquired technique*) Fertigkeit *f*; (*ability*) Fähigkeit *f*. **to learn new ~s** etwas Neues lernen.
skilled [skɪld] *adj* (*skilful*) geschickt, gewandt (*at* in +*dat*); (*trained*) ausgebildet, Fach-; (*requiring skill*) Fach-, fachmännisch. **he's ~ in persuading people** er versteht es, andere zu überreden; **a man ~ in diplomacy** ein geschickter Diplomat.

MAKE YOUR OWN JOB

Wouldn't it be nice to make money at a job that you like doing? But wanting a job and getting it are two different things, right? Here are some ideas that should help.
To start with, ask yourself two questions: What do I do best? And what else can I do? Think about it. Certainly you have skills. Some of those skills are worth money to someone. Decide how much time you have. Next, talk about your ideas with your parents, friends and neighbors. If you don't find anyone who is ready to give you a job, advertise! Most supermarkets have a notice-board where you could put up an ad – like this:

> NEED HELP AROUND YOUR PLACE?
> PHONE KERRY: 442-3062
> FRIENDLY!!! QUICK!!! CAREFUL!!!

Here are some jobs you might do in your community:
- Cleaning and tidying garages.
- Washing windows on the outside. Use a hose, a sponge and a ladder.
- Cooking or doing the shopping for elderly neighbors.
- Looking after pets/taking dogs for a walk. (You might tell your local vet that you can help his customers if they need your service.)
- Collecting and bringing back library books for people who are busy or unable to get out.
- Vacation services: Offer to mow lawns and empty mail boxes while families are away.

To start with, let the customers decide what to pay you!

Stopover D

[NEW FRONTIERS]

Timeline:
- 1770
- Declaration of Independence
- 1780
- Independence (end of war)
- 1790 — First President
- 1800
- "Louisiana Purchase" of land from France (for $15 million they doubled U.S. territory)
- 1810
- 1820
- Spain has to give Florida to the U.S.
- 1830
- 1840
- Gold found in California
- 1850 — End of 2-year Mexican War: Texas, New Mexico and California now U.S. territory
- 1860
- First railroad from San Francisco to New York completed
- 1870

The Americans are very restless. As you know, the average American family moves to a new town or neighborhood more often than the average European family. Many Americans start a new life in a new community every five or ten years.

When did the restlessness start?
With the first colonists, of course. They were the first "pioneers". They had come across the Atlantic to America. The pioneers knew: It was almost certain that one day the United States would stretch from the Atlantic to the Pacific. *(Look at the time line on the left and the map on page 87 to see how more and more of the continent became U.S. territory.)*

Why go west?
"Why not?" many thought. There was room for everybody, it seemed, even for the Indians. Back in Europe, millions of poor, and often hungry people heard about the American West. More and more arrived.

Who were the pioneers?
Many of the people who opened up the west were people from Europe – from Germany, from Ireland, from Sweden ... They had suffered hardship in their home countries, and were ready to suffer hardship in the wilderness. They hoped for a better life, or at least more freedom.
The first group certainly found freedom. They were trappers and hunted animals. Some of them went back to the east and showed the next group of pioneers how they could find the way west.

How did they travel?
The first hunters and trappers crossed the Appalachians on foot and on horseback, then sometimes by canoe along the river valleys. Later, pioneers could travel some of the way by riverboat – or by train. When it became possible to travel all the way by train, the West was already won.

US TERRITORY AND FRONTIER

US territory
- - - - at Independence 1776
.... after Louisiana Purchase 1803

Settlement
- 1820
- 1850

The Frontier — *None of the lines on this map show "the frontier". The American frontier was wherever civilization met the wilderness. And this was changing all the time.*

These were the people who wanted to find a piece of land in the West and become farmers. Whole families traveled together, built wooden houses and started to grow fruit and vegetables. Sometimes they had to fight off Indians who were trying to save their hunting grounds.

In the 1830s and 1840s, all kinds of people went west: the ranchers who had huge herds of cattle; the people who hoped to find gold and get rich; but also railroad workers, business people, doctors, teachers and many, many others.

For people who wanted to go all the way to California around 1850, there were three main routes:
- Some traveled by sea around South America. The journey was more comfortable than the other routes, but it took longer and was very expensive.
- Others sailed from the east coast to Panama, crossed the land on foot, and then sailed up the west coast to San Francisco. Many who chose this route died of terrible diseases.
- Most people (especially families) chose the different land routes, and traveled most of the journey by wagon train. In summer it was hot, in winter cold, in spring there was deep mud. And often there was the danger of Indians.

Slowly the settlers pushed the "frontier" further west.

Stopover D

(When the white man came)

The first Americans were the Indians. There were about one million of them. They belonged to many different tribes, each with its own way of life and language. At first the Indians and whites lived peacefully together. But for many whites, peace was a sign of weakness. The English colonists were glad for the help that they got from the Indians, but they did not like them. They wanted to trade with them, but cheated them where they could. The colonists thought that they had a right to take the land away from the Indians.

Not all whites were like this. When William Penn founded the State of Pennsylvania, he made a treaty with the Delaware tribe. After Penn had died, the whites broke the treaty. During the next 150 years the Delawares had to move seven times because the whites took more and more Indian land. Almost all the other tribes had the same story to tell.

Here is how one Indian chief tried to explain why the Indians and the whites didn't understand each other:

> "We know that the Earth doesn't belong to Man, Man belongs to the Earth. But the white man does not understand. For him, one part of the country is like another, because he is a stranger who comes in the night and takes away from Earth what he needs … He treats his mother, the Earth, and his father, the Sky, like things – things that he can buy and sell like sheep …"

From Little Big Horn to Wounded Knee

Of all the Indian tribes that fought bravely, none was braver than the Sioux. They had a good reason to fight. As the whites went further and further west, they killed all the buffalo that the Sioux hunted for food and clothing. The whites broke their treaties with the Sioux again and again. This was too much for the Sioux. Under Chief Sitting Bull, the Sioux and Cheyenne won a great victory over General Custer and his men at the Little Big Horn River, in 1876. To the whites this was a massacre. They had their chance for revenge 14 years later – or was it a terrible mistake? American soldiers killed 300 Sioux men, women and children as they prepared to surrender at Wounded Knee, in December 1890.

The Indians have never forgotten Wounded Knee. In 1973 a group of Indians declared the area a Sioux state; after three months they had to surrender to the police. They were fighting for better living conditions on their reservation.

General Custer and his men fighting the Sioux and Cheyenne

In 1890 the Indians were a broken people. In less than 300 years there were only 60,000 Indians left out of one million!
Now the Indians live in peace, and their numbers are growing again. There are about a million Indians today. Since 1928 they have been U.S. citizens. But they have not forgotten their history and traditions.

Stopover D

A quiz about the USA

It's time for the super quiz! The solution* to the quiz is a whole sentence. Take the correct letter from every question and write it down on a piece of paper. Write the question-number next to it. Then put the letters in the following order:

Question-number 1, 9, 26, 15, 14, 25, 30, 24, 29, 21, 31, 6, 18, 28, 22, 2, 5, 33, 23, 16, 20, 13, 11, 4, 3, 17, 7, 32, 27, 19, 10, 12, 34, 8.

1. The American flag has:
   a) twenty stars
   b) thirty stars
   c) fifty stars
   d) seventy stars

   (5th letter of the 1st word)

2. Americans call Father Christmas …
   (4th letter of the first word)
3. Which language – after English – is spoken most in the USA? (1st letter)
4. It is the 5th word in line 1 on page 49. (8th letter)
5. Who said: "Buenos días! Welcome to Texas."? (6th letter of surname)
6. This is part of a photo in *Orange Line 4*. What does it show? (8th letter of 1st word)
7. Which state borders upon** the most lakes? (8th letter)
8. The Germans call it "Bürgersteig", the British "pavement", and the Americans call it … (6th letter)
9. Which American city has cable cars? (9th letter of 2nd word)  
10. New York City has … boroughs. (4th letter)
11. In 1850 Louis Nusbaumer crossed a valley. What was it later called? (3rd letter of 1st word)
12. This is part of a drawing in *Orange Line 4*. What does it show? (3rd letter)

* [sə'luːʃn] – Lösung   ** [ˌbɔːdə ə'pɒn] – grenzt an

Stopover D

13. Where did Mrs Donahue collect Tracey after she had finished work at the supermarket? (3rd letter)
14. Nashville is in the state of …. (4th letter)
15. Denver is in the … Mountains. (4th letter)
16. Today most Indians live there. (5th letter)
17. What is the world's biggest department store? (2nd letter)
18. The American word for Underground is … (3rd letter)
19. Marco's father is a steelworker in this city. (10th letter)
20. 56% of the population of Miami are … (7th letter)
21. There are 38 modern schools in the community of … (5th letter)
22. What do you call this person? (2nd letter)
23. Santa Claus, of course, comes down the … (6th letter)
24. The state of California is
    a) as big as the Federal Republic of Germany, Switzerland and Austria together.
    b) as big as the Federal Republic of Germany.
    c) not as big as the Federal Republic of Germany. (pick a, b or c)
25. How do Americans write "colour"? (4th letter)
26. A big bird that Americans eat for Christmas dinner. (2nd letter)
27. What do the Cherokees call their terrible journey west? (1st letter of 4th word)
28. In 1836, a famous American was killed here. His name was … (3rd letter of surname)
29. A white singer who sang like a black. (5th letter of surname)
30. The film industry in … isn't what it was in the old days! (6th letter)
31. Who said: "I've always liked the way the Rolling Stones mix white and black music."? (1st letter of surname)
32. What is the famous bridge in San Francisco called? (4th letter of 3rd word)
33. People in Britain write "programme", and Americans write … (7th letter)
34. Look at the map of the USA. What is the longest river? (7th letter)

Grammar

Stopover A

1 Übersicht über die Zeiten   Revision of tenses

a) simple present

> Every day we **hear** voices from America.
> In San Antonio most people **speak** Spanish.

- Das *simple present* wird verwendet, wenn man ausdrücken will, daß etwas regelmäßig, oft, immer, manchmal oder nie geschieht.
- Es wird auch verwendet, um über Tatsachen und reine Sachverhalte zu berichten.

present progressive

> What **are** you **doing** at the moment?
> I**'m writing** a letter.

- Mit dem *present progressive* werden Vorgänge beschrieben, die noch nicht abgeschlossen sind oder gerade ablaufen.

b) simple past

> Birgit **went** to the USA last year.

- Das *simple past* drückt Ereignisse oder Handlungen aus, die in der Vergangenheit liegen und abgeschlossen sind.

past progressive

> She met a lot of young people while she **was staying** there.

- Das *past progressive* betont, daß ein Vorgang gerade ablief und noch nicht abgeschlossen war.

c) present perfect (simple)

I**'ve** just **read** an interesting article. (I can tell you all about it.) **Have** you *ever* **been** to the USA? Yes, I have. But I**'ve** *never* **been** to California. I **haven't had** the time *yet*.	Ich habe gerade einen interessanten Artikel gelesen. (Ich kann dir alles darüber erzählen.) Bist du schon einmal in den USA gewesen? Ja. Aber ich bin noch nie in Kalifornien gewesen. Bis jetzt habe ich die Zeit (dazu) noch nicht gehabt.

- Mit dem *present perfect simple* drückt man aus, daß eine Handlung, die in der Vergangenheit stattgefunden hat (z. B. das Lesen des Artikels), in der Gegenwart noch von Bedeutung ist (Man weiß noch genau, was darin stand.).
- In Fragen mit *ever* und Antworten mit *never* und *not yet* drückt das *present perfect simple* aus, daß bis jetzt etwas geschehen oder noch nicht geschehen ist.

d) past perfect (simple)

> When they got to the cinema at last the film **had** already **started**.
> (Als sie schließlich am Kino ankamen, hatte der Film schon angefangen.)

- Sollen zwei Vorgänge der Vergangenheit in einer Erzählung zeitlich abgestuft werden, so wird der Vorgang, der weiter zurückliegt, durch das *past perfect* ausgedrückt.

Grammar: Stopover A/Unit 1

e) will-future

> Harry **won't be** in Enid much longer.
> *I hope* I **will get** my driver's license soon.
> I know what I'**ll do** – I'**ll lend** you my bike.

- Man kann das *will*-Futur verwenden, um Vorhersagen zu machen oder Vermutungen anzustellen.
- Hoffnungen und Vermutungen werden häufig mit *I think, I hope, probably* + *will*-Futur ausgedrückt.
- Es kann auch verwendet werden, um einen spontanen Entschluß auszudrücken.

going to

> My mother **is going to get** me a new guitar.

- *Going to* wird verwendet, um Absichten, Vorhaben oder Pläne auszudrücken. Der Gebrauch von *going to* deutet darauf hin, daß die Absicht schon länger besteht.

f) conditional sentences

Typ I Erfüllbare Bedingungen

>   *present*   *will-future*
> If Marc **wants** to go to Florida, he **will need** some money.
> Wenn Marc nach Florida fahren möchte, dann braucht er etwas Geld.

- Der if-Satz im *simple present* drückt aus, daß die Bedingung erfüllbar ist.
- Der Hauptsatz im Futur drückt aus, was passiert oder passieren kann, falls diese Bedingung Wirklichkeit wird.

Unit 1

§ 2 Das Gerund   The gerund   Unit 1 Step A

Das Gerund wird aus der Stammform des Verbs und der Endung '-ing' gebildet.

| play + ing = playing | ridé + ing = riding | run + n = running |
| work + ing = working | také + ing = taking | sit + t = sitting |

1. Das Gerund als Subjekt

Riding is fun.	Reiten macht Spaß.
Playing basketball keeps you fit.	Basketball spielen hält dich fit.
Helping in the garden can be hard work.	Im Garten (zu) helfen kann harte Arbeit sein.
Working all day isn't always nice.	Den ganzen Tag lang zu arbeiten, ist nicht immer schön.

- Das Gerund verhält sich teils wie ein Nomen und teils wie ein Verb.
  Wie ein Nomen kann es Subjekt des Satzes sein.
  Vergleiche: **Horses** are nice. } subject
                Riding is fun.   }
- Wie ein Verb kann das Gerund aber auch ein Objekt (Playing **football** …), eine Ortsangabe (Helping **in the garden** …) oder eine Zeitangabe (Working **all day** …) bei sich haben.

Grammar: Unit 1

2. Das Gerund als Objekt

a) Nach bestimmten Verben

Birgit **loves traveling** around.	Birgit reist sehr gern herum.
She **enjoys talking** to American teenagers.	Sie spricht gern mit amerikanischen Jugendlichen.
And she **likes taking** photos of them.	Und sie macht gern Fotos von ihnen.
But she **can't stand driving** in city traffic.	Aber sie kann es nicht ausstehen, im Stadtverkehr zu fahren.
And she **hates going** on the subway at night.	Und sie fährt sehr ungern nachts mit der U-Bahn.

- Das Gerund kann auch – wie ein Nomen – Objekt im Satz sein. Nach bestimmten Verben kann somit entweder ein Nomen oder ein Gerund als Objekt stehen.
  Vergleiche: I like **books.** ⎫
  　　　　　　I like **reading.** ⎭ *object*
  He loves **the mountains.** He loves **climbing mountains.**

- Häufig verwendet man *Verb + Gerund*, um auszudrücken, was man gern oder ungern tut.

b) Nach Präpositionen

verb + preposition + gerund	
I **am looking forward to going** to America one day.	Ich freue mich darauf, eines Tages nach Amerika zu fahren.
I **dream of seeing** all those fantastic sights.	Ich träume davon, all jene phantastischen Sehenswürdigkeiten zu sehen.
I often **think of traveling** around the USA.	Ich denke oft daran, durch die USA zu reisen.
My friends and I sometimes **talk about going** there together.	Meine Freunde und ich sprechen manchmal darüber, gemeinsam dorthin zu fahren.

adjective + preposition + gerund	
Ted is **used to doing** things in the kitchen.	Ted ist es gewöhnt, in der Küche zu arbeiten.
He is **interested in cooking.**	Er ist am Kochen interessiert.
And he is very **good at making** chili con carne.	Und er kann sehr gut 'Chili con carne' kochen.
Tracey isn't **crazy about helping** him.	Tracey ist nicht verrückt darauf, ihm zu helfen.
She is always **afraid of doing** things wrong.	Sie hat immer Angst, etwas falsch zu machen.
She sometimes goes out in the evenings – but she is always **worried about walking** home in the dark.	Sie geht manchmal abends aus – aber sie hat immer Angst, allein im Dunkeln nach Hause zu gehen.

⚠️ to　Das Wort **to** kann sowohl Teil des Infinitivs wie auch Präposition sein:
　　　　　He was allowed **to go** home.　He had **to help** in the garden.
　　In diesen Sätzen ist **to** Teil des Infinitivs.

　　Sobald nach **to** ein Nomen oder das Pronomen *it* stehen kann, handelt es sich um eine Präposition, es muß also ein Gerund folgen:
　　　　　She looks forward to **it**.
　　　　　She looks forward **to spending** her holiday in France.
　　　　　I'm not used to it/the traffic. – I'm not used to driving.

Grammar: Unit 2

Unit 2

§ 3 **Bedingungssätze**   Conditional sentences   Unit 2 Step A

Typ II Nicht erfüllbare oder nur theoretisch erfüllbare Bedingungen
(Zu Typ I Erfüllbare Bedingungen vgl. § 1)

if-Satz *(if-clause)*	Hauptsatz *(main clause)*
If I **worked** really hard,	I **would** soon **be** a great magician.
Wenn ich wirklich hart arbeitete,	würde ich bald ein großer Zauberer sein.
If I **became** a great magician,	I **wouldn't stay** in Enid – or Oshkosh.
Wenn ich ein großer Zauberer würde,	würde ich nicht in Enid – oder Oshkosh – bleiben.
If I **was/were** really famous,	I **would go** all over the world.
Wenn ich richtig berühmt wäre,	würde ich überall hinfahren.
If I **went** all over the world,	I **would make** a lot of money.
Wenn ich überall hinfahren würde,	würde ich eine Menge Geld verdienen.
And if I **had** a lot of money,	I **might send** you a present, Herbie.
Und wenn ich viel Geld hätte,	würde ich dir vielleicht ein Geschenk schicken, Herbie.
If you **didn't dream** all day,	you **might have** more time for your magic.
Wenn du nicht den ganzen Tag träumtest,	würdest du (vielleicht) mehr Zeit für deine Zauberei haben.
And if you **practiced** more often,	you **could get** quite good.
Und wenn du öfter übtest,	könntest du ganz gut werden.
If I **were** you,	I **would go** and **practice** some new tricks.
An deiner Stelle	würde ich ein paar neue Tricks üben.

- Steht im *if*-Satz das *past tense*, so steht im Hauptsatz *would* + Infinitiv *(conditional)*. Neben *would* können – mit entsprechendem Bedeutungsunterschied – auch *might* und *could* verwendet werden.
- Hält der Sprecher die Bedingung für wahrscheinlich nicht erfüllbar oder den Tatsachen widersprechend, so steht im *if*-Satz das *past tense*.
- Bei den Personen *I, he, she* und *it* wird neben dem *past tense* von *be (was)* auch die Form *were* verwendet, (vgl. die Redewendung *If I were you ...*)

⚠ *Would* ist im *if*-Bedingungssatz falsch.

§ 4 **Verben mit zwei Objekten**   Verbs with two objects   Unit 2 Step B

Zahlreiche Verben können (oder müssen) zwei Objekte haben.
Zu ihnen gehören: *bring, give, lend, pass, read, send, show, take, teach, tell.*

subject	verb	indirect object	direct object
Mr Hopper	has shown	everybody	his stained glass windows.
Harry	has taught	his new friends	some fantastic tricks.
They	have told	him	some new jokes.
Ben	is going to send	Harry	his magic book.
And perhaps Herbie	will write	Linda	a letter.

- Das indirekte Objekt (meistens eine Person) steht im allgemeinen vor dem direkten Objekt (meistens eine Sache).

subject	verb	direct object	indirect object
Harry	had lent	his book	**to** Ben.
Herbie	gave	his telephone number	**to** a girl in his new class.

- Wenn das indirekte Objekt jedoch stärker betont werden soll oder wenn es sehr lang ist, steht es hinter dem direkten Objekt, dann allerdings mit *to*.

verb	direct object	indirect object
You can give	it	**to** him.
Show	them	**to** her.

- Wenn beide Objekte Pronomen sind, wird im allgemeinen die Reihenfolge 1. direktes Objekt 2. indirektes Objekt vorgezogen.

Unit 3

5 Das 'conditional perfect'

I **would have stopped** in time.	Ich **hätte** rechtzeitig **angehalten**.
He **should have seen** the boy.	Er **hätte** den Jungen **sehen sollen**.
He **shouldn't have driven** so fast.	Er **hätte** nicht so schnell **fahren sollen**.
It **could have been** much worse.	Es **hätte** viel schlimmer **sein können**.
He **might have killed** the boy.	Er **hätte** den Jungen (vielleicht sogar) **töten können**.

- Das *conditional perfect (conditional II)* wird gebildet aus *would + have + past participle*.
- Anstelle von *would* können – mit entsprechendem Bedeutungsunterschied – auch *could*, *might* und *should* verwendet werden.

⚠ Alle *'perfect'* Zeiten werden mit *has/have* oder *had* gebildet:
present perfect: You have seen it/She has seen it.
past perfect: She had seen it.
conditional perfect: She would have seen it.

Grammar: Unit 3

§6 Bedingungssätze mit dem 'conditional perfect' im Hauptsatz
Conditional sentences with the conditional perfect in the main clause

Typ III Nicht erfüllbare Bedingungen

if-Satz (if-clause)	Hauptsatz (main clause)
If Victoria **hadn't invited** Harry to her party,	things **would have been** different.
Wenn Victoria Harry nicht zu ihrer Party eingeladen hätte,	wären die Dinge anders gewesen.
If the car **hadn't stopped**,	Harry **would have gone** to Victoria's party.
Wenn das Auto nicht angehalten hätte,	wäre Harry zu Victorias Party gegangen.
If he **had gone** to her party,	he **could have shown** his magic tricks.
Wenn er zu ihrer Party gegangen wäre,	hätte er seine Zaubertricks zeigen können.
If Victoria **had been** nicer to him,	she **might have become** Harry's girlfriend.
Wenn Victoria netter zu ihm gewesen wäre,	hätte sie (vielleicht) Harrys Freundin werden können.
past perfect	conditional perfect

- Steht im *if*-Satz das *past perfect*, so steht im Hauptsatz das *conditional perfect*.
- Der Sprecher weiß, daß die im *if*-Satz genannte Bedingung nicht mehr verwirklicht werden kann, da die Handlung in der Vergangenheit nicht wirklich stattfand:
    If he had gone to Victoria's party = He didn't go to Victoria's party.
- Steht im Bedingungssatz der *if*-Satz zuerst, so setzt man ein Komma.
- Falls die Folge einer Handlung in der Gegenwart noch gilt, kann im Hauptsatz anstelle des *conditional perfect* auch *would* + Infinitiv *(conditional)* verwendet werden:
    If you had only taken your medicine every day, you would feel much better now.
                                                                would + Infinitiv
    Wenn du nur deine Medizin täglich eingenommen hättest, würdest du dich jetzt viel besser fühlen.

⚠ *'d* ist die Kurzform von *had* und *would*:
   He**'d** come if he**'d** known. = He **would** have come if he **had** known.

§7 Das Present perfect simple mit 'for' und 'since'
The present perfect simple with 'for' and 'since'

(Zum resultativen Gebrauch des *present perfect simple* und zur Verwendung mit *ever*, *never* und *not yet* vgl. §1)

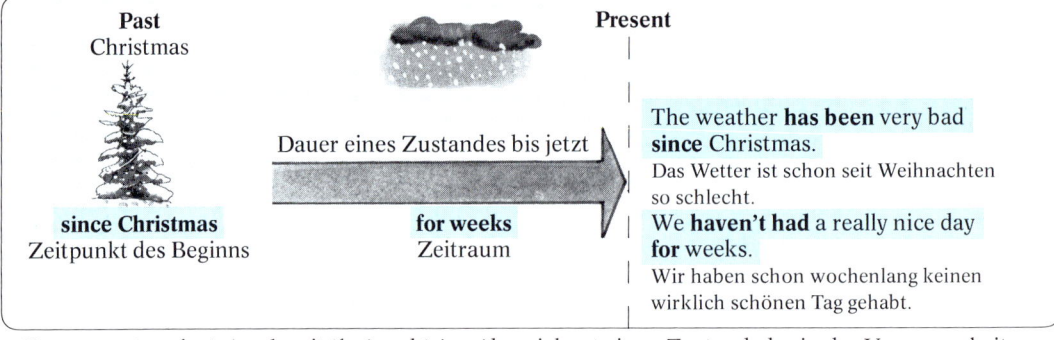

Past — Christmas — since Christmas (Zeitpunkt des Beginns) — Dauer eines Zustandes bis jetzt — for weeks (Zeitraum) — **Present**

The weather **has been** very bad **since** Christmas.
Das Wetter ist schon seit Weihnachten so schlecht.

We **haven't had** a really nice day **for** weeks.
Wir haben schon wochenlang keinen wirklich schönen Tag gehabt.

- Das *present perfect simple* mit *'for'* und *'since'* bezeichnet einen Zustand, der in der Vergangenheit anfing und bis zur Gegenwart andauert.
- Vor allem Verben wie *be, belong to, have, know*, die einen Zustand und keine Handlung im Verlauf ausdrücken, werden im *present perfect simple* mit *'for'* und *'since'* gebraucht.
- Im Deutschen benutzen wir meist das Präsens und unterstreichen die Dauer des Zustands häufig mit *'schon'*.

Grammar: Unit 3/4

'for' und 'since'

How long?	My dad **has been** in Arizona	**for** a long time now.	Mein Papa ist jetzt *schon lange* in A.
	He**'s had** that guitar	**for** twenty years.	Er hat die Gitarre *seit zwanzig Jahren*.
	The house **has belonged to us**	**for** many years.	Das Haus gehört uns *schon seit vielen Jahren*.

Since when?	We **haven't had** any news from him	**since** 1986.	Wir haben schon *seit 1986* keine Nachricht von ihm.
	I**'ve known** him	**since** I was a child.	Ich kenne ihn schon *seit meiner Kindheit*.
	But I **haven't seen** him	**since** last year.	Aber ich habe ihn *seit letztem Jahr* nicht mehr gesehen.

- *For* bezieht sich auf den ‎Zeitraum‎, den ein Zustand bereits andauert:

  for { *ten minutes / three hours / a few months / a long time* }

- *Since* bezieht sich auf den ‎Zeitpunkt‎, an dem der Zustand begann:

  since { *half past one / last Monday / November / Christmas / 1986 / I was ten* }

Unit 4

8 Der Gebrauch des bestimmten Artikels
The use of the definite article

Unit 4 Step B

Der bestimmte Artikel zeigt an, daß Dinge oder Personen näher bezeichnet werden:

Horses are beautiful animals.

Hier geht es um Pferde ganz allgemein.

The horses that you can see in the picture on page 56 were used to pull wagons.

Hier sind die Pferde (in diesem Fall durch einen Relativsatz) näher bezeichnet.

Ohne Artikel	Mit Artikel
Stoffbezeichnungen und abstrakte (allgemeine) Begriffe, die nicht näher bestimmt sind.	Stoffbezeichnungen und abstrakte (allgemeine) Begriffe, die näher bestimmt sind (oder bereits genannt wurden).
Water is a problem in Southern California. Where there's **smoke** there's **fire**. **Life** is too short.	‎The‎ water ‎in our rivers‎ is not very clean. ‎The‎ fire ‎that broke out in 1906‎ burned down many houses. I've just read a book on ‎the‎ life ‎of Christopher Columbus‎.
	• Der bestimmte Artikel steht, wenn die Stoffbezeichnung oder der abstrakte (allgemeine) Begriff durch eine Ergänzung *(in our rivers)* oder durch einen Relativsatz näher bestimmt wird.

Grammar: Unit 4

Personennamen im Singular	Familiennamen im Plural
Jolene and **Sandra** are pen pals. **Uncle Bernie** rang up last night. **Poor Jolene** wasn't allowed to go surfing. (Die arme Jolene …)	**The Donahues** and **the Robinsons** live in New York.
• Personennamen im Singular und Verwandtschaftsbezeichnungen, die wie Namen gebraucht werden, stehen ohne den bestimmten Artikel. Auch wenn dem Namen eine Adjektiv vorausgeht, steht kein Artikel (im Gegensatz zum Deutschen).	• Familiennamen im Plural werden mit dem bestimmten Artikel gebraucht.
Öffentliche Einrichtungen, Institutionen und Verkehrsmittel	**Öffentliche Gebäude, Institutionen und Verkehrsmittel**
Jolene doesn't like **school** much. A lot of people go to **church** on Sunday. Many American kids go to school by **bus**.	**The** school that she goes to isn't very modern. **The** church in Sundown Road is only 10 years old. **The** bus to Oshkosh leaves at 5.30.
• Wenn man an den Zweck einer Institution denkt (Unterricht, Gottesdienst usw.), steht der bestimmte Artikel nicht. Mit *by bus/by train* usw. ist die Verkehrsverbindung allgemein gemeint.	• Der bestimmte Artikel wird verwendet, wenn man an eine ganz bestimmte Schule, Kirche usw., ein bestimmtes Gebäude oder Fahrzeug denkt.

Geographische und andere Ortsbezeichnungen

Ohne Artikel	Mit Artikel
Ländernamen im Singular, Berggipfel **Mount Whitney** in **California** is about as high as **Mont Blanc** in **France**.	**Ländernamen im Plural, Gebirge** The pioneers that came to **the United States of America** found it difficult to cross **the Rocky Mountains**.
Parks, Seen, Straßen **Central Park** is New York's biggest park. Oshkosh lies on **Lake Winnebago**. Garth lives on **119th Street** in Harlem.	**Namen mit** *of-phrase* **The Statue of Liberty** is in New York harbor. **The Isle of Wight** is a popular place for a seaside holiday. **The Tower (of London)** is one of the city's famous sights.

§9 Der Gebrauch des unbestimmten Artikels
The use of the indefinite article

Unit 4 Step C

In bestimmten Wendungen unterscheidet sich der Gebrauch des unbestimmten Artikels im Englischen vom Deutschen.

Berufsbezeichnungen	
Tracey's father is **a policeman**.	Traceys Vater ist Polizist.
Tessie Ferranti is **a truck driver**.	Tessie Ferranti ist Lastwagenfahrerin.
Zeitangaben	
Tessie drives down to Florida once **a month**.	Tessi fährt einmal im Monat herunter nach Florida.
She is not allowed to go faster than 55 miles **an hour**.	Sie darf nicht schneller als 55 Meilen in der Stunde fahren.
The motel room is 30 dollars **a night**.	Das Zimmer im Motel kostet 30 Dollar pro Nacht.
Mengenangaben	
These apples are 50 cents **a pound**.	Diese Äpfel kosten 50 Cents das Pfund.
Nach *half, quite, such*	
Can I have **half a** pound of butter, please?	Kann ich bitte ein halbes Pfund Butter haben?
This is **quite a** good story.	Dies ist eine ganz gute Geschichte.
I've never read **such an** interesting book.	Ich habe noch nie ein so interessantes Buch gelesen.

- Bei Berufsbezeichnungen, Zeitangaben und bei Mengenangaben steht im Englischen der unbestimmte Artikel. Im Gegensatz dazu steht im Deutschen kein Artikel bzw. der bestimmte Artikel.
- Beachte die Stellung des unbestimmten Artikels nach Wörtern wie *quite, half, such*.

Unit 5

10 Das Passiv   The passive

Unit 5 Step A

Simple present
Das Passiv des *simple present* wird gebildet aus *am/is/are* und dem *past participle*.

active voice	passive voice
subject verb object	subject verb
They make these cameras in Japan.	These cameras **are made** in Japan.

- Das Objekt des Aktivsatzes wird im Passivsatz zum Subjekt.
- Oft wird in Passivsätzen der Verursacher einer Handlung nicht genannt, weil er unwichtig oder unbekannt ist: In dem Satz *These cameras are made in Japan* wird nicht gesagt, von wem die Kameras hergestellt werden. (Vgl. § 11)
- Passivsätze kommen häufig in Zeitungsberichten, in historischen Berichten und in technischen Beschreibungen vor.
- Passivsätze stellen eine Handlung aus anderer Sicht dar als Aktivsätze.
  In dem Satz *They make these cameras …* ist *They* Subjekt des Aktivsatzes und somit besonders betont, während im Passivsatz die Betonung auf dem Subjekt *These cameras* liegt.

Grammar: Unit 5/6

§ 11 Das Simple Past des Passivs Unit 5 Step B

Das Passiv des *simple past* wird gebildet mit *was/were* und dem *past participle*.

active:	On Friday	someone	**stole**	a car in George Street.
passive:	On Friday	a car	**was stolen**	in George Street.
passive:	**Was**	anything	**taken**	out of the car?
active:	This morning	the police	**arrested**	two men.
passive:	This morning	two men	**were arrested**.	

Das Passiv mit 'by-agent'

Will man besonders betonen, **von wem** etwas getan wird, ergänzt man den Passivsatz durch das *by-agent*.

Vergleiche:	ohne 'by-agent'	mit 'by-agent'
	This morning two men were arrested.	This morning two men were arrested **by Sergeant Donahue.**

- In diesem Satz ist es klar, wer der Handelnde war *(police)*. Er braucht deshalb nicht erwähnt zu werden.
- In diesem Satz wird besonders betont, daß es nicht irgendein Polizist war, sondern Sergeant Donahue.

§ 12 Der Infinitiv des Passivs   The passive infinitive   Unit 5 Step C

active			passive		
	auxiliary	infinitive		auxiliary	infinitiv
You	must	**shut**	These doors	must	**be shut.**
You	can easily	**do**	This	can easily	**be done.**
You	should	**open**	The windows	should	**be opened.**

- Nach Hilfsverben steht im Aktivsatz der Infinitiv Aktiv *(shut, do, open)*, im Passivsatz steht der Infinitiv Passiv *(be shut, be done, be opened)*.
- Im Deutschen ist das Passiv weniger gebräuchlich als im Englischen. Im Deutschen bevorzugt man statt des Passivs oft eine unpersönliche Konstruktion mit „man".

The windows should be opened.
Man sollte die Fenster öffnen.
(Die Fenster sollten geöffnet werden.)

Lots of things can be done with a computer.
Man kann vieles mit einem Computer machen.
(Mit einem Computer kann vieles gemacht werden.)

Unit 6

§ 13 Verben mit Adverbien und Präpositionen   Unit 6 Step A
Phrasal verbs and prepositional verbs

Viele Verben können mit unterschiedlichen Adverbien oder Präpositionen fest verbunden sein. Zu ihnen gehören z.B. *come, get, go, look, take*. Durch diese Verbindungen entstehen eine Vielzahl von Begriffen.
Die folgenden Adverbien und Präpositionen sind in *Orange Line* in Verbverbindungen erschienen:

talk **about**	show **around**	fall **down**	look **like**	come **round**
look **after**	stare **at**	wait **for**	take **off**	put **through**
play **against**	bring **back**	believe **in**	turn **on**	listen **to**
throw **away**	leave **behind**	break **into**	fill **out**	clear **up**

Grammar: Unit 6

1. Verben mit Adverbien Phrasal verbs

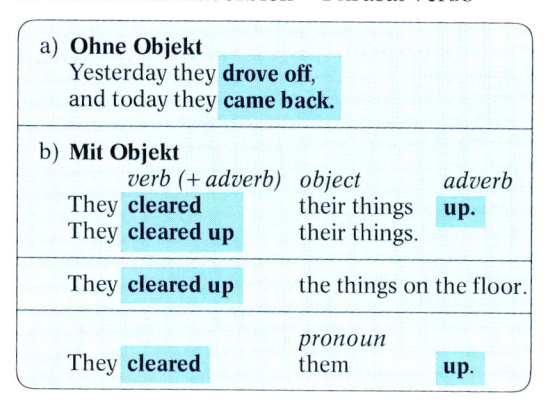

a) **Ohne Objekt**
Yesterday they **drove off**,
and today they **came back**.

b) **Mit Objekt**

verb (+ adverb)	object	adverb
They **cleared**	their things	**up.**
They **cleared up**	their things.	
They **cleared up**	the things on the floor.	
	pronoun	
They **cleared**	them	**up.**

- *Phrasal verbs* können mit oder ohne Objekt gebraucht werden.
- Ist das Objekt des *phrasal verb* ein Nomen, so kann das Adverb vor oder hinter dem Objekt stehen.
- Ist das Objekt sehr lang, so steht das Adverb vor dem Objekt.
- Ist das Objekt ein Personalpronomen, so steht das Adverb hinter dem Objekt.

2. Verben mit Präpositionen Prepositional verbs

	verb + preposition	*obj.*	
I'll	**wait for**	you	at the station.
I kept	**looking at**	my watch.	
I was	**listening to**	a cassette	while I was waiting.
But I	**thought of**	you	all the time.

- *Prepositional verbs* haben im Aktivsatz immer ein Objekt bei sich.
- Die Präposition steht vor dem Objekt.

4 Die Wortstellung im englischen Satz
Word order in the English sentence

Unit 6 Step B

1. Aussagesätze Statements

	subject	*verb*	*object*	
	Tommy	found	a real book.	
	He	didn't want to throw	it	away.
	The mechanical teacher	had given	Margie	test after test.
When	Margie and Tommy	turned	the page,	it had the same words on it.
Margie had done worse and worse until	her mother	had phoned	the County Inspector.	

- Die normale Wortstellung im englischen Satz lautet: Subjekt – Verb – Objekt.
- Auch bei zusammengesetzten Zeiten wird diese Wortstellung beibehalten.
- Anders als im Deutschen wird das Satzmuster S – V – O auch in Nebensätzen beibehalten.

Grammar: Unit 6

2. Fragesätze   Questions

question word	auxiliary	subject	verb	object
–	Are	you	doing	your homework?
–	May	I	read	the book?
–	Do	all the kids	learn	the same things?
How	can	anyone	write	a book about school?
Where	did	you	find	the book?

- In Fragesätzen stehen Hilfsverben vor dem Subjekt.
- Die Stellung S – V – O wird auch in Fragesätzen beibehalten.

3. Die Stellung von Orts- und Zeitangaben   The position of adverbials of place and time

adverbial	subject	verb	object	adverbial
	Tommy	had found	the book	**in the attic.**
	They	had	that type of school	**hundreds of years ago.**
On Saturdays and Sundays	Margie	didn't have to do	any work.	
In the old schools	all the children	learnt	the same things.	
	Margie	had to put	her homework	*place* *time* **in the same slot** **every day.**

- Orts- und Zeitangaben können am Anfang oder am Ende eines Satzes stehen.
- Anders als im Deutschen bleibt das Satzmuster S – V – O auch in Sätzen mit Orts- und Zeitangaben erhalten.
- Stehen Orts- oder Zeitangaben am Anfang des Satzes, so sind sie stärker betont.
- Stehen eine Orts- und eine Zeitangabe am Ende des Satzes, so gilt: **Ort vor Zeit**.

4. Die Stellung von Adverbien der Häufigkeit   The position of adverbs of frequency

subject	auxiliary	adverb	verb	object	
Margie	–	**always**	hated	school.	
The mechanical teacher	–	**sometimes**	broke down.		
Margie	had	**never**	seen	a book	before.
She	could	**usually**	do	her homework	in the evening.
She was **often** late.					

- *Always, never, often, sometimes* und *usually* sind Adverbien der Häufigkeit; d. h. sie drücken aus, wie oft etwas geschieht. Sie stehen normalerweise zwischen Subjekt und Verb.

- Enthält der Satz ein Hilfsverb, so steht das Adverb der Häufigkeit nach dem Hilfsverb; besteht das Verb aus mehreren Hilfsverben, dann steht das Adverb nach dem 1. Hilfsverb.
- Besteht das Verb nur aus einer Form von *be*, steht das Verb meist hinter dieser Form.
- Das Adverb *sometimes* kann auch am Ende oder am Anfang des Satzes stehen: *Sometimes the mechanical teacher broke down. The mechanical teacher broke down sometimes.*

⚠ Im Deutschen stehen Adverbien der Häufigkeit oft zwischen Verb und Objekt bzw. nach dem Verb: Er fährt oft Ski.
Im Englischen hingegen darf das Adverb der Häufigkeit nie zwischen Verb und Objekt stehen.

5. Die Stellung der Adverbien der Art und Weise

front position	subject	auxiliary	mid position	verb + object		end position
	Margie			looked at	the mechanical teacher	**angrily.**
	Each child	should		be taught		**differently.**
	The mechanical teacher		**quickly**	calculated	Margie's marks.	
	The Inspector	could	**easily**	repair	the mechanical teacher.	
Excitedly	Margie			turned	the pages of the old book.	

- Die Adverbien der Art und Weise *(adverbs of manner)* stehen sehr häufig am Ende des Satzes.
- Stehen sie in der Mitte des Satzes, so stehen sie direkt vor dem Vollverb oder zwischen Hilfsverb und Vollverb.
- Nur wenn sie stark betont werden sollen, erscheinen Adverbien der Art und Weise am Anfang des Satzes.

⚠ Adverbien stehen **nie** zwischen Vollverb und Objekt.

Register des Grammatikanhangs

	Seite
Artikel (§§ 8, 9)	97–99
bestimmter Artikel (§ 8)	97/98
unbestimmter Artikel (§ 9)	99
Bedingungssätze (§§ 1f), 3, 5, 6)	92, 94, 95, 96
conditional sentences (§§ 1f), 3)	92, 94
conditional perfect (§§ 5, 6)	95, 96
definite article (§ 8)	97/98
'for' and 'since' (§ 7)	96/97
Das Gerund (§ 2)	92/93
Das Gerund als Subjekt (§ 2)	92
Das Gerund als Objekt (§ 2)	93
indefinite article (§ 9)	99
infinitive, passive (§ 12)	100
Passiv (§§ 10, 11, 12)	99/100
simple present (§ 10)	99
simple past (§ 11)	100
passive infinitive (§ 12)	100

	Seite
phrasal verbs (§ 13)	100/101
position of adverbs of frequency (§ 14)	102
position of adverbials of place and time (§ 14)	102
position of adverbs of manner (§ 14)	103
present perfect simple with 'for' and 'since' (§ 7)	96//97
prepositional verbs (§ 13)	100/101
questions (word order) (§ 14)	102
statements (word order) (§ 14)	101
tenses (§ 1, *revision*)	91/92
Verben mit zwei Objekten (§ 4)	94/95
Verben mit Adverbien und Präpositionen (§ 13)	100/101
Wortstellung (§ 14)	101–103
Zeiten (§ 1, Übersicht)	91/92

Useful grammatical terms

active voice [ˈæktɪv vɔɪs]	Aktiv
adjective [ˈædʒɪktɪv]	Adjektiv
adverb [ˈædvɜːb]	Adverb
adverb of manner [ˈædvɜːb əv ˈmænə]	Adverb der Art und Weise
auxiliary [ɔːˈɡzɪljərɪ]	Hilfsverb
cardinal number [ˌkɑːdɪnl ˈnʌmbə]	Grundzahl
clause [klɔːz]	Nebensatz
comparison [kəmˈpærɪsn]	Steigerung
conditional sentence [kənˈdɪʃənl ˈsentəns]	Bedingungssatz
contact clause [ˈkɒntækt klɔːz]	Relativsatz ohne Relativpronomen
definite article [ˈdefənɪt ˈɑːtɪkl]	bestimmter Artikel
future [ˈfjuːtʃə]	Futur
gerund [ˈdʒerənd]	„Gerund"
if-clause [ˈɪfklɔːz]	if-Satz
indefinite article [ɪnˈdefənɪt]	unbestimmter Artikel
infinitive [ɪnˈfɪnətɪv]	Infinitiv
main clause [ˈmeɪn klɔːz]	Hauptsatz
noun [naʊn]	Nomen
passive voice [ˈpæsɪv vɔɪs]	Passiv
past participle [ˈpɑːst ˈpɑːtɪsɪpl]	Partizip Perfekt
past perfect [ˈpɑːst ˈpɜːfɪkt]	Plusquamperfekt
past progressive [ˈpɑːst prəˈɡresɪv]	Verlaufsform Imperfekt
past tense [ˈpɑːs_tens]	Imperfekt
position [pəˈzɪʃn]	Stellung (eines Satzteils)
end position [ˈend pəˈzɪʃn]	am Ende eines Satzes
front position [ˈfrʌnt pəˈzɪʃn]	am Anfang eines Satzes
mid position [ˈmɪd pəˈzɪʃn]	in der Mitte eines Satzes
possessive determiner [pəˈzesɪv dɪˈtɜːmɪnə]	Possessivbegleiter
possessive pronoun [pəˈzesɪv ˈprəʊnaʊn]	Possessivpronomen
preposition [ˌprepəˈzɪʃn]	Präposition
present perfect [ˌpreznt ˈpɜːfɪkt]	Perfekt
present progressive [ˌpreznt prəʊˈɡresɪv]	Verlaufsform Präsens
present tense [ˈpreznt tens]	Präsens
prop-word [ˈprɒpwɜːd]	Stützwort
question tag [ˈkwestʃən tæɡ]	Bestätigungsfrage
question word [ˈkwestʃən wɜːd]	Fragewort
reciprocal pronoun [rɪˈsɪprəkl ˌprəʊnaʊn]	reziprokes (rückbezügliches) Pronomen
relative clause [ˈrelətɪv klɔːz]	Relativsatz
sentence [ˈsentəns]	Satz
simple past [ˌsɪmpl ˈpɑːst]	Imperfekt
subject [ˈsʌbdʒɪkt]	Subjekt
substitute [ˈsʌbstɪtjuːt]	Ersatzverb
tense [tens]	Zeit
verb [vɜːb]	Vollverb
will-future [ˈwɪl ˌfjuːtʃə]	*will*-Futur

Vocabulary

Lautzeichen (Phonetic Symbols)

Vokale (Vowels)
[ɑː]   father
[ʌ]   brush
[e]   pen
[ə]   away
[ɜː]   turn
[æ]   bank
[ɪ]   this
[iː]   piece
[ɒ]   shop
[ɔː]   door
[ʊ]   pullover
[uː]   blue

Doppellaute (Diphthongs)
[aɪ]   right
[aʊ]   house
[eə]   their
[eɪ]   late
[ɪə]   idea
[ɔɪ]   boy
[əʊ]   road
[ʊə]   sure

Konsonanten (Consonants)
[j]   your
[l]   listen
[ŋ]   sing
[ŋg]   England
[r]   red
[s]   sister
[z]   has
[ʒ]   garage
[dʒ]   German
[ʃ]   she
[tʃ]   child
[st/sp] story, special
[ð]   them
[θ]   thanks
[v]   leave
[w]   week

ˈ = Hauptbetonung   ˌ = Nebenbetonung
‿ = besonders enge Bindung zweier Wörter aneinander

~ Dieses Zeichen in der mittleren Spalte ersetzt das neue Wort.
° Die mit ° gekennzeichneten Wörter gehören zum rezeptiven Wortschatz. In Bundesländern, in denen ein rezeptiver Wortschatz nicht ausdrücklich verlangt wird, werden diese Wörter genauso behandelt wie der übrige Wortschatz.
⟨ ⟩ Stücke, deren Überschriften, und Übungen, deren Ziffern in Winkelklammern stehen, sind fakultativ.

s.th. = something
s.o. = someone
s.b. = somebody
n. = noun (Nomen)
AE = American English
BE = British English
sl. = slang
sing./pl. = singular/plural

Stopover A: Voices of America

°stopover [ˈstɒpəʊvə]	a stop between flights	°Zwischenlandung
movie (AE) [ˈmuːvɪ]	film that you see at a cinema or on TV	Film
°politician [ˌpɒlɪˈtɪʃn]	~s play an important role in public life.	°Politiker(in)
teenager [ˈtiːnˌeɪdʒə]	boy or girl between the age of 13 and 19	Teenager
Paul Christiansen [ˈkrɪstjənsn]	a boy's name	Personenname (männlich)
Sarah Rosenbaum [ˌseərə ˈrəʊzənbaʊm]	a girl's name	Personenname (weiblich)
°cello [ˈtʃeləʊ]	Tom plays the guitar. Kate plays the ~.	°Cello
country [ˈkʌntrɪ]	A ~ group plays ~ music.	Country(musik)
Jolene Clarke [dʒəʊˈliːn ˈklɑːk]	a girl's name	Personenname (weiblich)
Bryan Schulz [ˌbraɪən ˈʃʊlts]	a boy's name	Personenname (männlich)

Stopover A

to be **divorced** [dɪˈvɔːst]	not to be husband and wife any longer	geschieden sein
Tracey Donahue [ˌtreɪsɪ ˈdɒnəjuː]	a girl's name	Personenname *(weiblich)*
apartment (AE) [əˈpɑːtmənt]	BE: flat	Wohnung
to **babysit** [ˈbeɪbɪsɪt]	to look after a baby or young child when the parents are out	babysitten, auf kleine Kinder aufpassen
Garth Robinson [ˌgɑːθ ˈrɒbɪnsn]	a boy's name	Personenname *(männlich)*
basketball [ˈbɑːskɪtbɔːl]	a ball game (very popular in the USA)	Basketball
block [blɒk]	area of buildings with a street on each side	Häuserblock
Sheena [ˈʃiːnə]	a girl's name	*Vorname (weiblich)*
Spanish [ˈspænɪʃ]	In Madrid people speak ~.	spanisch; Spanisch
Carmen García [ˌkɑːmən gɑːˈsiə]	a girl's name	Personenname *(weiblich)*
Mexico [ˈmeksɪkəʊ]	a country in America	Mexiko
all my life	I've lived here ~ = I've always lived here.	mein ganzes Leben
°**driver's license** (AE) [ˈlaɪsns]	You are not allowed to drive without a ~.	°Führerschein
Marco Ferranti [ˌmɑːkəʊ fəˈræntɪ]	a boy's name	Personenname *(männlich)*
Tessie [ˈtesɪ]	a girl's name	*Vorname (weiblich)*
truck (AE) [trʌk]	BE: lorry	Lastwagen, Lieferwagen
°to **do a paper route** [ˈpeɪpəruːt]	to take (news)papers to people's houses	°Zeitungen austragen

The USA – facts and figures

°**figure** [ˈfɪgə]	~s are numbers.	°Ziffer, Zahl
population [ˌpɒpjʊˈleɪʃn]	all the people who live in a country or town	Bevölkerung
% = **per cent** [pəˈsent]	1 ~ = the hundredth part of s.th.	Prozent
°**Asian** [ˈeɪʃn]	China and India are ~ countries.	°asiatisch; Asiate, Asiatin
°**Eskimo** [ˈeskɪməʊ]	~s live in the far north of North America.	°Eskimo
°**Hispanic** [hɪˈspænɪk]	of Spanish-speaking countries; s.o. from there	°*jemand aus einem spanischsprachigen Land*
Puerto Rico [ˌpwɜːtəʊ ˈriːkəʊ]	a small island near the USA	Puerto Rico
Cuba [ˈkjuːbə]	a large island near the USA	Kuba
flag [flæg]	The American ~ is red, white, and blue.	Fahne, Flagge
star [stɑː]	At night, you can often see ~s in the sky.	Stern
state [steɪt]	Oklahoma is one of the ~s of the USA.	(Bundes-)Staat
the **Federal Republic of Germany** (FRG) [ˈfedərəl rɪˈpʌblɪk əv ˈdʒɜːmənɪ]	= West Germany	die Bundesrepublik Deutschland
Switzerland [ˈswɪtsələnd]	a country in Europe	die Schweiz
to **die** [daɪ]	At the end of our lives, we all must ~.	sterben
each [iːtʃ]	"I've got seven pullovers – one for ~ day of the week".	jede(-r, -s) (einzelne)
hot dog [ˈhɒt dɒg]	hot sausage with bread	Hot Dog *(heißes Würstchen im Brötchen)*
times [taɪmz]	3 ~ 3 is 9.	mal

twice [twaɪs]	two times	zweimal
the **European Community** [ˌjʊərəˈpiːən kəˈmjuːnəti]	Britain, France, Germany, etc. are in the ~.	die Europäische Gemeinschaft
°**area** [ˈeərɪə]	how big a field, country etc. is	°Fläche, Gebiet
km² [ˌskweə kɪˈlɒmɪtə], BE: [~ˈkɪləʊmiːtə]	= square kilometer (AE)/~ kilometre (BE)	Quadratkilometer
TV set [set]	If your ~ is broken, you can't watch TV.	Fernsehgerät
size [saɪz]	What ~ is it = How big is it?	Größe
°**statistics** [stəˈtɪstɪks]	~ tell you lots of facts.	°Statistik(en)

⟨This land is your land⟩

chorus [ˈkɔːrəs]	part of a song which you sing again and again	Refrain
redwood [ˈredwʊd]	~ trees get very old and very big.	Mammutbaum (kalifornischer Nadelbaum)
Gulf Stream [ˈɡʌlf ˌstriːm]	The ~ is in the Atlantic Ocean.	Golfstrom
was made [meɪd]	This car ~ in Germany = They made this car in Germany.	wurde gemacht, hergestellt
ribbon [ˈrɪbən]	A road can look like a long ~.	Band
highway (AE) [ˈhaɪweɪ]	main road	autobahnähnliche Landstraße
endless [ˈendlɪs]	without end	endlos
skyway [ˈskaɪweɪ]	here: sky	Himmel
valley [ˈvælɪ]	low land between mountains	Tal
to roam [rəʊm]	to travel or walk about	herumstreunen
to ramble [ˈræmbl]	to walk around	herumwandern
footstep [ˈfʊtstep]	When you walk, you make ~s.	Schritt, Fußstapfen
to sparkle [ˈspɑːkl]	Pieces of glass often ~ in the sun.	funkeln, glitzern
diamond [ˈdaɪəmənd]	~s are small and very expensive stones.	Diamant
desert [ˈdezət]	very dry land where almost nothing can grow	Wüste
to stroll [strəʊl]	to ramble	herumbummeln
to wave [weɪv]	here: to move in the wind	hier: wogen
dust [dʌst]	When it's dry, there's a lot of ~ on the roads.	Staub
to roll [rəʊl]	to turn over and over	hier: wirbeln
to chant [tʃɑːnt]	to sing	singen
to lift [lɪft]	They had a wonderful view from the top of the mountain when the fog ~ed.	hier: sich lichten
Woody Guthrie [ˌwʊdɪ ˈɡʌθrɪ]	an American folksinger	amerikanischer Folksänger
Louisiana [luːˌiːzɪˈænə]	a state in the South of the USA	amerikanischer Bundesstaat
newsboy [ˈnjuːzbɔɪ]	a boy who sells newspapers	Zeitungsjunge
hobo (AE) [ˈhəʊbəʊ]	s.o. without a home who travels a lot	Vagabund, Wanderarbeiter
Pete Seeger [ˌpiːt ˈsiːɡə]	an American folksinger	amerikanischer Folksänger
Bob Dylan [ˌbɒb ˈdɪlən]	an American rock and folksinger	amerikanischer Rock- und Folksänger
Odetta [əʊˈdetə]	an American folksinger	amerikanische Folksängerin
national anthem [ˌnæʃənl ˈænθəm]	a country's national song	Nationalhymne
collage [kɒˈlɑːʒ]	You put photos, newspaper articles etc. together to make a ~.	Collage

Exercises

1. **interest** [ˈɪntrɪst] — Football is Tom's main ~. — Interesse
   duty [ˈdjuːtɪ] — what s.o. must do — Pflicht; Aufgabe
   in fact [ɪn ˈfækt] — really — in der Tat, tatsächlich
   whether [ˈweðə] — I don't know ~ he's got a brother. — ob
2. °**bowling center** (AE)/~ **centre** (BE) [ˈbəʊlɪŋ ˌsentə] — Some people like to go to a ~ a few times every month. — °Bowling-/Kegelzentrum
3. **mailman** (AE) [ˈmeɪlmən] — BE: postman — Briefträger
5. °**tense** [tens] — — °Tempus, Zeitform
   °**cholera** [ˈkɒlərə] — Even today people can die of ~. — °Cholera
6. **Stan** [stæn] — a boy's name, short for Stanley — Vorname (männlich)

Baltimore [ˈbɔːltɪmɔː] — Stadt im Osten der USA
Brooklyn [ˈbrʊklɪn] — Stadtbezirk von New York
Denver [ˈdenvə] — Stadt in Colorado
Harlem [ˈhɑːləm] — Stadtteil von New York
Miami [maɪˈæmɪ] — Stadt in Florida
Pittsburgh [ˈpɪtsbɜːg] — Stadt in Pennsylvania
San Antonio [ˌsæn ˌænˈtəʊnɪəʊ] — Stadt in Texas
San Francisco [ˌsæn frənˈsɪskəʊ] — Stadt in Kalifornien
Seattle [sɪˈætl] — Stadt im Nordwesten der USA
Arizona [ˌærɪˈzəʊnə] — Staat im Südwesten der USA
California [ˌkælɪˈfɔːnjə] — Staat im Westen der USA
Colorado [ˌkɒləˈrɑːdəʊ] — Staat im Westen der USA
Florida [ˈflɒrɪdə] — Staat im Südosten der USA
Pennsylvania [ˌpensɪlˈveɪnjə] — Staat im Osten der USA
Texas [ˈteksəs] — Staat im Südwesten der USA

Unit 1

A What New York means to me

crime [kraɪm] — It is a very serious ~ if you steal s.o.'s car. — Verbrechen
maybe [ˈmeɪbiː] — = perhaps — vielleicht
race [reɪs] — Black and white people belong to two different ~s. — Rasse
°**skyscraper** [ˈskaɪˌskreɪpə] — very high building — °Wolkenkratzer
smell [smel] — I don't like the ~ of that cheese. — Geruch, Duft
poverty [ˈpɒvətɪ] — There's a lot of ~ = A lot of people are poor. — Armut
°**sidewalk** (AE) [ˈsaɪdwɔːk] — Cars drive on the road, people walk on the ~. — °Bürgersteig
place [pleɪs] — This is the right ~ for a picnic. — Platz, Stelle, Ort
café [ˈkæfeɪ], AE: [kæˈfeɪ] — small restaurant — Imbißstube, Café
kid [kɪd] — child or teenager — Kind, Jugendliche(r)
skateboard [ˈskeɪtbɔːd] — It's like a board with 4 small wheels. — Skateboard, Rollbrett
rollerskate [ˈrəʊləskeɪt] — It's like a shoe with 4 small wheels. — Rollschuh
°**to watch the world go by** [ˌgəʊ ˈbaɪ] — to watch what is going on around you — °alles um sich herum beobachten
whole [həʊl] — the ~ world = all the countries in the world — ganze(-r, -s)
°**wonder** [ˈwʌndə] — s.th. which is strange or beautiful — °Wunder

Exercises

3. **to keep fit** [ˌkiːp ˈfɪt] — Swimming, running etc. will ~ you ~. — (sich) gesund, fit erhalten
   to take part (in) [ˌteɪk ˈpɑːt] — "Did you ~ in the competition?" – "Yes, I even won a prize." — teilnehmen (an)
   to jog [dʒɒg] — to run slowly — einen Dauerlauf machen, joggen

Unit 1

⟨**The Big Apple**⟩

the Big Apple	People often call New York ~.	*andere Bezeichnung für New York*
Washington, D.C. [ˈwɒʃɪŋtən ˌdiːˈsiː]	the capital of the USA	*Hauptstadt der USA*
borough [ˈbʌrə]	a part of a city	*Bezirk*
subway (AE) [ˈsʌbweɪ]	BE: the Underground	*U-Bahn*
harbor (AE)/ harbour (BE) [ˈhɑːbə]	port; the Port of Dover = Dover ~	*Hafen*
immigrant [ˈɪmɪgrənt]	~s leave their own country to live in another one.	*Einwanderer, Einwanderin*
to pass [pɑːs]	*here:* to go or travel past	*passieren, vorbeifahren*
Irish [ˈaɪərɪʃ]	people from Ireland; adjective of "Ireland"	*Iren, irisch*
Dublin [ˈdʌblɪn]	the capital of Ireland	*Hauptstadt Irlands*
Jew [dʒuː]	More ~s live in the USA than in Israel.	*Jude*
Tel Aviv [ˌtel əˈviːv]	largest city in Israel	*größte Stadt Israels*
The New York Times [taɪmz]	name of a newspaper	*Name einer Zeitung*
Peter Minuit [ˈmɪnjʊɪt]	a man's name	*holländischer Siedler*
Dutchman [ˈdʌtʃmən]	Dutchmen come from Holland.	*Holländer*
homeless [ˈhəʊmlɪs]	without a home	*obdachlos*

1 ⟨**Streets in Manhattan**⟩

avenue [ˈævənjuː]	a street, especially one with trees on each side	*Allee, Boulevard*
to include [ɪnˈkluːd]	The tour ~s the main sights = You can see the main sights on the tour.	*einschließen, enthalten*

2 ⟨**A heart in New York**⟩

tall [tɔːl]	Giants are very ~.	*groß, hoch*
skyline [ˈskaɪlaɪn]	the buildings against the sky	*Skyline, Silhouette*
to wander [ˈwɒndə]	to walk around	*herumbummeln*
dark (n.) [dɑːk]	noun of 'dark' (adj.)	*Dunkelheit*
heart beat [ˈhɑːt ˌbiːt]	When you're very excited, you can sometimes feel your ~.	*Herzschlag*
to have s.th. on your mind [maɪnd]	to think about s.th. a lot	*(gedanklich) sich mit etwas beschäftigen*
not a dime's worth of difference [ˈdaɪmz ˌwɜːθ ˌɒv ˈdɪfrəns]	It doesn't make ~ = It doesn't change anything.	*hier:* kein *Unterschied*
to touch down [ˌtʌtʃ ˈdaʊn]	to land	*landen, aufsetzen*

3 Almost the best

Ted [ted]	a boy's or man's name	*Vorname (männlich)*
to **be used to** [juːst]	This is nothing new to me – I'm ~ it.	*an etwas gewöhnt, gewohnt sein*
to **clear** [klɪə]	They ~ed the streets of snow.	*auf-, abräumen, freimachen*
to **coach** [kəʊtʃ]	Ted Donahue ~es a football team.	*trainieren*

Unit 1

°**chili con carne** [ˈtʃɪlɪ kɒn ˈkɑːnɪ]	meal of meat and beans, with chili	°*scharf gewürztes Gericht mit Peperoni*
Mary [ˈmeərɪ]	a girl's or woman's name	*Vorname (weiblich)*
YMCA [ˌwaɪemˌsiˈeɪ]	a club for young people (Young Men's Christian Association)	CVJM
Buick [ˈbjuːɪk]	an American car	*amerikanische Automarke*
garbage can (AE) [ˈgɑːbɪdʒ kæn]	Put the empty tins in the ~.	Müll-, Abfalleimer
°**modest** [ˈmɒdɪst]	They have lots of money, but they live ~ly.	°bescheiden

Exercises

1	**text** [tekst]	the words on the page	Text
2	**can't stand** [stænd]	I can't stand it = I hate it.	nicht ausstehen können
3	**zoo** [zuː]	a place where you can see lots of different animals	Zoo
	ice-skating [ˈaɪsˌskeɪtɪŋ]	I like ~ better than roller-skating.	Eislauf, Schlittschuhlaufen
	baseball [ˈbeɪsbɔːl]	an American ball game	Baseball
5	°**pronunciation** [prəˌnʌnsɪˈeɪʃn]	how you say a word or words	°Aussprache
	difference [ˈdɪfrəns]	The ~ between 2 and 5 is 3. (noun of "different")	Unterschied, Differenz
	to **pronounce** [prəˈnaʊns]	You don't ~ the 'k' in 'knife'.	aussprechen
	°**silent** [ˈsaɪlənt]	In 'knife' the 'k' is ~ – you can't hear it.	°stumm; schweigend
	°**recording** [rɪˈkɔːdɪŋ]	If you record s.th., you make a ~.	°Aufnahme, Aufzeichnung

C Up on 119th Street

°**cop** [kɒp] (sl.)	policeman	°Polizist
to **remind** s.o. of s.th. [rɪˈmaɪnd]	These photos ~ me of our holiday.	jdn. an etwas erinnern
partner [ˈpɑːtnə]	s.o. who works, plays, dances with you etc.	Partner(in)
Wayne Ellis [ˌweɪn ˈelɪs]	a man's name	*Personenname (männlich)*
°**Irish coffee** [ˌaɪərɪʃ ˈkɒfɪ]	a drink that looks black and white	°*Irish Coffee (Kaffee mit Whisky und Schlagsahne)*
honey [ˈhʌnɪ]	I like marmalade better than ~. *Here:* 'dear'	Honig; *hier: liebevolle Anrede*
to **push** [pʊʃ]	She ~ed the child to the door.	schieben, stoßen
gang [gæŋ]	group of people (especially in crime)	Bande, Gang
to be **out of school**	not to go to school any more	nicht (mehr) zur Schule gehen
to be **out of money/work**	not to have any money/work	kein Geld/ keine Arbeit haben
shop-lifter [ˈʃɒpˌlɪftə]	A ~ steals things from shops.	Ladendieb(in)
°to **go on to**	I'm afraid that he will ~ more serious crimes.	°zu etwas übergehen
to **break in(to)**	Burglars have broken in and taken all the money.	einbrechen
°**warehouse** [ˈweəhaʊs]	They keep the goods in a ~.	°Lager(halle)
°**watchman** [ˈwɒtʃmən]	A night ~ looks after buildings at night.	°Wächter
gun [gʌn]	British policemen don't usually carry ~s.	Schußwaffe

to **step on the gas** [gæs] (AE)	to drive very quickly		Gas geben
alarm [əˈlɑːm]	The fire ~ rang and everyone left the building.		Alarm(anlage)
although [ɔːlˈðəʊ]	They liked the meal ~ Ted hadn't cooked it himself.		obwohl, obgleich
chance [tʃɑːns]	You have no ~ against a man with a gun.		Chance, Aussicht(en), Möglichkeit
°to **slam** into [slæm]	He hadn't noticed the door and ~med ~ it.		°gegen etwas 'knallen'
°**jail** [dʒeɪl]	prison		°Gefängnis
(to do) a "**job**"	*here:* a crime		ein „Ding" (drehen)
smart [smɑːt]	clever		schlau, gewitzt
(a) **born** (teacher) [bɔːn]	He's very good at teaching. = He's a ~ teacher.		(der) geborene (Lehrer)
brave [breɪv]	Robin Hood was a very ~ man.		mutig, tapfer

Exercises

1 **reason** [ˈriːzn]	What is the ~? = Why?		Grund, Anlaß
2 **Lincoln** [ˈlɪŋkən]	a boy's name		*Vorname (männlich)*
Donna [ˈdɒnə]	a girl's name		*Vorname (weiblich)*
Joel [dʒəʊəl]	a boy's name		*Vorname (männlich)*
Julie [ˈdʒuːlɪ]	a girl's name		*Vorname (weiblich)*
Ruth [ruːθ]	a girl's name		*Vorname (weiblich)*
Al [æl]	a boy's name		*Vorname (männlich)*
Leroy [ˈliːrɔɪ]	a boy's name		*Vorname (männlich)*
blues [bluːz]	= sad feeling; slow black American music		Blues *(Musikrichtung)*
Sam [sæm]	a boy's name		*Vorname (männlich)*
blue [bluː]	*here:* very sad		*hier:* trübsinnig
Zara [ˈzærə]	a girl's name		*Vorname (weiblich)*
4 °to **stand in line** (AE)	to wait behind other people		°sich anstellen
souvenir [ˌsuːvəˈnɪə]	A ~ reminds you of your holiday.		Andenken, Souvenir
5 **Roberto Fernandez** [rəˌbɜːtəʊ fɜːˈnændez]	a boy's name		*Personenname (männlich)*
°**messenger** [ˈmesɪndʒə]	A ~ brings messages.		°Bote, Botin
agency [ˈeɪdʒənsɪ]	We booked our holiday at a travel ~.		Agentur, Büro
UN [juːˈen] = **United Nations** [juːˌnaɪtɪd ˈneɪʃnz]	More than 150 states belong to the ~.		die Vereinten Nationen
to **deliver** [dɪˈlɪvə]	A mailman ~s letters, postcards etc.		zustellen, (aus)liefern
°**beeper** [ˈbiːpə]	Policemen or doctors often carry ~s.		°Funkrufempfänger
international [ˌɪntəˈnæʃnəl]	This is a phone box for national and ~ calls.		international
°**call box** [ˈkɔːl bɒks]	= (tele)phone box		°Telefonzelle
to **commute** [kəˈmjuːt]	to travel between your home and your place of work		pendeln

Unit 1 / Unit 2

NEW YORK

Broadway ['brɔːdweɪ]	Straße in Manhattan	Manhattan [mænˈhætn]	Insel zwischen dem Hudson und dem East River; heute einer der fünf Stadtbezirke New Yorks
Brooklyn ['brʊklɪn]	einer der fünf Stadtbezirke New Yorks		
the Bronx [brɒŋks]	einer der fünf Stadtbezirke New Yorks	Museum of Modern Art	Museum für moderne Kunst
Central Park [ˌsentrəl ˈpɑːk]	Park in Manhattan	⟨Queens [kwiːnz]	einer der fünf Stadtbezirke New Yorks⟩
Chinatown ['tʃaɪnətaʊn]	Chinesenviertel New Yorks	Rockefeller Center [ˌrɒkəfelə ˈsentə]	Komplex von Bürogebäuden und Unterhaltungszentren
Coney Island [ˌkəʊnɪ ˈaɪlənd]	Vergnügungspark	Shea Stadium [ˌʃeɪ ˈsteɪdɪəm]	großes Stadion
⟨Empire State Building [ˌempaɪə ˈsteɪt ˌbɪldɪŋ]	weltberühmtes Hochhaus (381 m hoch)⟩	⟨Staten Island [ˌsteɪtn ˈaɪlənd]	einer der fünf Stadtbezirke New Yorks⟩
⟨Fifth Avenue [ˌfɪfθ ˈævənjuː]	elegante Einkaufsstraße⟩	Statue of Liberty [ˌstætʃuː_əv ˈlɪbətɪ]	Wahrzeichen der Stadt New York und Symbol der Freiheit
⟨Grand Central Station ['grænd ˌsentrəl ˈsteɪʃn]	größter Bahnhof New Yorks⟩	⟨Times Square [ˌtaɪmz ˈskweə]	belebter Platz am Broadway⟩
Greenwich Village [ˌgrɪnɪdʒ ˈvɪlɪdʒ]	Künstlerviertel im Süden Manhattans	⟨Wall Street [ˈwɔːl striːt]	Finanzzentrum an der Südspitze Manhattans⟩
Harlem ['hɑːləm]	Stadtteil (nördlich vom Central Park)	Washington Square [ˌwɒʃɪŋtən ˈskweə]	belebter Platz in Manhattan
Little Italy [ˌlɪtl ˈɪtəlɪ]	Viertel mit vielen italienischen Einwanderern	⟨World Trade Center [ˌwɜːld ˈtreɪd ˌsentə]	Welthandelszentrum⟩
Macy's ['meɪsiːz]	größtes Kaufhaus der Welt (West 34th Street)		
⟨Madison Square Garden ['mædɪsn ˌskweə ˈgɑːdn]	riesige Halle für Musik- und Sportveranstaltungen⟩		

Unit 2

A Should they or shouldn't they?

°to take over	to take (or buy) s.th. from s.o.	°übernehmen
°stained glass [steɪnd]	A ~ glass window has lots of different colors in it.	°Buntglas
Bernie ['bɜːnɪ]	a boy's or man's name (short for 'Bernard')	Vorname (männlich)
Wisconsin [wɪsˈkɒnsɪn]	a state in the North of the USA	amerikanischer Bundesstaat
Oshkosh ['ɒʃkɒʃ]	a town in Wisconsin	Stadt in Wisconsin
change [tʃeɪndʒ] (n.)	s.th. different or new	(Ver)änderung, Wechsel
to take a chance [tʃɑːns]	to do s.th. that might be very good (or very bad) for you	eine Gelegenheit ergreifen; etwas riskieren
Herbie ['hɜːbɪ]	a boy's or man's name (short for 'Herbert')	Vorname (männlich)
Big Boggles [ˌbɪg ˈbɒglz]	a funny name for a teacher (Mr Bogg)	ein Spitzname

Unit 2

Exercises

1	**correct(ly)** [kəˈrekt(lɪ)]	right, in the right way	richtig
	magic [ˈmædʒɪk]	s.th. that is (or looks) impossible	Zauberei, Magie
	°**e.g.** [iːˈdʒiː]	You say 'for example', but you can also write '~'.	°z.B. (zum Beispiel)
	to **make new friends**	to meet new people and to become friends with them	neue Freundschaften schließen
2	°**community** [kəˈmjuːnətɪ]	When people live in the same town and know each other, they are a ~.	°Gemeinschaft, Gemeinde
	friendly [ˈfrendlɪ]	If you are always nice to people, you are ~.	freundlich
	°**tax** [tæks]	People who earn money must pay ~ (for new roads, schools, hospitals, etc.).	°Steuer
	Mercy Medical Center Hospital (BE: centre) [ˌmɜːsɪ ˈmedɪkl ˌsentə ˈhɒspɪtl]	name of a hospital	*Name eines Krankenhauses*
	Park Plaza Shopping Center [ˌpɑːk ˌplɑːzə ˈʃɒpɪŋ ˌsentə]	name of a shopping center	*Name eines Einkaufszentrums*
	church [tʃɜːtʃ]	a building where people meet to say prayers	Kirche
	local [ˈləʊkl]	Your ~ newspaper reports on things that happen near where you live.	lokal, örtlich
	radio station [ˈreɪdɪəʊ ˌsteɪʃn]	The music that you hear on your radio comes from a ~.	Radiosender
	°**climate** [ˈklaɪmɪt]	Africa has a hot ~: it's usually very hot there.	°Klima
	Lake Winnebago [ˌwɪnəˈbeɪɡəʊ]	a lake in Wisconsin	*See in Wisconsin*
	°**sailboat** (AE) [ˈseɪlbəʊt]	a boat that you can sail in (BE: sailing boat)	°Segelboot
3	**So long** [ˌsəʊ ˈlɒŋ] ⎫		bis später
	Take care [ˌteɪk ˈkeə] ⎬ more ways to say		mach's gut
	Good luck [ˌɡʊd ˈlʌk] ⎪ goodbye (= I'll see you…)		alles Gute
	See you [ˈsiːjə] ⎭		bis dann, tschüß

3 A telex from Harry

°**telex** [ˈteleks]	You need a special machine to send a ~.	°Fernschreiben, Telex(gerät)
it's me	= It is I. But people often say '~'.	ich bin's
to **airmail** [ˈeəmeɪl]	to send a letter by airmail	mit Luftpost schicken
°**broken-hearted** [ˌbrəʊkənˈhɑːtɪd]	very sad	°untröstlich
if I were you	If you think that you know what someone should do, you say "~, I would…"	(ich) an deiner Stelle…
ice-hockey [ˈaɪsˌhɒkɪ]	a winter sport	Eishockey
to **ski** [skiː]	You can ~ down a snowy mountain.	skifahren
°**cross-country skiing** [ˈkrɒsˌkʌntrɪ ˌskiːɪŋ]	skiing across the countryside, not down mountains	°Skilanglauf

Exercises

2 °**talk** [tɔːk]	When people are talking, what you hear is ~.	°Gespräch, Unterhaltung
°to **know one's way around**	to know a place (e.g. a town) very well	°sich auskennen *(örtlich)*

Marvin [ˈmɑːvɪn]	a boy's or man's name		*Vorname (männlich)*
Wes [wes]	a boy's or man's name		*Vorname (männlich)*
3 **neighborhood** (AE) (BE: neighbourhood) [ˈneɪbəhʊd]	Everything near your home is in your ~.		Nachbarschaft
member [ˈmembə]	The people in a club are its ~s.		Mitglied
°**newsletter** [ˈnjuːzˌletə]	a small newspaper		°Mitteilungsblatt
to **join** [dʒɔɪn]	to become a member of a group, or to come together with other people to do s.th.		Mitglied werden, mit-, hinzukommen
meeting [ˈmiːtɪŋ]	People have a ~ to talk about something important.		Treffen, Besprechung
°**PTA meeting** [ˌpiːtiːˈeɪ]	a meeting of parents and teachers (PTA = Parents' Teachers' Association)		°Elternabend

C Magic – real magic

Sandy [ˈsændɪ]	a girl's or woman's name		*Vorname (weiblich)*
Victoria [vɪkˈtɔːrɪə]	a girl's or woman's name		*Vorname (weiblich)*
Cabot [ˈkæbət]	a surname		*Familienname*
blond [blɒnd]	yellow (hair)		blond
Anne-Marie [ˌænməˈriː]	a girl's or woman's name		*Vorname (weiblich)*
to **seem** [siːm]	to ~ to be tired = to look tired		scheinen
°**loser** [ˈluːzə]	s.o. who always loses		°Verlierer(in), „Niete"
to **make fun of s.o.**	to say or do s.th. so that other people laugh at s.o.		sich über jdn. lustig machen
fool [fuːl]	s.o. who is silly		Narr, Dummkopf
°to **stare** [steə]	to look hard and long		°starren
seventeen-year-old	A ~ brother is seventeen years old.		siebzehnjährig
Bret [bret]	a boy's or man's name		*Vorname (männlich)*
to **look and sound sorry**	to seem to be sorry		so aussehen und so klingen, als ob es einem leid täte
pretty [ˈprɪtɪ]	nice to look at		hübsch
on the phone [fəʊn]	= on the telephone		am Telefon
to **nod** [nɒd]	what you do with your head when you say 'yes'		nicken
not even [ˌnɒt ˈiːvn]	"Is the water hot?" – "No, it's ~ warm!"		nicht einmal

Exercises

1 to **divide** [dɪˈvaɪd]	to break into different parts		(ein)teilen, gliedern
⟨6⟩ **greeter** [ˈgriːtə]	a card you can use to say 'hello' to s.o.		Grußkarte
to **kiss** [kɪs]	If you ~ someone, you usually like him or her very much.		küssen
frog [frɒg]	In some stories the ~ is really a prince.		Frosch
to **try** [traɪ]	I've never eaten blue cheese, but I'd like to ~ it.		(aus)probieren
gold [gəʊld]	s.th. hard and yellow that is very expensive		Gold
Who cares? [huːˈkeəz]	This question really means 'it doesn't matter'.		Was soll's?
to **call** [kɔːl]	to ring up, to telephone		anrufen
in a hurry [ˈhʌrɪ]	When you are ~, you do not have much time.		in Eile
⟨8⟩ **phone-in** [ˈfəʊnɪn]	People can ring up the radio station during a ~.		*Radiosendung, an der sich Hörer telefonisch beteiligen können*
exchange student [ɪksˈtʃeɪndʒ ˌstjuːdnt]	s.o. who goes to school or university in a different country for a short time		Austauschschüler(in), -student(in)
Phil [fɪl]	a boy's or man's name (short for 'Philip')		*Vorname (männlich)*

to take a part [pɑːt]	to play a role	eine Rolle übernehmen
Philpott [ˈfɪlpɒt]	a surname	*Familienname*
caller [ˈkɔːlə]	s.o. who calls on the phone	Anrufer
prefix [ˈpriːfɪks]	*Un-*, *in-* and *dis-* are ~es.	Vorsilbe, Präfix
honest [ˈɒnɪst]	He is very ~: he always tells the truth.	ehrlich
°to **get** s.th. **out**	to take s.th. out	°etwas herausholen
dictionary [ˈdɪkʃənrɪ]	a book that explains what words mean	Wörterbuch
to **look up**	to look in a book for information about s.th.	etwas nachschlagen
prob'ly	= probably	
to **provide** [prəˈvaɪd]	to give, to let s.o. have	liefern, bereitstellen
opportunity [ˌɒpəˈtjuːnətɪ]	Many people call the USA the land of ~.	Gelegenheit
educated [ˈedjuːkeɪtɪd]	Someone who has learned a lot is well ~.	erzogen
taught the fear of Jesus [ˌtɔːt ðə fɪər_əv ˈdʒiːzəs]	= They taught me to love Jesus.	(mir wurde) Ehrfurcht vor Jesus beigebracht
to **daydream** [ˈdeɪdriːm]	to dream while you are awake	(mit offenen Augen) träumen
romantic [rəʊˈmæntɪk]	s.o. who likes to dream	Romantiker
to have a ball (sl.) [bɔːl]	to have a good time	sich amüsieren
to **marry** [ˈmærɪ]	to make s.o. one's wife/husband	heiraten
L. A. = Los Angeles	city in California	*Stadt in Kalifornien*
doll (AE, sl.) [dɒl]	*here:* a pretty girl	Puppe, *hier:* hübsches Mädchen
hayseed (AE, sl.) [ˈheɪsiːd]	like s.o. from the country	tölpelhaft, naiv
to **breathe** [briːð]	*here:* to feel free	(frei) atmen
gonna die (sl.) [ˌgɒnə ˈdaɪ]	= (I'm) going to die	
to **bury** [ˈberɪ]	When people die, someone must ~ them.	beerdigen
John Cougar Mellencamp [ˌdʒɒn ˌkuːgə ˈmelənkæmp]	a singer	*ein Sänger*

Prefixes

un-		im-, in-, ir-,		dis-	
uncomfortable	unbequem	imperfect	unvollkommen	to disbelieve	etwas nicht glauben
unemployed	arbeitslos	improbable	unwahrscheinlich	dishonest	unehrlich
unfriendly	unfreundlich	incorrect	falsch	to dislike	etwas nicht mögen
unhappy	unglücklich	inexpensive	preiswert	displeased	verärgert
to unlock	etw. aufschließen	irregular	unregelmäßig	to disqualify	disqualifizieren
to untie	etwas lösen, losbinden				

Stopover B: Christmas in the USA

merry [ˈmerɪ]	full of fun	fröhlich
°**tradition** [trəˈdɪʃn]	s.th. that you do because people have done it like that for a long time	°Tradition
°**holly** [ˈhɒlɪ]	a tree	°Stechpalme
°**decorations** [ˌdekəˈreɪʃnz]	You can use colored paper to make Christmas ~.	°Dekoration, Schmuck
°**carol** [ˈkærəl]	a Christmas song	°Weihnachtslied
Christmas Eve [ˌkrɪsməs ˈiːv]	December 24th	Heiligabend
midnight [ˈmɪdnaɪt]	twelve o'clock at night	Mitternacht
Christmas Day [ˌkrɪsməs ˈdeɪ]	December 25th	1. Weihnachtstag

Santa Claus (AE) [ˈsæntə ˌklɔːz]	the man who brings presents to children on Christmas Day (BE: Father Christmas)	der Weihnachtsmann, *auch:* Nikolaus
stocking [ˈstɒkɪŋ]	Socks are short, but ~s are long.	Strumpf
to **hang up** [ˌhæŋ ˈʌp], **hung, hung** [hʌŋ]	When you come home, you ~ your coat in the hall.	aufhängen
fireplace [ˈfaɪəpleɪs]	place in a room for an open fire	Kamin
chimney [ˈtʃɪmnɪ]	The smoke from the fireplace goes out through the ~.	Schornstein
°**reindeer** [ˈreɪnˌdɪə]	an animal like a deer that lives in northern countries	°Rentier
roof [ruːf]	the top of a house	Dach
°**turkey** [ˈtɜːkɪ]	a big bird that people in Britain and America often eat at Christmas	°Truthahn
oven [ˈʌvn]	You put your turkey in the ~ for about three hours.	Backofen
°**catalogue** [ˈkætəlɒg]	a book with pictures and a list of things that you can buy	°Katalog

Aunt Mabel comes for Christmas dinner

My! [maɪ]	If you say "~" like Aunt Mabel, you are surprised at something.	*(Ausruf) etwa:* Meine Güte! Oh!
°to **shrink** [ʃrɪŋk], **shrank** [ʃræŋk], **shrunk** [ʃrʌŋk]	to get smaller	°schrumpfen, einlaufen
Gee! (AE) [dʒiː]	If you say "~", you are excited or happy about something.	*(Ausruf) etwa:* Mensch!
°**delicious** [dɪˈlɪʃəs]	I love pineapples because they are so ~.	°köstlich, lecker
three cheers [tʃɪəz]	another way to say "hooray"	ein dreifaches Hoch!
cook [kʊk]	s.o. who cooks (or has cooked s.th.)	Koch, Köchin
angel [ˈeɪndʒəl]	Some people put an ~ on top of their Christmas tree.	Engel
°**plum pudding** [ˌplʌm ˈpʊdɪŋ]	s.th. like a cake that you eat hot on Christmas Day, after the turkey	°Plumpudding *(kuchenartiger Pudding mit Rosinen etc.)*
to be **full**	I'm ~: I can't eat any more.	satt, voll
to **burst** [bɜːst], **burst, burst**	to get very big and then break	platzen, bersten
Gosh! [gɒʃ]	If you say "~" you are very surprised or excited.	*(Ausruf) etwa:* Mensch!
to be **in a bad mood**	to feel unhappy and angry with everyone	schlechter Laune sein

Exercises

1	to **offer** [ˈɒfə]	to say that s.o. can have s.th.	anbieten

⟨Unwanted guests⟩

unwanted [ˌʌnˈwɒntɪd]	S.o. or s.th. that you don't want is ~.	unerwünscht
guest [gest]	We invited four ~s to dinner.	Gast
Bernadette [ˌbɜːnəˈdet]	a girl's or woman's name	*Vorname (weiblich)*
Father		*Anrede für einen Priester*
O'Reilly [əʊˈraɪlɪ]	a surname	*Familienname*
Philadelphia [ˌfɪləˈdelfjə]	a town in Pennsylvania	*Stadt in Pennsylvania*
Vietnam [ˌvjetˈnæm]	a country near China	Vietnam
Fitzgerald [fɪtsˈdʒerəld]	a surname	*Familienname*
Jack [dʒæk]	a boy's or man's name	*Vorname (männlich)*

refugee [ˌrefjʊˈdʒiː]	a person who has to leave a country because of trouble	Flüchtling
Gary [ˈgærɪ]	a boy's or man's name	*Vorname (männlich)*
fair [feə]	"I didn't break the glass. It isn't ~ if I have to pay for it!"	fair, gerecht
footstep [ˈfʊtstep]	what you hear when s.o. walks	Schritt
smile	noun of 'to smile'	Lächeln
pregnant [ˈpregnənt]	expecting a baby	schwanger
stranger [ˈstreɪndʒə]	s.o. that you don't know	Fremde/r
Conti [ˈkɒntɪ]	a surname	*Familienname*
"Teen-Glam" [ˈtiːnˌglæm]	a name for make-up (not real)	*(erfundener) Produktname*
make-up [ˈmeɪkʌp]	You put ~ on your face to make yourself more beautiful.	Make-up, Schminke
gold [gəʊld]	s.th. hard and yellow that is very expensive	Gold
necklace [ˈneklɪs]	"That ~ looks nice with your blue dress."	Halskette
to wish s.o. s.th. [wɪʃ]	to hope that s.o. will have s.th.	jdm. etwas wünschen
mass [mæs]	Some people go to ~ every Sunday.	Messe
Western [ˈwestən]	a film about cowboys and Indians	Western
to knock (on a door) [nɒk]	to make a noise with your hand on a door	klopfen
the rest [rest]	the other part(s)	der Rest, der übrige Teil
heater [ˈhiːtə]	When you switch on a ~, it makes the room warm.	Heizgerät
mattress [ˈmætrɪs]	the part of a bed that you lie on	Matratze
Wagner [ˈwægnə]	a surname	*Familienname*
I guess (AE) [ges]	BE: I think	ich denke
sleep	noun of 'to sleep'	Schlaf

Exercises

6	°to **decorate** [ˈdekəreɪt]	to put decorations on	°schmücken
7)	egg nog [ˈegnɒg]	a drink that you can make with eggs	*amerikanisches Getränk*
	tablespoon [ˈteɪblspuːn]	a large spoon (full of s.th.)	Eßlöffel
	cl = centiliter (AE) [ˈsentɪˌliːtə] (BE: centilitre)		Zentiliter
	whipping cream [ˈwɪpɪŋ ˌkriːm]	the best part of the milk	Schlagsahne
	liquid [ˈlɪkwɪd]	Water is ~, but ice isn't.	flüssig
	extract [ˈekstrækt]	Coffee ~ tastes like very strong coffee.	Extrakt, Auszug
	nutmeg [ˈnʌtmeg]	You sometimes put a little ~ in cakes.	Muskatnuß
	(it) serves four [sɜːvz]	It is enough for four people.	für vier Personen
	to separate [ˈsepəreɪt]	to break into different parts	trennen
	egg yolk [ˈegˌjəʊk]	the yellow part of an egg	Eigelb
	to beat [biːt], beat [biːt], beaten [ˈbiːtn]	to hit quickly with a spoon or fork	schlagen
	to whip [wɪp]	to beat	schlagen
	mixture [ˈmɪkstʃə]	s.th. that has a lot of different things in it	Mischung
	separately [ˈseprətlɪ]	on its own, not together with anything else	getrennt
	to pour [pɔː]	You ~ tea from the teapot into your cup.	gießen
	cranberry sauce [ˈkrænbərɪ ˌsɔːs]	~ is nice with turkey.	Preiselbeersoße
	roast potatoes [ˌrəʊst pəˈteɪtəʊz]	You can put your ~ in the oven with the turkey.	Röstkartoffeln
	brandy butter [ˌbrændɪ ˈbʌtə]	~ is nice with plum pudding.	Weinbrandbutter

Stopover B

Eating and drinking

bacon	Speck	coffee	Kaffee
baked beans	*weiße Bohnen in Tomatensoße*	juice	Saft
biscuit	Keks, Plätzchen	lemonade	Limonade
chili con carne	*scharf gewürztes Gericht mit Peperoni*	milk	Milch
		tea	Tee
chips	Pommes frites	to **be hungry/thirsty**	hungrig/durstig sein
crisps	Kartoffelchips	to **be full**	satt sein
fish fingers	Fischstäbchen	to **boil**	(in Wasser) kochen
fruit	Obst	to **cook**	kochen
hot dog	Hot Dog *(Würstchen im Brötchen)*	to **drink**	trinken
		to **eat**	essen
ice-cream	Eis(krem)	to **have breakfast/ lunch/supper**	frühstücken/zu Mittag/ zu Abend essen
mashed potatoes	Kartoffelbrei		
meat	Fleisch	it's **delicious**	es ist lecker
plum pudding	Plumpudding *(kuchenartiger Pudding mit Rosinen etc.)*		
		freezer	Tiefkühltruhe
roast potatoes	Röst-, Bratkartoffeln	refrigerator	Kühlschrank
sandwich	Butterbrot, Sandwich	oven	Backofen
sausage	Wurst	stove	Herd
stew	Eintopfgericht		
sweets	Süßigkeiten	café	Café, Imbißstube
turkey	Truthahn	cafeteria	Kantine, Cafeteria
vegetable	Gemüse	restaurant	Restaurant
whipping cream	Schlagsahne	snack bar	Imbißstube

Unit 3

A At the truck stop

truck stop [trʌk ˌstɒp]	a place where truck drivers stop for a meal		Raststätte *(überwiegend für LKW-Fahrer)*
hamburger [ˈhæmbɜːgə]	A ~ has meat in it, and it's cheap.		Hamburger
Steve [stiːv]	a boy's or man's name		*Vorname (männlich)*
McDuck's [məkˈdʌk]	the name of a snack bar (not real)		*(erfundener) Name*
°**C'mon = come on**	Sometimes "~" means "Surely you're not serious!"		°Sei/Seien Sie doch nicht so!
gas (AE) [gæs]	You can't drive a car without ~.		Benzin
(gas) station	a place where drivers stop to get gas		Tankstelle
highway [ˈhaɪweɪ]	main road		*autobahnähnliche Landstraße*
to **order** [ˈɔːdə]	to ask for s.th. in a restaurant or snack bar		bestellen
trucker [ˈtrʌkə]	truck driver		Lastwagenfahrer(in)

Exercises

2 °**motel** [məʊˈtel]	a hotel for drivers		°Motel
4 to **depend on** [dɪˈpend]	"Can we have a picnic tomorrow?" – "It ~s ~ the weather."		abhängen von
°**emphasis** [ˈemfəsɪs]	In the word "newspaper", the ~ is always on "news".		°Betonung

5 °air-conditioning ['eəkənˌdɪʃənɪŋ]	In hot countries, many buildings have ~.	°Klimaanlage
shower ['ʃaʊə]	In hot weather, a ~ is nicer than a bath.	Dusche
to pay **in cash** [kæʃ]	to pay with money	bar bezahlen
to pay **by**...	to use s.th. to pay	mit ... bezahlen
°credit card ['kredɪt ˌkɑːd]	You don't need to have any money with you if you have a ~.	°Kreditkarte
traveler (AE) (BE: traveller) ['trævlə]	a person who travels	Reisende/r
(traveler's) check (AE) [tʃek] (BE: cheque)	When you write your name on a ~, it is as good as money.	(Reise)scheck
vacancy ['veɪkənsɪ]	*here:* hotel room which no one is using	freies Zimmer; *auch:* freie Stelle
°receptionist [rɪ'sepʃənɪst]	the person at the desk in a hotel	°Empfangschef(-in)
to be **full (up)**	We have no rooms = We're ~.	voll, belegt sein
gimme (sl.) ['gɪmɪ]	= give me	
quarter pounder ['paʊndə]	a hamburger that weighs a quarter of a pound	Viertelpfünder
cheeseburger ['tʃiːzˌbɜːgə]	a hamburger with cheese	Cheeseburger
side order ['saɪd ˌɔːdə]	s.th. that you order to eat with your food (e.g. salad, vegetables)	Beilage
French fries (AE) [fraɪz]	BE: chips	Pommes frites
Doc Pepper [ˌdɒk 'pepə]	an American drink	*amerikanisches Colagetränk*
to go	*here:* to take away	*hier:* zum Mitnehmen
Martyn Wiley [ˌmɑːtɪn 'waɪlɪ]	the name of an English writer	*englischer Autor*
rhythm ['rɪðəm]	The music has got ~ – it's easy to dance to it.	Rhythmus
poem ['pəʊɪm]	Goethe wrote a lot of ~s.	Gedicht
to snap one's fingers [snæp]	to make a noise with your fingers	mit den Fingern schnippen
in time	together with the music	im Takt

My crazy dad

Boston ['bɒstən]	an important city in the East of the USA	*Stadt im Osten der USA*
as [æs]	because; when	weil, da; als, wie
to **bite** [baɪt], **bit** [bɪt], **bitten** ['bɪtn]	Watch out! That dog likes to ~ people.	beißen
desert ['dezət]	very dry land where almost nothing can grow	Wüste
°mobile home [ˌməʊbaɪl]	a large caravan that you can live in	°Wohnmobil
Utah [juːtɔː]	a state in the West of the USA	*amerikanischer Bundesstaat*
Bluff City [ˌblʌf 'sɪtɪ]	a small town in Utah	*kleine Stadt in Utah*
°to **take to pieces**	to break into small parts	°in Einzelteile zerlegen
to **marry** s.o. ['mærɪ]	to become s.o.'s husband/wife	jdn. heiraten
since [sɪns]	"I haven't met him ~ Monday." = "I met him on Monday, but not after that."	seit
in some ways	in some points	in mancher Hinsicht
°canyon ['kænjən]	Sometimes a river cuts deep into the rocks and makes a ~.	°Canyon, Schlucht
San Juan [ˌsæn 'hwʌn]	a river in the USA	*Fluß in den USA*
movie theater (AE) [ˌmuːvɪ 'θɪətə]	BE: cinema	Kino
high school ['haɪskuːl]	a school for older children	*weiterführende Schule in den USA*

Unit 3

Exercises

3	**Redwood High** [ˌredwʊd ˈhaɪ] = **Redwood High School**	the name of a school	*Name einer Schule*
5	**tooth** [tu:θ], pl. **teeth** [ti:θ]	The baby has got no ~ yet.	Zahn, Zähne
	toothbrush [ˈtu:θbrʌʃ]	You clean your teeth with a ~.	Zahnbürste
	toothpaste [ˈtu:θpeɪst]	You put ~ on the toothbrush.	Zahnpasta
	nail [neɪl]	You have a ~ at the end of every finger.	Nagel
	nailbrush [ˈneɪlbrʌʃ]	You clean your nails with a ~.	Nagelbürste
	shampoo [ʃæmˈpu:]	You wash your hair with ~.	Haarwaschmittel, Shampoo
	comb [kəʊm]	To make your hair nice, you need a brush or a ~.	Kamm
	towel [ˈtaʊəl]	When you have washed yourself and are wet, you need a ~.	Handtuch
	underwear [ˈʌndəweə]	the clothes that you put on first	Unterwäsche
	pyjamas [pəˈdʒɑ:məz]	a pair of trousers and jacket that you wear in bed	Schlafanzug
	walkman [ˈwɔ:kmən]	small cassette-recorder with headphones	Walkman
	to **dry** [draɪ]	to make s.th. dry	(ab)trocknen
6	the **Pacific** [pəˈsɪfɪk]	sea between America, Asia and Australia	Pazifik

C On the road with Tessie

to **roll** [rəʊl]	*here:* to drive slowly	*hier:* langsam fahren; rollen
°**depot** [ˈdepəʊ]	place where the trucks (or buses) start from and come back to	°Depot, Zentrale
Tennessee [ˌtenəˈsi:]	a state in the Southeast of the USA	*amerikanischer Bundesstaat*
Nashville [ˈnæʃvɪl]	the capital of Tennessee	*Hauptstadt von Tennessee*
°**ton** [tʌn]	If something weighs a ~, it is very heavy.	°Tonne *(Gewicht)*
°**gear** [gɪə]	When a car goes faster or slower, the driver must change ~s.	°Gang
°to **flash by** [flæʃ]	to go past very fast	°vorbeisausen
to **save** [seɪv]	Doctors always try to ~ people's lives.	retten
speed [spi:d]	how fast s.th. is	Geschwindigkeit
speed limit [ˈspi:d ˌlɪmɪt]	If there is a ~, you cannot drive as fast as you like.	Geschwindigkeitsbegrenzung
John Trimble [ˌdʒɒn ˈtrɪmbl]	the name of a radio announcer	*Personenname (männlich)*
Jarell [dʒəˈrel]	a surname	*Familienname*
°**truck plaza** [ˈtrʌk ˌplɑ:zə]	a big truck stop with shops, a radio station etc.	°*große Raststätte mit Läden etc.*
Virginia [vəˈdʒɪnjə]	a state in the Southeast of the USA	*amerikanischer Bundesstaat*
Doswell [ˈdɒswel]	a small town in Virginia	*Kleinstadt in Virginia*
°**oldie** [ˈəʊldɪ]	an old song	°Oldie *(alter Schlager)*
Dave Dudley [ˌdeɪv ˈdʌdlɪ]	an American country music singer	*amerikanischer Countrysänger*
°to **wheel** [wi:l]	to drive	°fahren
awake [əˈweɪk]	opposite of 'asleep'	wach
to **take a rest** [rest]	to stop for a short time and perhaps sleep	eine Pause machen, sich ausruhen
Bible [ˈbaɪbl]	a great religious book	Bibel
God [gɒd]	The Bible is the word of ~.	Gott

Unit 3

Sesame Street ['sesəmɪ ˌstriːt]	a TV program for children		Sesamstraße *(Kindersendung)*
the **President** ['prezɪdənt]	~ of the USA is an important politician.		Präsident(in)
Frankenstein ['fræŋkənstaɪn]	In the film, Dr ~ made a 'man' in his lab.		Frankenstein *(Figur aus einem Gruselfilm)*
°**whisk(e)y** ['wɪskɪ]	Some people like drinking ~, but too much is bad for you.		°Whisky
Georgia ['dʒɔːdʒjə]	a state in the Southeast of the USA		amerikanischer Bundesstaat
Atlanta [ət'læntə]	a city in Georgia		Stadt in Georgia
start [stɑːt]	noun of 'to start'		Start, Beginn

Exercises

5) Hamburger Dan [dæn]	the name of a snack bar	Name einer Imbißstube
juke box ['dʒuːk bɒks]	You put money in the ~, choose a record, and then you can hear the record.	Musikbox
a-playing [ə'pleɪɪŋ] (sl.)	= playing	
waitress ['weɪtrɪs]	a woman who brings the food to the tables in a restaurant	Kellnerin, Bedienung
done brought (sl.)	= brought	
to fit s.o. [fɪt]	to be just right for s.o.	zu jdm./auf jdn. passen
it sure do fit me (sl.)	= it certainly fits me	
chorus ['kɔːrəs]	part of a song that you sing many times	Refrain
to pour [pɔː]	You ~ tea from the teapot into your cup.	(ein)gießen, einschenken
quarter ['kwɔːtə]	a quarter of a dollar	Vierteldollar; 25-Cent-Stück
aboard [ə'bɔːd]	on (a ship, a bus, a truck)	an Bord; *hier:* in
semi = semitrailer ['semɪ]	a big truck with two parts	Sattelschlepper
like a flash [flæʃ]	very fast	wie ein Blitz
them big wheels (sl.)	= these/those big wheels	
a-rollin' [ə'rəʊlɪn] (sl.)	= rolling	
expression [ɪk'spreʃn]	word or phrase	Ausdruck
to head for [hed]	to be on the way to	fahren (in Richtung)
4 situation [ˌsɪtjʊ'eɪʃn]	how things are at a certain place and time	Situation, Lage
Macon ['meɪkən]	a town in Georgia	*Stadt in Georgia*
Albany ['ɔːlbənɪ]	a town in Georgia	*Stadt in Georgia*
sick [sɪk]	ill	krank
off one's route [ruːt]	not on the road that one wants to travel on	nicht auf jds. Weg
Frank [fræŋk]	a boy's or man's name	*Vorname (männlich)*
°CB radio [ˌsiːˌbiː 'reɪdɪəʊ]	Truck drivers can talk to each other over CB radio (CB = Citizen's Band).	°CB-Funk *(Radiofrequenzen, die von Privatpersonen benutzt werden können)*

⟨Getting around in the USA⟩

to be grown-up [grəʊn'ʌp]	to be a child no longer	erwachsen sein
drive-in store (AE) [ˌdraɪv_ɪn 'stɔː]	shop where you can buy goods while you are sitting in your car	*Laden, in dem man vom Auto aus einkaufen kann*
Washington, D.C. ['wɒʃɪŋtən ˌdiː'siː]	capital of the USA	*Hauptstadt der USA*

Unit 3/Unit 4

Greyhound ['greɪhaʊnd]	name of an American bus company	amerikanische Busgesellschaft
old-fashioned [ˌəʊldˈfæʃənd]	the opposite of 'modern'	altmodisch
San Francisco Zephyr ['zefə]	name of a modern train	Name eines Zuges
pioneer [ˌpaɪəˈnɪə]	s.o. who goes somewhere where nobody has been before	Pionier(in)
6 **Wyoming** [waɪˈəʊmɪŋ]	a state in the West of the USA	amerikanischer Bundesstaat
Bell [bel]	a surname	Familienname
Cheyenne [ʃaɪˈæn]	capital of Wyoming	Hauptstadt von Wyoming
⟨7⟩ Tammy [ˈtæmɪ]	a girl's or woman's name	Vorname (weiblich)
summary [ˈsʌmərɪ]	A ~ has all the important facts, but is very short.	Zusammenfassung
8 **Debbie Preston** [ˌdebɪ ˈprestən]	name of a country singer (not real)	Personenname (weiblich)
Janey [ˈdʒeɪnɪ]	a girl's or woman's name	Vorname (weiblich)
Denver Dreamers [ˈdriːməz]	name of a country group (not real)	Name einer Country-Band

Differences between American and British English

AE:		BE:		AE:	BE:	
-er	**center**	-re	**centre** Zentrum	**apartment**	**flat**	Wohnung
	meter		**metre** Meter	**fall**	**autumn**	Herbst
	theater		**theatre** Theater	**French fries**	**chips**	Pommes frites
-o	**color**	-ou	**colour** Farbe	**I guess**	**I think**	ich denke
	favorite		**favourite** Lieblings-	**mailman**	**postman**	Briefträger
	harbor		**harbour** Hafen	**movie star**	**film star**	Filmstar
	neighbor		**neighbour** Nachbar/in	**movie theater**	**cinema**	Kino
-l	**traveler**	-ll	**traveller** Reisende/r	**Santa Claus**	**Father Christmas**	Weihnachtsmann
	she **dialed**		she **dialled** sie wählte	**sidewalk**	**pavement**	Bürgersteig
-m	**program**	-mme	**programme** Programm	**store**	**shop**	Laden
-ck	**check**	-que	**cheque** Scheck	**subway**	**Underground**	Untergrundbahn
-c	to **practice**	-s	to **practise** üben	**truck**	**lorry**	Lastwagen

What you find in cities

air-conditioning	Klimaanlage	**crime**	Verbrechen	**motel**	Motel
block	Häuserblock	**department store**	Kaufhaus	**population**	Bevölkerung
café	Imbiß, Café	**depot**	Depot, Zentrale	**poverty**	Armut
call box	Telefonzelle	**factory**	Fabrik	**radio station**	Radiosender
chimney	Schornstein	**garbage can**	Mülleimer	**shop-lifter**	Ladendieb(in)
church	Kirche	**gas station**	Tankstelle	**skyscraper**	Wolkenkratzer
community	Gemeinde	**jail**	Gefängnis	**warehouse**	Lager(halle)

Unit 4

A This is California

kind [kaɪnd]	An anorak is a ~ of jacket.	Art, Sorte
landscape [ˈlænskeɪp]	countryside	Landschaft
huge [hjuːdʒ]	very large	riesig

°**pleasant** [ˈpleznt]	nice	°angenehm
Golden Gate Bridge [ˌɡəʊldən ˈɡeɪt]	a bridge near San Francisco	*Brücke bei San Francisco*
Los Angeles [lɒs ˈændʒɪliːz]	city in California	*Stadt in Kalifornien*
pollution [pəˈluːʃn]	Air ~ comes from cars and factories.	Verschmutzung
°**clear** [klɪə]	If the glass of a window is ~, you can see through it.	klar
°**wilderness** [ˈwɪldənɪs]	wild land with no houses or farms on it	°Wildnis
further [ˈfɜːðə]	It's a long way from London to New York, but it's ~ to San Francisco.	weiter
tall [tɔːl]	(growing) very high	hoch (gewachsen), groß
°**giant redwood** [ˈredwʊd]	a very big tree	°Mammutbaum
Mount Whitney [ˌmaʊnt ˈwɪtnɪ]	a mountain in California	*Berg in Kalifornien*
°**above sea-level** [ˈsiːlevl]	higher than the sea	°über dem Meeresspiegel
kilometer (AE) [kɪˈlɒmɪtə] (BE: kilometre) [ˈkɪləʊˌmiːtə]	a thousand meters	Kilometer
valley [ˈvælɪ]	low land between mountains	Tal
Death Valley [ˌdeθ ˈvælɪ]	a desert in a valley in California	*Tal in Kalifornien*
below [bɪˈləʊ]	opposite of "above"	unter, unten
Hollywood [ˈhɒlɪwʊd]	suburb of Los Angeles, center of the film industry	*Vorort von Los Angeles*
°**agricultural** [ˌæɡrɪˈkʌltʃərəl]	to do with farms	°landwirtschaftlich
production [prəˈdʌkʃn]	noun of 'to produce'	Produktion
such a (thing) [ˈsʌtʃə]	a thing like that	solch ein/e…, so ein/e…
°**system** [ˈsɪstəm]	The USA has a very good telephone ~.	°System, Anlage
°**billion** (AE) [ˈbɪljən]	a thousand millions	°Milliarde
liter (AE) (BE: litre) [ˈliːtə]	You can buy lemonade in one-~ bottles.	Liter
daily [ˈdeɪlɪ]	every day	täglich
record [ˈrekɔːd]	It's a record = It's the biggest/fastest/highest/…	Rekord

B A letter to a pen pal

°**pen pal** [ˈpenˌpæl]	= pen-friend	°Brieffreund(in)
°**temblor** [ˈtemblə]	When the earth moves a little bit, you call this a ~.	°leichtes Erdbeben
grade (AE) [ɡreɪd]	BE: form, class	Klasse
Walt Disney [ˌwɔːlt ˈdɪznɪ]	a famous American film director	*amerikanischer Filmregisseur* (1901–1966)
cartoon [kɑːˈtuːn]	*here:* a kind of film	Zeichentrickfilm, Cartoon
cable [ˈkeɪbl]	a strong rope, usually made of wire	Kabel, Drahtseil
cable car	a car that goes up and down a hill on a cable	Straßenbahn *(in San Francisco)*
°**wagon** [ˈwæɡən]	a car that is pulled by an engine or a horse	°Waggon; (Plan-)Wagen
to **invent** [ɪnˈvent]	to make for the first time	erfinden
°**law** [lɔː]	A ~ tells people that they must (or mustn't) do something.	°Gesetz
to **park** [pɑːk]	to stop driving and leave your car somewhere	parken

Unit 4

Exercises

earthquake [ˈɜːθkweɪk]	In an ~, the earth moves and sometimes houses fall down.	Erdbeben
°tremor [ˈtremə]	When the earth moves a little, you feel a ~.	°Beben, Erschütterung
they	~ say that English is easier than French.	man
3 °box number	a number that you can put on an envelope instead of an address	°Chiffre, Postfach
Hernandez [hɜːˈnændəz]	a surname	Familienname
Laramie [ˈlærəmɪ]	a city in Wyoming	Stadt in Wyoming
5 Frisco [ˈfrɪskəʊ]	short for San Francisco	

⟨**California**⟩

Disneyland [ˈdɪznɪˌlænd]		Vergnügungspark in Kalifornien
pioneer [ˌpaɪəˈnɪə]	one of the first white people who lived in the West	Pionier(in)
reunion [ˌriːˈjuːnjən]	a meeting of friends who haven't been together for a long time	Treffen, Zusammenkunft

C Death Valley

°wagon train	wagons that travel together	°Planwagenkolonne, Treck
°to set off	to start on a trip	°aufbrechen, losfahren
Salt Lake City [ˌsɔːlt leɪk ˈsɪtɪ]	the capital of Utah	Hauptstadt von Utah
journey [ˈdʒɜːnɪ]	trip	Reise
ox [ɒks], pl. oxen [ˈɒksn]	a kind of bull	Ochse(n)
gold [gəʊld]	s.th. hard and yellow that is very expensive	Gold
gold rush [ˈgəʊld rʌʃ]	Lots of people rushed to California to look for gold in 1849.	Goldrausch
trail [treɪl]	path	Pfad, Weg
on horseback [ˈhɔːsbæk]	riding on a horse	zu Pferd
short cut [ˈʃɔːt kʌt]	a shorter way	Abkürzung
among these [əˈmʌŋ]	in this group	unter, zwischen diesen
Louis Nusbaumer [ˌluːɪs ˈnʊsbaʊmə]	a man's name	Name eines deutschen Einwanderers
°to emigrate [ˈemɪgreɪt]	to leave one's country and live in another	°auswandern
the Black Forest	a forest in Germany	Schwarzwald
°to fall behind	to become slower and slower and then be the last	°zurückfallen, -bleiben
ground [graʊnd]	here: earth	(Erd)boden
leather [ˈleðə]	Most shoes are made of ~.	Leder
°mirage [ˈmɪrɑːʒ]	s.th. that you see when it is very hot, but it isn't real	°Luftspiegelung, Fata Morgana
to go on foot	to walk	zu Fuß gehen
to exchange [ɪksˈtʃeɪndʒ]	to give s.th. so that you get s.th. else for it	(aus)tauschen
blood [blʌd]	If you cut your finger, you see ~.	Blut
Ehrhardt [ˈerhɑːt]	a surname	Familienname
Mojave River [məʊ ˈhɑːvɪ]	a river in California	Fluß in Kalifornien
ranch [rɑːntʃ]	a big farm with lots of cows and bulls	Ranch, Viehfarm
safety [ˈseɪftɪ]	noun of 'safe'	Sicherheit

Exercises

3 **mechanic** [mɪˈkænɪk]	a person who works with machines, cars, etc.		Mechaniker
) **translation** [trænsˈleɪʃn]	I can't understand stories in Spanish – I need a German ~.		Übersetzung
5 **cent** = ¢ [sent]	There are a hundred ~s in a dollar.		Cent
) **Calico Ghost Town** [ˈkælɪkəʊ]	a town where nobody lives any more		*Geisterstadt in Kalifornien*
Las Vegas [ˌlæs ˈveɪgəs]	a city in the West of the USA		*Stadt im Westen der USA*
Walter Knott [ˌwɔːltə ˈnɒt]	a man's name		*Personenname (männlich)*

I have **no** milk.	keine Milch	●	I have **no** apples.		keine Äpfel
I have**n't** got **any** milk.	keine Milch		I have**n't** got **any** apples.		keine Äpfel
little water	wenig Wasser		**few** cars		wenige Autos
a little water	ein bißchen Wasser	●	**a few** cars		ein paar Autos
some water	etwas Wasser		**some** cars		einige Autos
How **much** money?	Wieviel Geld?		Do you have **many** friends?		… viele Freunde?
I have**n't** got **much** money.	nicht viel Geld.	●	I have**n't** got **many** friends.		nicht viele Freunde.
She has got **a lot of** money.	… viel Geld.		I have got **a lot of** books.		… viele Bücher.
… **lots of** money.	… viel Geld.		… **lots of** books.		… viele Bücher.

Stopover C: America: Land of the Indians?

1 **tear** [tɪə]	~s come from your eyes when you cry.		Träne
Cherokee [ˌtʃerəˈkiː]	a group of Indians		*Indianerstamm*
°to **settle** [ˈsetl]	to go somewhere and live there		°(sich an)siedeln
°**settler** [ˈsetlə]	s.o. who settles somewhere		°Siedler(in)
Sequoya [sɪˈkwɔɪə]	an Indian's name		*Name eines Indianers*
to **develop** [dɪˈveləp]	verb of 'development'		(sich) entwickeln
government [ˈgʌvnmənt]	The ~ makes laws for a country.		Regierung
peaceful [ˈpiːsfʊl]	quiet and friendly		friedlich, friedliebend
soldier [ˈsəʊldʒə]	~s wear uniform and carry guns.		Soldat
to **escape** [ɪˈskeɪp]	to get away from s.th. bad or dangerous		entkommen
Smoky Mountains [ˌsməʊkɪ ˈmaʊntɪnz]	mountains in the East of the USA		Gebirgszug (Teil der Appalachen)
°**Indian Territory** [ˈterɪtərɪ]	part of the USA which the whites left for the Indians		°Indianerterritorium, -gebiet
cold [kəʊld]	noun of 'cold'		Kälte
hunger [ˈhʌŋgə]	noun of 'hungry'		Hunger
°**summary** [ˈsʌmərɪ]	a short text with all the main facts of a long text		°Zusammenfassung
2 **reservation** [ˌrezəˈveɪʃn]	a place especially for the Indians		Reservat
°to **drive** s.o./s.th. [draɪv]	The whites wanted the Indians' land – so they decided to ~ them away.		°(ver)treiben
South Dakota [dəˈkəʊtə]	a state in the North of the USA		*amerikanischer Bundesstaat*
Navajos [ˈnævəhəʊz]	a group of Indians		*Indianerstamm*
education [ˌedjuːˈkeɪʃn]	Schools are there to give you an ~.		Erziehung; Ausbildung
to **prepare** [prɪˈpeə]	to get s.o. or s.th. ready		vorbereiten
to **give up hope** [həʊp]	not to hope any more		die Hoffnung aufgeben

Stopover C

unemployment [ˌʌnɪmˈplɔɪmənt]	~ is high: lots of people are without work.	Arbeitslosigkeit
°**alcoholic** [ˌælkəˈhɒlɪk]	s.o. who drinks too much and cannot stop	°Alkoholiker(in)
°**suicide rate** [ˈsuːɪsaɪd ˌreɪt]	the number of people who kill themselves	°Selbstmordrate

⟨3 **Alone against Apaches**⟩

Apaches [əˈpætʃɪz]	a group of Indians	*Indianerstamm*
New Mexico [ˌnjuːˈmeksɪkəʊ]	a state in the Southwest of the USA	*amerikanischer Bundesstaat*
pioneer [ˌpaɪəˈnɪə]	one of the first people who settled in the West	Pionier(in)
to fight [faɪt], fought, fought [fɔːt]	Peaceful people do not want to ~.	(be)kämpfen
Mexican [ˈmeksɪkən]	s.o. from Mexico; adjective of 'Mexico'	Mexikaner(in); mexikanisch
to trust [trʌst]	to believe that s.o. is good	(ver)trauen
to break out	*here:* to start	ausbrechen
chief [tʃiːf]	the man who leads a group of Indians	Häuptling
Cochise [kəˈtʃiːz]	the name of an Indian chief	*Name eines Häuptlings*
peace [piːs]	They do not want to fight: what they want is ~.	Frieden
warrior [ˈwɒrɪə]	s.o. who is good at fighting	Krieger
to attack [əˈtæk]	to come suddenly and fight	angreifen
settlement [ˈsetlmənt]	place where people have settled	Siedlung
Western [ˈwestən]	*here:* story about the American West	Western *(Erzählung)*
Louis L'Amour [ləˈmʊə]	an American writer	*amerikanischer Autor*
Angie Lowe [ˈændʒɪ ˈləʊ]	a woman's name	*Personenname (weiblich)*
cabin [ˈkæbɪn]	little wooden house	Hütte
shotgun [ˈʃɒtgʌn]	} kinds of guns	Schrotflinte
Winchester [ˈwɪntʃestə]		Winchestergewehr
Walker Colt [ˈwɔːkə ˈkəʊlt]		Colt *(Revolver)*
to lift [lɪft]	If something is heavy, it is hard to ~ it.	(hoch)heben
corral [kɒˈrɑːl]	a field for horses with fences round it	umzäunte Weide; Korral
to turn s.o. back [tɜːn]	*here:* to fight hard so that the attackers give up and go away	zurückschlagen; abwehren
army [ˈɑːmɪ]	Soldiers are part of an ~.	Armee
to outnumber [ˌaʊtˈnʌmbə]	to be more than	zahlenmäßig überlegen sein
El Paso [elˈpæsəʊ]	city in Texas	*Stadt in Texas*
steady [ˈstedɪ]	Hold the ladder ~ = Hold it so that it does not move.	fest, ruhig
to recognize [ˈrekəgnaɪz]	to know who s.o. is when you look at him or her	(wieder)erkennen
description [dɪˈskrɪpʃn]	She gave me a ~ of him = She told me what he looked like.	Beschreibung
dead [ded]	"Is he ~?" – "Yes, he died last year."	tot
to beat, beat, [biːt] beaten [ˈbiːtn]	Your heart ~s faster if you are afraid.	schlagen
to guess (AE) [ges]	BE: to think	*hier:* vermuten
Ed [ed]	a boy's or man's name (short for 'Edward')	*Vorname (männlich)*
surprise [səˈpraɪz]	s.th. that makes you surprised	Überraschung
spring [sprɪŋ]	a place where water comes out of the ground	Quelle
to raise (hope) [reɪz]	to lift, to allow to grow	(hoch)heben; großziehen; *hier:* (Hoffnung) wecken
proud [praʊd]	If you do something well, you can be ~ of yourself.	stolz

	prickly pear [ˌprɪklɪ ˈpeə]	Some Indians eat the ~ fruit.	Feigenkaktus
	yard [jɑːd]	A ~ is a bit shorter than a meter.	Yard *(ca. 91,4 cm)*
	to fire [ˈfaɪə]	to shoot	feuern, schießen
	to tremble [ˈtrembl]	If you are afraid, your hands might ~.	zittern
	to return s.th. [rɪˈtɜːn]	to give or bring s.th. back	zurückgeben
	gift [gɪft]	a present	Geschenk
	Geronimo [dʒəˈrɒnɪməʊ]	an Indian chief	*Name eines Häuptlings*
	to adapt [əˈdæpt]	*here:* to change s.th. so that you can understand it more easily	bearbeiten, adaptieren
6	**Western** [ˈwestən]	a story or film about the American West	Western *(Film, Roman)*
	Mexican [ˈmeksɪkən]	s.o. from Mexico; adjective of 'Mexico'	Mexikaner(in); mexikanisch
	cattle [ˈkætl]	cows and bulls	Vieh
	°**bandit** [ˈbændɪt]	robber, outlaw	°Bandit, Räuber
	to **fight** [faɪt], **fought**, **fought** [fɔːt]	Peaceful people do not want to ~.	kämpfen
	°to **round up** [raʊnd]	to bring the cattle together	°zusammentreiben
	°**slaughterhouse** [ˈslɔːtəhaʊs]	a place where they kill animals for meat	°Schlachthof
	Kansas City [ˌkænzəs ˈsɪtɪ]	a city in Missouri (near the state of Kansas)	*Stadt in Missouri*
9	**Pardon?** [ˈpɑːdn]	If you haven't understood what someone has said, you say '~'.	Wie bitte?
	How are you? [ˌhaʊ_ə ˈjuː]		Wie geht es dir/Ihnen?
10	**westward** [ˈwestwəd]	towards the west	westwärts
	Horizon Holidays [həˈraɪzn]	the name of a company that plans holidays (not real)	*erfundener Name eines Reiseunternehmens*
	Elvis Presley Boulevard [ˌelvɪsˌpreslɪ ˈbuːləvɑː]	the name of a street	*Straßenname*
	Memphis [ˈmemfɪs]	a city in Tennessee	*Stadt in Tennessee*
	Madam [ˈmædəm]	In situations where you say 'Sir' to a man you say '~' to a woman.	höfliche Anrede für eine Frau
	to **attack** [əˈtæk]	to come suddenly and fight	angreifen
	waste [weɪst]	It is a ~ to throw away things that you could use again.	Verschwendung
	°to **refund a payment** [ˌriːfʌnd_ə ˈpeɪmənt]	to give back the money which s.o. has paid	°eine Zahlung zurückerstatten
	Yours faithfully [ˈfeɪθfəlɪ]	s.th. that you can write to s.o. that you don't know	Mit freundlichem Gruß; Hochachtungsvoll
	Casey [ˈkeɪsɪ]	a surname	*Familienname*
	nurse [nɜːs]	s.o. who helps a doctor or looks after people in hospital	Krankenschwester
	°**zipper** (AE) [ˈzɪpə], (BE: **zip**) [zɪp]	Most trousers and some jackets have ~s to close them.	°Reißverschluß
⟨11⟩	**poem** [ˈpəʊɪm]	Goethe wrote a lot of ~s.	Gedicht
	root [ruːt]	The ~s of a tree are under the ground.	Wurzel
	to **plant** [plɑːnt]	to put s.th. (a tree, etc.) in the ground so that it can grow	pflanzen
⟨12⟩	**Sitting Bull**	name of an Indian chief	*Name eines Indianerhäuptlings*

Back to nature!

cattle	Vieh	field	Feld	leaf	Blatt	river	Fluß
climate	Klima	fog	Nebel	map	(Land)karte	rock	Fels
country(side)	Land(schaft)	forest	Wald	mountain	Berg	root	Wurzel
desert	Wüste	ground	Erdboden	mouse, mice	Maus, Mäuse	trail	Spur, Weg
deer	Hirsch(e), Reh(e)	hill	Hügel	national park	Nationalpark	tree	Baum
		island	Insel	path	Pfad	tremor	Erdbeben
eagle	Adler	lake	See	ranch	Viehfarm	valley	Tal
earthquake	Erdbeben	landscape	Landschaft	reindeer	Rentier(e)	wilderness	Wildnis

once	einmal	one hundred	hundert	10 per cent	10 Prozent
twice	zweimal	one thousand	tausend	a quarter of a pound of tea	ein Viertelpfund Tee
three times	dreimal	one million	Million	half a pound of ...	ein halbes Pfund ...
twice as much as	doppelt so viel wie	one billion	Milliarde	a pound of ...	ein Pfund ...
meter (AE)/metre (BE)	Meter	foot	Fuß (30,48 cm)	a kilo of ...	ein Kilo ...
(square) kilometer (AE)/ (square) kilometre (BE)	(Quadrat-)kilometer	yard	Yard (91,44 cm)	a ton of ...	eine Tonne ...
		mile	Meile (1,609 km)	a liter (AE)/a litre (BE) of ...	ein Liter ...

Unit 5

A How is it done?

Fizz [fɪz]	name of a magazine (not real)	*erfundener Name einer Zeitschrift*
effect [ɪˈfekt]	A red sky in the evening is just an ~ of the light and the air.	Effekt, Wirkung
photography [fəˈtɒɡrəfi]	Her hobby is ~: She loves taking photos.	Fotografie
°**screen** [skriːn]	A film is shown on a ~.	°Leinwand, Bildschirm
method [ˈmeθəd]	a special way to do s.th.	Methode
°**separately** [ˈseprətli]	not together	°getrennt
to **mix** [mɪks]	to put different things together	mischen
electronically [ˌɪlekˈtrɒnɪkli]	adverb of 'electronics'	elektronisch
°**newsreader** [ˈnjuːzˌriːdə]	s.o. who reads the news on the radio or on TV	°Nachrichtensprecher(in)
background [ˈbækɡraʊnd]	what is behind s.th. that you are looking at	Hintergrund
°to **filter** [ˈfɪltə]	to keep some things back and let other things through	°filtern
monster [ˈmɒnstə]	a huge animal – King Kong, for example	Ungeheuer, Monster
to **chase** [tʃeɪs]	to run after	jagen
ape [eɪp]	a big monkey, but without a tail	Menschenaffe
person [ˈpɜːsn]	a man, woman or child	Person

Exercises

2 **movies** (AE) [ˈmuːvɪz]	BE: cinema	Kino
3 °**passive** [ˈpæsɪv]	'It is done' is the ~ form of 'They do it'.	°passiv, Passiv
position [pəˈzɪʃn]	exactly where s.th. or s.o. is	Position, Lage
to **draw** [drɔː], **drew** [druː] **drawn** [drɔːn]	to make a picture with a pencil or pen	zeichnen
4 **studio** [ˈstjuːdɪəʊ]	Films and records are often made in a ~.	Studio
spaceship [ˈspeɪʃɪp]	You can leave earth in a ~.	Raumschiff

to **photograph** [ˈfəʊtəɡrɑːf]	to take photos	fotografieren
and so on [ənd ˈsəʊ ˌɒn]	etc.	und so weiter
realistic [ˌrɪəˈlɪstɪk]	It's ~ = It looks or sounds real.	realistisch
Greg [ɡreɡ]	a boy's or man's name	*Vorname (männlich)*
5 **quite a surprise** [ˌkwaɪt ə səˈpraɪz]	I was quite surprised = It was ~ to me.	eine ziemliche Überraschung

B A helicopter crash

helicopter [ˈhelɪkɒptə]	A ~ is s.th. like a plane, but it can land almost everywhere.	Hubschrauber
crash [kræʃ]	a bad accident in a car, plane, etc.	Unfall, Absturz
Shane West [ˌʃeɪn ˈwest]	a man's name	*Personenname (männlich)*
pilot [ˈpaɪlət]	a person who flies a plane or helicopter	Pilot(in)
to **crash** [kræʃ]	verb of 'crash'	verunglücken, abstürzen
°**expert** [ˈekspɜːt]	a person who knows a lot about s.th.	°Experte, Expertin
cause [kɔːz]	Fast driving is the ~ of many accidents.	Ursache
blind [blaɪnd]	*here:* without the help of the pilot	blind
°**avionics** [ˌeɪviˈɒnɪks]	all the instruments that a pilot needs in a plane or helicopter	°Fluginstrumente
to **cause** [kɔːz]	to be the cause of (verb of 'cause')	verursachen
fault [fɔːlt]	s.th. that is wrong with s.th.	Fehler
°**equipment** [ɪˈkwɪpmənt]	machines etc. that are needed for s.th.	°Ausrüstung

Exercises

3 °to **knock down** [nɒk]	to hit s.o. so that he or she falls down	°anfahren; umstoßen
mouse [maʊs], **mice** [maɪs]	very small animal(s)	Maus, Mäuse
4 **robot** [ˈrəʊbɒt]	a computer-controlled 'worker machine', usually with arms, legs, etc.	Roboter
5) to **replace** [rɪˈpleɪs]	to take the place of s.o. or s.th.	ersetzen

C The fun they had

the fun they had	= the fun that they had	
Margie [ˈmɑːdʒɪ]	a girl's or woman's name	*Vorname (weiblich)*
°to **print** [prɪnt]	Today, books are ~ed by machines.	°drucken
mechanical [mɪˈkænɪkl]	like a machine	mechanisch
county [ˈkaʊntɪ]	a special part of a country or state	Bezirk *(USA)*, Grafschaft *(GB)*
°**County Inspector** [ˌkaʊntɪ ɪnˈspektə]	a person who examines schools and/or teachers in a county	°Bezirksschulrat
ugly [ˈʌɡlɪ]	opposite of 'beautiful'	häßlich
°**slot** [slɒt]	When you buy something from a machine, you put money in a ~.	°Schlitz
°**sector** [ˈsektə]	part	°Sektor, Abschnitt
progress [ˈprəʊɡres]	development	Fortschritt(e)
disappointed [ˌdɪsəˈpɔɪntɪd]	sad because s.th. is not what you had hoped or expected	enttäuscht
°**altogether** [ˌɔːltəˈɡeðə]	completely	°ganz
shoulder [ˈʃəʊldə]	Your ~s are at the top of your arms.	Schulter
sigh [saɪ]	When you are sad, tired, or disappointed, you sometimes give a ~.	Seufzer

schoolyard [ˈskuːljɑːd]	where children play at school		Schulhof
°to flash [flæʃ]	(of a light) to go on and off		°(auf)blinken
Isaac Asimov [ˌaɪzək ˈæzɪmɒf]	a famous American writer		amerikanischer Schriftsteller
°to adapt [əˈdæpt]	to change, to make s.th. easier to understand		°bearbeiten

Exercises

1 science fiction [ˌsaɪəns ˈfɪkʃn]	stories about the future		Science Fiction
2 °bleeding [ˈbliːdɪŋ]	blood that comes out if you cut yourself		°Blutung
3 °diagram [ˈdaɪəgræm]			°Diagramm, graphische Darstellung
personal computer [ˈpɜːsnl]	computer for one person		PC, Personal Computer
°to store [stɔː]	to keep in a special place		°speichern, lagern
to save [seɪv]	to keep, not to use		sparen; retten
UniTV [ˈjuːniː] AstroTV [ˈæstrəʊ]	names of TV stations		Namen von Fernsehstationen
4 energy [ˈenədʒi]	Lights, machines, and cars all use ~.		Energie
°to cut [kʌt]	to make less		°verringern; senken
costs [kɒsts]	the money that you have to pay for s.th.		Kosten
bottle bank [ˈbɒtl ˌbæŋk]	a place that you can take empty bottles back to		Altglascontainer
⟨6⟩ moon [muːn]	You can see the ~ in the sky at night.		Mond
race [reɪs]	In a ~, the fastest person wins.		Rennen
to press [pres]	to push with your finger		drücken
I guess (AE) [ges]	BE: I think		ich denke
to steer [stɪə]	You must ~ a car so that it goes the right way.		steuern
9 alarm clock [əˈlɑːm klɒk]	a clock that wakes you in the morning		Wecker
to set the alarm	to switch the alarm clock on so that it will ring at a certain time		den Wecker stellen
TV dinner	a meal which you only have to warm up		Fertiggericht
⟨10⟩ poem [ˈpəʊɪm]	Goethe wrote lots of ~s.		Gedicht
Teevee [tiːˈviː]	= TV		
spouse [spaʊz]	wife or husband; here: a surname		Gemahl(in); hier: Familienname
How do you do? [ˌhaʊdjuˈduː]	You can say this when you meet s.o. for the first time.		guten Tag/Abend (förmliche Begrüßung)
to come right about	here: to be all right again		wieder funktionieren

⟨Song: In the year 2525⟩

man [mæn]	opposite of 'woman'; also: mankind		Mann; Menschheit
to be alive [əˈlaɪv]	to live		leben, am Leben sein
to survive [səˈvaɪv]	to be still alive		überleben
ain't gonna need (sl.) [ˌeɪnt gɒnə ˈniːd]	= I'm not going to need		
lie [laɪ]	s.th. which isn't true; opposite of 'truth'		Lüge
pill [pɪl]	When you are ill, the doctor sometimes gives you ~s to take.		Tablette, Pille
to chew [tʃuː]	to use your teeth on		kauen
limp [lɪmp]	without energy		schlaff, kraftlos
to pick [pɪk]	to choose		(aus)wählen
bottom [ˈbɒtəm]	opposite of 'top'		Boden
tube [tjuːb]	here: a thin glass		Röhre
a-coming (sl.)	= coming		
he oughta make it (sl.)	= he ought to manage it		er sollte es schaffen

Unit 5 / Unit 6

(I) guess (AE) [ges]	BE: I think	ich denke
judgement day ['dʒʌdʒmənt]	the day when God comes again	der Tag des Jüngsten Gerichts
to shake [ʃeɪk], shook [ʃʊk], shaken [ʃeɪkn]	You sometimes ~ your head when you say no.	(sich) schütteln
mighty ['maɪtɪ]	powerful	mächtig
to tear down [teə], tore [tɔː], torn [tɔːn]	to pull down, to break up	abreißen
I'm kind a wond'rin' (sl.)	= I'm wondering. I'm trying to find an answer.	
he ain't put back nothing (sl.)	= He hasn't given anything back.	
reign [reɪn]	time when s.o. is powerful	Herrschaft
eternal [iːˈtɜːnl]	If something is ~, it will never end.	ewig
twinkling ['twɪŋklɪŋ]	the kind of light that comes from stars	Glitzern, Funkeln
to describe [dɪˈskraɪb]	to say what s.th. is like	beschreiben
danger ['deɪndʒə]	noun of 'dangerous'	Gefahr
depressed [dɪˈprest]	sad	deprimiert, niedergeschlagen
pessimistic [pesɪˈmɪstɪk]	A ~ person always thinks that the worst will happen.	pessimistisch
thoughtful ['θɔːtfʊl]	A ~ person thinks a lot.	nachdenklich

Nouns and verbs

number	Nummer	**name**	Name	**film**	Film
to **number**	numerieren	to **name**	benennen	to **film**	filmen
list	Liste	**change**	(Ver)änderung	**crash**	Zusammenstoß, Absturz
to **list**	auflisten	to **change**	(ver)ändern	to **crash**	zusammenstoßen, abstürzen
cause	Ursache	**photograph**	Fotografie		
to **cause**	verursachen	to **photograph**	fotografieren	**program(me)**	Programm
question	Frage	**control**	Kontrolle	to **program(me)**	programmieren
to **question**	(be)fragen	to **control**	kontrollieren, steuern		

What you can say about people

blind	blind	**(dis)honest**	(un)ehrlich	**sensible**	vernünftig
blond	blond	**interesting**	interessant	**smart**	schlau, gewitzt
boring	langweilig	**modest**	bescheiden	**strong**	stark
brave	tapfer, mutig	**peaceful**	friedliebend	**stupid**	dumm
careful	vorsichtig	**pessimistic**	pessimistisch	**tall**	groß
careless	nachlässig	**pleasant**	angenehm	**thoughtful**	nachdenklich
clever	schlau	**pretty**	hübsch	**ugly**	häßlich
crazy	verrückt	**quiet**	ruhig	**(un)friendly**	(un)freundlich
cruel	grausam	**romantic**	romantisch	**(un)popular**	(un)beliebt

Unit 6

A The exchange

exchange [ɪksˈtʃeɪndʒ]	In an ~, two people change places for a while, or visit each other at different times.	Austausch
Barnaby Stubbs [ˈbɑːnəbɪ ˈstʌbz]	a man's or boy's name	*Personenname (männlich)*

Unit 6

Barney [ˈbɑːnɪ]	a boy's or man's name (short for 'Barnaby')	*Vorname (männlich)*
to **fill out**	to write in the empty lines	ausfüllen
°to **put down**	to write	°aufschreiben
to **pick up** (a language)	*here:* to learn	*hier:* lernen, aufschnappen
shorts [ʃɔːts]	short trousers	Shorts, kurze Hose

Exercises

2 **Hemisfair** [ˈhemɪsˌfeə]	name of a world fair	*Name einer Weltausstellung*
El Mercado [ˌel merˈkɑːdəʊ]	a market in San Antonio	*Marktviertel in San Antonio*
La Villita [lʌ vɪˈliːtə]	a part of San Antonio	*Stadtviertel von San Antonio*
the **Institute of Texan Cultures** [ˈɪnstɪtjuːt ˌəv ˌteksn ˈkʌltʃəz]		*Institut für texanische Kulturen*
proud of [praʊd]	If you do something well, you can be ~ yourself.	stolz auf
the **Alamo** [ˈæləməʊ]	a building where Americans fought against Mexican soldiers	*spanisches Missionsgebäude aus dem 18. Jh.*
Davy Crockett [ˌdeɪvɪ ˈkrɒkɪt]	a famous hero of the American West	*amerikanischer Abenteurer und Pionier (1786–1836)*
the **Hertzberg Collection** [ˈhɜːtsbɜːg kəˈlekʃn]		*Sammlung von Gegenständen aus dem Zirkusleben*

B He's here!

°**opera** [ˈɒpərə]	Mozart and Wagner wrote a lot of ~s.	°Oper
I guess (AE) [ges]	BE: I suppose, I think	ich denke
specialty (AE) [ˈspeʃltɪ] (BE: speciality) [ˌspeʃɪˈælətɪ]	s.th. special; s.th. that is typical of a certain place	Spezialität
the **Sunken Gardens** [ˌsʌŋkən ˈgɑːdənz]	a park in San Antonio	*Gartenanlage in San Antonio*

Exercises

⟨2⟩ **ebony** [ˈebənɪ]	a kind of dark wood	Ebenholz
ivory [ˈaɪvərɪ]	A lot of elephants are hunted for their ~.	Elfenbein
harmony [ˈhɑːmənɪ]	When two voices are in ~, they sound good together.	Harmonie
piano [pɪˈænəʊ]	an instrument	Klavier, Piano
keyboard [ˈkiːbɔːd]	the part of the piano that you play on	Klaviatur, Tastatur
Lord [lɔːd]	God	der Herr, Gott
wherever [weərˈevə]	= it doesn't matter where	wo(hin) auch immer
to **survive** [səˈvaɪv]	She ~d the crash = She didn't die.	überleben
alive [əˈlaɪv]	opposite of 'dead'	lebendig
3 **Tina Turner** [ˌtiːnə ˈtɜːnə]	an American singer	*amerikanische Sängerin*
°**cover** [ˈkʌvə]	Please put the record back in its ~.	°Hülle, Umschlag
Anna "Tina" Mae Bullock [ˌænə ˌtiːnə ˌmeɪ ˈbʊlək]	Tina Turner's real name	*richtiger Name Tina Turners*
Nutbush [ˈnʌtbʊʃ]	a town in Tennessee	*Stadt in Tennessee*

Unit 6

gospel music [ˈgɒspl]		a kind of black music	Gospel *(religiös geprägte Musik)*
St. Louis [snt ˈluːɪs]		an American city	*amerikanische Großstadt*
Ike Turner [ˌaɪk ˈtɜːnə]		an American singer	*amerikanischer Sänger*
soul [səʊl]		a kind of black music	Soul *(Musikrichtung)*
°**revue** [rɪˈvjuː]		a big show with music	°Revue, Musikshow
band [bænd]		a group of people that play music together	Musikgruppe, Band
tour [tʊə]		*here:* journey with concerts in different places	Tournee
Las Vegas [ˌlæs ˈveɪgəs]		an American city	*amerikanische Großstadt*
comeback [ˈkʌmbæk]		She had a ~ = She became popular again.	Comeback
private [ˈpraɪvət]		opposite of 'public'	privat
copy [ˈkɒpɪ]		one thing that looks like another	Kopie; Exemplar
the **Rolling Stones** [ˌrəʊlɪŋ ˈstəʊnz]		an English rock group	*englische Rockgruppe*
°**repeatedly** [rɪˈpiːtɪdlɪ]		again and again	°wiederholt
finally [ˈfaɪnəlɪ]		in the end	schließlich, endlich
4 **guest** [gest]		a visitor in another person's home	Gast

Ramona's Radio Show

DJ [ˈdiːˌdʒeɪ] = **disc jockey** [ˈdɪsk ˌdʒɒkɪ]		the person who plays and talks about the records on a radio show	Diskjockey
Ramona Díaz [rəˈməʊnə ˈdɪas]		a woman's name	*Personenname (weiblich)*
KFAQ [ˌkeɪ ˌef ˌeɪ ˈkjuː]		the name of a radio station in San Antonio	*Radiostation in San Antonio*
°**winner** [ˈwɪnə]		the person who wins	°Gewinner(in)
°**phone-in** [ˈfəʊnɪn]		(part of) a radio program when people can phone the station	°Radiosendung, an der die Hörer sich telefonisch beteiligen
rhythm [ˈrɪðəm]		Music with a strong ~ is good to dance to.	Rhythmus
the **Chapman Familiy** [ˈtʃæpmən]		a family of gospel singers	*amerikanische Gospelgruppe*
°**shield** [ʃiːld]		In the old days, soldiers carried swords and ~s.	°(Schutz)schild
influence [ˈɪnflʊəns]		It was an ~ on me: it changed the way I think/make music/etc.	Einfluß
root [ruːt]		The ~s of a tree are under the ground.	Wurzel
blues [bluːz]		a kind of black music	Blues *(Musikrichtung)*
Ray Charles [ˌreɪ ˈtʃɑːlz]		an American singer	*amerikanischer Sänger und Musiker*
Aretha Franklin [əˌriːθə ˈfræŋklɪn]		an American singer	*amerikanische Sängerin*
respect [rɪˈspekt]		You should always have ~ for other people.	Respekt, Achtung
Martin Luther King [ˌmɑːtɪn ˌluːθə ˈkɪŋ]		black people's leader in the 60s	*Führer der Bürgerrechtsbewegung in den USA (1929–1968)*
James Brown [ˌdʒeɪmz ˈbraʊn]		an American singer	*amerikanischer Sänger*
°**slave** [sleɪv]		a worker who could be bought and sold	°Sklave, Sklavin
simple [ˈsɪmpl]		It's ~ = It's easy to understand.	einfach

feeling [ˈfiːlɪŋ]	Love is a ~.	Gefühl
°**guy** (AE) [gaɪ]	another word for 'man'	°Typ, Kerl
Robert Johnson [ˌrɒbət ˈdʒɒnsn]	an American singer	*amerikanischer Blues-Musiker*
Delta Blues [ˌdeltə ˈbluːz]	a kind of blues	*Blues aus der Region des Mississippideltas*
Detroit [dəˈtrɔɪt]	an American city	*amerikanische Großstadt*
°**beat** [biːt]	*here:* rhythm	°*hier:* Rhythmus
Muddy Waters [ˌmʌdɪ ˈwɔːtəz]	an American singer	*amerikanischer Sänger*
the **Beatles** [ˈbiːtlz]	an English pop group	*englische Musikgruppe*
Fats Domino [ˌfæts ˈdɒmɪnəʊ] **Little Richard** [ˌlɪtl ˈrɪtʃəd] **Chuck Berry** [ˌtʃʌk ˈberɪ]	American singers	*amerikanische Rock 'n' Roll-Musiker*
to **copy** [ˈkɒpɪ]	to do s.th. in the same way as s.o. else	nachmachen; kopieren
Boogie [ˈbuːgɪ]	a kind of fast blues with piano	Boogie *(Musikrichtung)*
Moose Gregson [ˌmuːs ˈgregsn]	a boy's name	*Personenname (männlich)*
°**producer** [prəˈdjuːsə]	the person who is in charge of making a record/film etc.	°Produzent(in)
⟨2⟩ queen [kwiːn]	*here:* most important woman	Königin
⟨4⟩ to have the blues [bluːz]	to feel sad all the time	niedergeschlagen sein

⟨San Antonio⟩

Governor's Palace [ˌgʌvənəz ˈpælɪs]	a big building in San Antonio	Gouverneurspalast
villa [ˈvɪlə]	a large country house	Villa
Paseo del Rio [pæˌseɪəʊ del ˈriːəʊ]	Spanish for 'path along the river'	*Uferpromenade in San Antonio*
the Mission Concepción [ˌmɪʃn ˌkɒnsepsˈjɒn]		*Missionsgebäude Concepción*
battle [ˈbætl]	Davy Crockett and his friends fought at the ~ of the Alamo.	Schlacht, Kampf

[Working with your dictionary]

1 **in alphabetical order** [ˌælfəˈbetɪkl]	The names Alan, Betty, Bob, Cathy are in ~.	in alphabetischer Reihenfolge
headword [ˈhedwɜːd]	a main word in a dictionary	Stichwort
derivative [dɪˈrɪvətɪv]	'Watcher' is a derivative of 'watch'.	*hier:* Ableitung
compound [ˈkɒmpaʊnd]	'Watchdog' is a compound of 'watch' and 'dog'.	zusammengesetztes Wort
part of speech [spiːtʃ]	noun, verb, adjective, etc.	Wortart
abbreviation [əˌbriːvɪˈeɪʃn]	short form of a word	Abkürzung
Columbus [kəˈlʌmbəs]	= Christopher Columbus	*Entdecker Amerikas (1451–1506)*
to **translate** (into) AE: [ˈtrænsleɪt] BE: [trɑːnsˈleɪt]	to put into another language	übersetzen (in)
to **hurt, hurt, hurt** [hɜːt]	He ~ his leg when he fell off his bike.	verletzten, wehtun

2 **symphony** [ˈsɪmfənɪ]	a piece of music for an orchestra			Symphonie
3 **everyday** [ˈevrɪdeɪ]	~ words are the kind of words that we use every day.			alltäglich
to **describe** [dɪˈskraɪb]	to say what s.th. is like			beschreiben

---

Feelings

angry	ärgerlich, zornig	lonely	einsam	to cry	weinen
in a good/bad mood	guter/schlechter Laune	nervous	nervös	to give a sigh	seufzen
broken-hearted	untröstlich	pleased	erfreut	to laugh	lachen
depressed	niedergeschlagen	proud	stolz	to hate	hassen
disappointed	enttäuscht	sad	traurig	I can't stand	ich kann …
displeased	verärgert	tired	müde	…	nicht ausstehen
excited	aufgeregt	(un)happy	(un)glücklich	to like	mögen
glad	froh	worried	besorgt	to love	lieben

Stopover D: (New frontiers)

frontier [ˈfrʌnˌtɪə]	place where you leave a country (and go into another)	Grenze *(zwischen besiedeltem und unbesiedeltem Land)*
Declaration of Independence [ˌdekləˈreɪʃn̩_əv ˌɪndɪˈpendəns]	The American ~ was on July 4, 1776.	Unabhängigkeitserklärung
war [wɔː]	fighting between countries	Krieg
Louisiana Purchase [luːˌiːzɪˈænə ˈpɜːtʃəs]		*Louisiana-Landkauf (1803)*
to **double** [ˈdʌbl]	to make twice as big	verdoppeln
territory [ˈterɪtrɪ] (BE), AE: [ˈterətɔrɪ]	land that belongs to a country or people	Territorium, Gebiet
New Mexico [ˌnjuːˈmeksɪkəʊ]	a state in the Southwest of the USA	*amerikanischer Bundesstaat*
railroad (AE) [ˈreɪlrəʊd]	BE: railway	Eisenbahn
restless [ˈrestlɪs]	A ~ person does not want to stay in the same place for a long time.	unruhig
colonist [ˈkɒlənɪst]	a person who settles in a new country and takes it over	Siedler(in)
pioneer [ˌpaɪəˈnɪə]	a person who does s.th. or goes somewhere for the first time	Pionier(in)
to **stretch** [stretʃ]	to go as far as	(sich er)strecken
to **open up** [ˈəʊpən]	They ~ed ~ the West = They made it easy for people to travel there after them.	erschließen
to **suffer** [ˈsʌfə]	to go through	(er)leiden
hardship [ˈhɑːdʃɪp]	Where there is poverty, people suffer ~.	Not, Elend
freedom [ˈfriːdəm]	noun of 'free'	Freiheit
trapper [ˈtræpə]	a person who catches animals	Fallensteller, Trapper
the **Appalachians** [ˌæpəˈleɪtʃjənz]	mountains in the East of the USA	die Appalachen *(Gebirge im Osten der USA)*
canoe [kəˈnuː]	a kind of boat	Kanu
riverboat [ˈrɪvəbəʊt]	a large boat that travels on rivers	Flußdampfer
settlement [ˈsetlmənt]	a place where people have settled	Siedlung
wherever [weərˈevə]	His dog follows him ~ he goes.	wo auch immer
civilization [ˌsɪvɪlaɪˈzeɪʃn]	opposite of 'wilderness'	Zivilisation

to **fight off** [faɪt], **fought, fought** [fɔːt]	to try to keep s.o. away	bekämpfen, abwehren
hunting grounds [ˈhʌntɪŋ ˌgraʊndz]	land where there are animals that can be hunted	Jagdgründe
rancher [ˈræntʃə] (AE), BE: [ˈrɑːntʃə]	a big farmer	Viehzüchter(in), Rancher
herd [hɜːd]	a lot of animals together	Herde
cattle [ˈkætl]	cows and bulls	Vieh
Panama [ˌpænəˈmɑː]	a country in Central America	*Land in Mittelamerika*
disease [dɪˈziːz]	Cholera is a ~.	Krankheit
danger [ˈdeɪndʒə]	noun of 'dangerous'	Gefahr
settler [ˈsetlə]	a person who settles in a new place	Siedler(in)

[When the white man came]

tribe [traɪb]	The Cherokees and the Navajos are Indian ~s.	Stamm
peace [piːs]	noun of 'peaceful'	Frieden
weakness [ˈwiːknəs]	Always agreeing is a sign of ~.	Schwäche
to **trade** [treɪd]	to buy and sell	handeln
to **cheat** [tʃiːt]	to play a trick on s.o.	betrügen; mogeln
William Penn [ˌwɪljəm ˈpen]	a famous colonist	*William Penn (1644–1718), Gründer Pennsylvanias*
to **found** [faʊnd]	William Penn ~ed Pennsylvania.	gründen
treaty [ˈtriːtɪ]	In a ~, two sides agree to something.	Vertrag
Delaware [ˈdeləweə]	an Indian tribe (also a US state)	*Indianerstamm*
chief [tʃiːf]	the man who leads an Indian tribe	Häuptling
man [mæn]	*here:* people	*hier:* der Mensch, die Menschheit
stranger [ˈstreɪndʒə]	a person that you don't know	Fremde(r)
to **treat** [triːt]	to ~ s.o. well = to be good to s.o.	behandeln
Little Big Horn [ˌlɪtl ˈbɪg ˌhɔːn]	a river in the Northwest of the USA	*Flußname*
Wounded Knee [ˌwuːndɪd ˈniː]	a place in South Dakota	*Ortsname*
Sioux [suː], pl. [suːz]	an Indian tribe	*Indianerstamm*
buffalo [ˈbʌfələʊ] (sing. and pl.)	wild cattle	Büffel
clothing [ˈkləʊðɪŋ]	clothes	Kleidung
Cheyenne [ʃaɪˈæn]	an Indian tribe	*Indianerstamm*
victory [ˈvɪktərɪ]	They won = It was a ~ for them.	Sieg
General Custer [ˌdʒenərəl ˈkʌstə]	an important American soldier	*amerikanischer General*
massacre [ˈmæsəkə]	In a ~, lots of people are killed.	Massaker, Gemetzel
revenge [rɪˈvendʒ]	He wants ~ = He wants to hit back.	Rache
to **prepare** [ˌprɪˈpeə]	to get ready, to make ready	(sich) vorbereiten
to **surrender** [səˈrendə]	to give up	sich ergeben
to **declare** [dɪˈkleə]	to say or name s.th. in public	erklären
living conditions [ˈlɪvɪŋ kənˌdɪʃnz]	what life is like in a place	Lebensbedingungen
a people [ˈpiːpl]	a group of people who have the same traditions, etc.	Volk
left [left]	There is nothing ~ = It is all gone.	übrig
citizen [ˈsɪtɪzn]	A ~ of a country has a right to live there.	(Staats)bürger(in)

Alphabetical word list

In dieser alphabetischen Wortliste ist das gesamte Vokabular von Orange Line 1–4 enthalten.

- Das Zeichen ˅ vor einer Angabe bedeutet, daß das Wort zum rezeptiven Wortschatz zählt.
- Das Zeichen * nach einem Verb bedeutet: unregelmäßiges Verb.
- Die hier angegebene Schreibweise entspricht dem *British English*. Abweichungen im *American English* sind in der **Revision Box** auf Seite 122 aufgelistet.

A

a [ə, eɪ]	ein(e)
a little [lɪtl]	ein bißchen
a lot [ɒt]	viel
⟨a-rollin'⟩ [əˈroʊlɪn]	rollend
[abbreviation] [əˌbriːviˈeɪʃn]	Abkürzung
to be able to [ˈeɪbl]	können
⟨aboard⟩ [əˈbɔːd]	an Bord
about [əˈbaʊt]	von, über; etwa, ungefähr
about two pounds	ungefähr zwei Pfund
to forget about s.th. [təˈget]	etw. vergessen
What about...?	Wie steht's mit...?
above [əˈbʌv]	über
accident [ˈæksɪdənt]	Unfall
⟨accident'ly⟩ [ˌæksɪˈdentlɪ]	versehentlich
to ache [eɪk]	weh tun
across [əˈkrɒs]	(quer) über, (hin)über, herüber
to act [ækt]	*(eine Rolle, ein Stück)* spielen, handeln
⟨action⟩ [ˈækʃn]	Bewegung
activities [ækˈtɪvɪtɪz]	Betätigungen
actor [ˈæktə]	Schauspieler
to adapt [əˈdæpt]	bearbeiten, adaptieren
to add [æd]	dazutun, addieren
address [əˈdres]	Adresse
adjective [ˈædʒɪktɪv]	Adjektiv
adventure [ədˈventʃə]	Abenteuer
adverb [ˈædvɜːb]	Adverb
advertisement [ədˈvɜːtɪsmənt]	Anzeige
to be afraid [əˈfreɪd]	Angst haben
I'm afraid	ich habe Angst, leider
after [ˈɑːftə]	nach, nachdem
after all	überhaupt, schließlich
after that	danach
to look after	aufpassen auf
to rush after	hinterhereilen
the day after tomorrow	übermorgen
afternoon [ˌɑːftəˈnuːn]	Nachmittag
again [əˈgen]	wieder
against [əˈgenst]	gegen
age [eɪdʒ]	(Zeit-)Alter
Iron Age [ˈaɪən]	Eisenzeit
agency [ˈeɪdʒənsɪ]	Agentur
a year **ago** [əˈgoʊ]	vor einem Jahr
to agree [əˈgriː]	übereinstimmen
agricultural [ˌægrɪˈkʌltʃərəl]	landwirtschaftlich
ahead [əˈhed]	voraus
air [eə]	Luft
air-conditioning [ˈeəkənˌdɪʃnɪŋ]	Klimaanlage
to airmail [ˈeəmeɪl]	per Luftpost schicken
airport [ˈeəpɔːt]	Flughafen
alarm [əˈlɑːm]	Alarm
alarm clock	Wecker
to set the alarm	den Wecker stellen
alcoholic [ˌælkəˈhɒlɪk]	Alkoholiker(in)
⟨alive⟩ [əˈlaɪv]	am Leben
all [ɔːl]	all(es)
all by myself	ganz alleine
all day	den ganzen Tag
all gone	alles weg
all my life	mein ganzes Leben
all round him	um ihn herum
after all	überhaupt, schließlich
let's all push	drücken wir alle
not ... at all	überhaupt nicht
three all	drei beide, drei zu drei
all right [ɔːlˈraɪt]	in Ordnung
to be allowed to [əˈlaʊd]	dürfen
almost [ˈɔːlməʊst]	fast
alone [əˈləʊn]	allein
along [əˈlɒŋ]	entlang
alphabet [ˈælfəbet]	Alphabet
[alphabetical order] [ˌælfəˈbetɪkl]	alphabetische Reihenfolge
already [ɔːlˈredɪ]	schon
also [ˈɔːlsəʊ]	auch
although [ɔːlˈðəʊ]	obwohl
altogether [ˌɔːltəˈgeðə]	ganz
always [ˈɔːlweɪz]	immer
am [æm]	bin
5 **am** [eɪˈem]	5 Uhr vormittags
ambulance [ˈæmbjʊləns]	Krankenwagen
American [əˈmerɪkən]	amerikanisch, Amerikaner(in)
among [əˈmʌŋ]	unter, zwischen
an [ən]	ein(e) *(siehe a)*
⟨anchor⟩ [ˈæŋkə]	Anker
and [ænd]	und
and so on	und so weiter
angel [ˈeɪndʒəl]	Engel
angry [ˈæŋgrɪ]	böse, verärgert
animal [ˈænɪml]	Tier
announcer [əˈnaʊnsə]	Ansager(in)
anorak [ˈænəræk]	Anorak
another [əˈnʌðə]	noch ein, ein anderes
answer [ˈɑːnsə]	Antwort
for an answer	als Antwort
to answer	antworten
⟨anthem⟩ [ˈænθəm]	Hymne
⟨anvil⟩ [ˈænvɪl]	Amboß
any [ˈenɪ]	(irgend)ein, -e, -es
Have we got any crisps?	Haben wir Kartoffelchips?
We haven't got any crisps.	Wir haben keine Chips.
anyone [ˈenɪwʌn]	(irgend) jemand, jede(r)
anything [ˈenɪθɪŋ]	(irgend)etwas
anyway [ˈenɪweɪ]	jedenfalls
anywhere [ˈenɪweə]	irgendwo
apartment (AE) [əˈpɑːtmənt]	Wohnung
ape [eɪp]	(Menschen-)Affe
⟨appendicitis⟩ [əˌpendɪˈsaɪtɪs]	Blinddarmentzündung
apple [ˈæpl]	Apfel
apple tree [ˈæpltriː]	Apfelbaum
appointment [əˈpɔɪntmənt]	Termin
to appreciate [əˈpriːʃɪeɪt]	schätzen, mögen
April [ˈeɪprəl]	April
are [ɑː]	bist, sind, seid
aren't [ɑːnt]	sind nicht
area [ˈeərɪə]	Gebiet, Fläche
arm [ɑːm]	Arm
⟨army⟩ [ˈɑːmɪ]	Armee
around [əˈraʊnd]	herum
to arrest [əˈrest]	verhaften
to arrive [əˈraɪv]	ankommen
arrow [ˈærəʊ]	Pfeil
art [ɑːt]	Kunst
article [ˈɑːtɪkl]	Artikel, Gegenstand
artificial [ˌɑːtɪˈfɪʃl]	künstlich
as [æz]	als, so, wie, weil
as a pet	als Haustier
as big as	so groß wie
as soon as	sobald
ash-tray [ˈæʃtreɪ]	Aschenbecher
Asian [ˈeɪʃn]	Asiat(in); asiatisch
to ask [ɑːsk]	fragen, bitten
to ask for	bitten um
to be asleep [əˈsliːp]	schlafen
Assembly [əˈsemblɪ]	Versammlung, Morgenandacht
assistant [əˈsɪstənt]	Assistent(in)
⟨assistant manager⟩ [ˈmænɪdʒə]	zweite(r) Geschäftsführer(in)
shop-assistant	Verkäufer(in)
at [æt]	bei, an
look at	anschauen
not ... at all	überhaupt nicht
at Barbara's house	bei Barbara zu Hause
at first	zuerst
at home	zu Hause
⟨at half price⟩	zum halben Preis
at last	endlich
at least	wenigstens
at night	nachts
at once	sofort
at the bottom (of)	unten, am Grund von
at the bus stop	an der Bushaltestelle
at the top of	oben auf
at the window	am Fenster
good at English	gut in Englisch
atmosphere [ˈætməsfɪə]	Atmosphäre, Stimmung
to attack [əˈtæk]	angreifen
attic [ˈætɪk]	Dachboden
August [ˈɔːgəst]	August
aunt [ɑːnt]	Tante
Austrian [ˈɒstrɪən]	Österreicher(in); österreichisch
⟨authentic⟩ [ɔːˈθentɪk]	echt, authentisch
autumn [ˈɔːtəm]	Herbst
⟨avenue⟩ [ˈævənjuː]	Allee
average [ˈævərɪdʒ]	Durchschnitt(s-), ,normal'
avionics [ˌeɪvɪˈɒnɪks]	Fluginstrumente
awake [əˈweɪk]	wach
away [əˈweɪ]	weg (von)
to ride away	wegreiten, -fahren
to run away	weglaufen
to throw away	wegwerfen
awful [ˈɔːfl]	schrecklich

B

baby [ˈbeɪbɪ]	Baby
to babysit [ˈbeɪbɪsɪt]	auf kleine Kinder aufpassen
baby brother	kleiner Bruder
back [bæk]	hinten, zurück; Rücken
⟨to go back home⟩	nach Hause zurückkehren
at the back (of the coach)	hinten (im Bus)
back brakes	Hinterradbremse
back door	Hintertür
background [ˈbækgraʊnd]	Hintergrund
backstage [ˈbæksteɪdʒ]	hinter den Kulissen
bacon [ˈbeɪkən]	Speck
bad [bæd]	schlecht, schlimm
bad luck [lʌk]	Pech
[badly]	schlecht
bag [bæg]	Tasche
baked beans [ˌbeɪkt ˈbiːnz]	weiße Bohnen in Tomatensauce
ball [bɔːl]	Ball
⟨to have a ball⟩ (sl.)	sich amüsieren
⟨balloon⟩ [bəˈluːn]	Luftballon
banana [bəˈnɑːnə]	Banane
band [bænd]	Schar, Bande, Band, Gruppe

Alphabetical word list

bandit ['bændɪt]	Bandit(in)	⟨bitty⟩	klitzeklein
bang [bæŋ]	Knall, ‚peng', ‚bums'	to **bite*** [baɪt]	beißen
to bang	(zu)knallen	**black** [blæk]	schwarz
bank [bæŋk]	Bank	⟨blackbird⟩	Amsel
bottle bank	Altglascontainer	['blækbɜ:d]	
bar [bɑ:]	Stange, Riegel; Bar	⟨to blare⟩ [bleə]	dröhnen
bar of chocolate	Tafel Schokolade	**blazer** ['bleɪzə]	Blazer
to **bark** [bɑ:k]	bellen	**bleeding** ['bli:dɪŋ]	Blutung
barn [bɑ:n]	Scheune	**blind** [blaɪnd]	blind
baseball ['beɪsbɔ:l]	Baseball	**block** [blɒk]	Häuserblock
basket ['bɑ:skɪt]	Korb	**blond** [blɒnd]	blond
basketball	Basketball	**blood** [blʌd]	Blut
bath [bɑ:θ]	Bad	**blouse** [blaʊz]	Bluse
to have a bath	baden	to **blow*** [bləʊ]	wehen, blasen
bathroom	Badezimmer	⟨to blow⟩	pfeifen
['bɑ:θrʊm]		⟨to blow out⟩	ausblasen
⟨battle⟩ ['bætl]	Schlacht, Kampf	**blue** [blu:]	blau
Bavarian	bayrisch; Bayer(in)	⟨blue⟩	traurig
[bə'veərɪən]		⟨blues⟩ [blu:z]	Blues
⟨bay⟩ [beɪ]	Bucht	blue with cold	blau vor Kälte
B.C. [ˌbi:'si:]	vor Christus	⟨to have the blues⟩	niedergeschlagen sein, den „Moralischen" haben
to **be*** [bi:]	sein		
[to be on]	laufen *(Film)*		
be quiet	sei(d) ruhig	**board** [bɔ:d]	Tafel; Brett
to be right	recht haben	on board	an Bord
⟨there'd be⟩ ['ðeəd bi:]	es wären	**boat** [bəʊt]	Boot, Schiff
		⟨body⟩ ['bɒdɪ]	Körper
beach [bi:tʃ]	Strand	⟨body fat⟩	Körperfett
beach bag	Strandtasche	to **boil** [bɔɪl]	kochen (in Wasser)
beans [bi:nz]	Bohnen	**bolt** [bəʊlt]	Bolzen, Schraube
beat [bi:t]	Rhythmus	**bone** [bəʊn]	Knochen
⟨to beat⟩	schlagen	**bonnet** ['bɒnɪt]	Haube, Häubchen; Kühlerhaube
⟨heart beat⟩	Herzschlag		
beautiful ['bju:tɪfʊl]	schön	⟨Bonnie⟩ ['bɒnɪ]	Geliebte(r)
because [bɪ'kɒz]	weil	⟨bonny⟩ ['bɒnɪ]	hübsch, schön
because of	wegen	**book** [bʊk]	Buch
to **become*** [bɪ'kʌm]	werden	exercise book	Heft
bed [bed]	Bett	textbook	Lehrbuch
to go to bed	ins Bett gehen	bookshop	Buchhandlung
to take ... to bed	... mit ins Bett nehmen	bookshelf	Bücherregal
bedroom ['bedrʊm]	Schlafzimmer	['bʊkʃelf]	
beeper ['bi:pə]	Funkrufempfänger	to book	buchen
before [bɪ'fɔ:]	vor *(einem Zeitpunkt)*	**boot** [bu:t]	Stiefel
		to **border** upon ['bɔ:də]	angrenzen an
the day before yesterday	vorgestern	⟨border⟩	Grenze, Grenzgebiet
to **begin*** [bɪ'gɪn]	anfangen	**boring** ['bɔ:rɪŋ]	langweilig
beginner [bɪ'gɪnə]	Anfänger(in)	**born** [bɔ:n]	geboren
behind [bɪ'haɪnd]	hinter	⟨borough⟩ ['bʌrə]	Stadtbezirk
to fall behind	zurückbleiben	to **borrow** ['bɒrəʊ]	sich borgen
to **believe** [bɪ'li:v]	glauben	**boss** [bɒs]	Chef(in)
to believe in	glauben (an)	**both** [bəʊθ]	beide
bell [bel]	Glocke	**bottle** ['bɒtl]	Flasche
to **belong to** [bɪ'lɒŋ]	gehören	bottle bank	Altglascontainer
⟨belongings⟩ [bɪ'lɒŋɪŋz]	Habseligkeiten	**bottom** ['bɒtəm]	Boden, unten, unterer Teil
below [bɪ'ləʊ]	unten, unter	to **bounce** [baʊns]	springen *(Ball)*
best [best]	der, die, das Beste; am besten	**bow** [bəʊ]	Bogen
		to **bow** [bəʊ]	sich verbeugen
bet [bet]	Wette	bowling centre	Bowling-, Kegelzentrum
to bet	wetten	['bəʊlɪŋ ˌsentə]	
You bet!	Darauf kannst du Gift nehmen!	**bowman** ['bəʊmən]	Bogenschütze
		box [bɒks]	Karton, Kiste, Schachtel
better ['betə]	besser		
between [bɪ'twi:n]	zwischen	call box	Telefonzelle
Bible ['baɪbl]	Bibel	juke box	Musikbox
bicycle ['baɪsɪkl]	Fahrrad	['dʒu:kbɒks]	
bicycle-pump [ˌpʌmp]	Fahrradpumpe	telephone box	Telefonzelle
		⟨box number⟩	Postfach, Chiffre
big [bɪg]	groß	**boy** [bɔɪ]	Junge
Big Wheel ['wi:l]	Riesenrad	Boy!	Ausdruck des Erstaunens *(Junge!)*
bike [baɪk]	Fahrrad		
billion (AE) ['bɪljən]	Milliarde	boyfriend ['bɔɪfrend]	(fester) Freund
binoculars [bɪ'nɒkjʊləz]	Fernglas	**brain** [breɪn]	Gehirn
Biology [baɪ'ɒlədʒɪ]	Biologie	brains	Intelligenz
bird [bɜ:d]	Vogel	**brakes** [breɪks]	Bremsen
bird-bath	Vogelbad	⟨brandy butter⟩ ['brændɪ ˌbʌtə]	Weinbrandbutter
bird seed [si:d]	Vogelfutter		
bird table	Vogelhäuschen	**brave** [breɪv]	mutig, tapfer
bird-watching ['wɒtʃɪŋ]	Beobachten von Vögeln	**bread** [bred]	Brot
		break [breɪk]	Pause
biro ['baɪrəʊ]	Kugelschreiber	to break	(zer)brechen
birthday ['bɜ:θdeɪ]	Geburtstag	to break down	kaputtgehen
⟨Happy birthday to you.⟩	Herzlichen Glückwunsch zum Geburtstag!	to break into	einbrechen
		⟨to break out⟩	ausbrechen
biscuit ['bɪskɪt]	Keks; Hundekuchen	nervous breakdown	Nervenzusammenbruch
a **bit** [bɪt]	ein bißchen	**breakfast** ['brekfəst]	Frühstück
a bit of	ein bißchen von	for breakfast	zum Frühstück

to have breakfast	frühstücken		
⟨out of breath⟩ [breθ]	außer Atem		
⟨to breathe⟩ [bri:ð]	atmen		
bridge [brɪdʒ]	Brücke		
bright [braɪt]	hell		
to **bring*** [brɪŋ]	(her)bringen		
⟨to bring back⟩	zurückbringen		
British ['brɪtɪʃ]	britisch		
⟨broad⟩ [brɔ:d]	breit		
broken ['brəʊkən]	gebrochen, kaputt		
broken-hearted [ˌbrəʊkən'hɑ:tɪd]	untröstlich		
brother ['brʌðə]	Bruder		
brown [braʊn]	braun		
brush [brʌʃ]	Besen, Bürste, Schrubber		
to brush	bürsten		
bucket ['bʌkɪt]	Eimer		
budgie ['bʌdʒɪ]	Wellensittich		
buffalo ['bʌfələʊ]	Büffel		
to **build*** [bɪld]	bauen		
building ['bɪldɪŋ]	Gebäude		
bull [bʊl]	Stier		
burglar ['bɜ:glə]	Einbrecher(in)		
to **burn*** [bɜ:n]	(ver)brennen		
to **burst*** [bɜ:st]	platzen		
⟨to bury⟩ ['berɪ]	beerdigen		
bus [bʌs]	Bus		
bus company	Busunternehmen		
bus driver	Busfahrer(in)		
bus station	Busbahnhof		
bus stop	Bushaltestelle		
by bus	mit dem Bus		
business ['bɪznɪs]	Geschäft		
businesswoman ['bɪznɪsˌwʊmən]	Geschäftsfrau		
busy ['bɪzɪ]	fleißig, beschäftigt		
but [bʌt]	aber		
butcher ['bʊtʃə]	Metzger		
butcher's	Metzgerei		
butter ['bʌtə]	Butter		
to **buy*** [baɪ]	kaufen		
by [baɪ]	bei, an		
by cheque	mit Scheck		
by nine o'clock	bis (spätestens) neun Uhr		
by radio	per Funk		
by train	mit dem Zug		
by myself	alleine, selbst		
a book by ...	ein Buch von		
bye-bye [ˌbaɪ'baɪ]	auf Wiedersehen! Tschüs!		

C

⟨cabin⟩ ['kæbɪn]	Hütte
cable ['keɪbl]	Seil
cable car ['keɪblˌkɑ:]	Seilbahn, (gezogene) Straßenbahn
café ['kæfeɪ]	Café, Imbißstube
cafeteria [ˌkæfɪ'tɪərɪə]	Kantine, Cafeteria
cage [keɪdʒ]	Käfig
cake [keɪk]	Kuchen
to **call** [kɔ:l]	(an)rufen; nennen
to call out	ausrufen
to be called [kɔ:ld]	genannt werden, heißen
telephone call	Anruf
call box	Telefonzelle
⟨caller⟩	Anrufer(in)
camera ['kæmərə]	Fotoapparat
camp [kæmp]	Lager
camping-site ['kæmpɪŋˌsaɪt]	Campingplatz
can [kæn]	Dose
can [kæn; kən]	kann, können
cannot ['kænɒt]	kann nicht
can't [kɑ:nt]	kann nicht
Canadian [kə'neɪdɪən]	Kanadier(in); kanadisch
⟨candle⟩ ['kændl]	Kerze
canoe [kə'nu:]	Kanu
canyon ['kænjən]	Cañon, Schlucht
capital ['kæpɪtl]	Hauptstadt
car [kɑ:]	Auto
police car	Polizeiwagen
toy car	Spielzeugauto

138

Alphabetical word list

car park	Parkplatz
cable car ['keɪbl ˌkɑː]	Seilbahn; (gezogene) Straßenbahn
caravan ['kærəvæn]	Wohnwagen
card [kɑːd]	Karte
cardigan ['kɑːdɪgən]	Strickjacke
careful ['keəfʊl]	vorsichtig
be careful	sei(d) vorsichtig
careless ['keəlɪs]	nachlässig, gedankenlos
caretaker ['keəˌteɪkə]	Hausmeister(in)
carol ['kærəl]	(Weihnachts-)Lied
carpet ['kɑːpɪt]	Teppich
(carrier bag) ['kærɪə ˌbæg]	Tragetasche
carrot ['kærət]	Möhre, Karotte
to carry ['kærɪ]	tragen
cartoon [kɑːˈtuːn]	Zeichentrickfilm, Cartoon
in cash [kæʃ]	bar
cassette [kəˈset]	Kassette
cassette-recorder [rɪˈkɔːdə]	Kassettenrekorder
castle ['kɑːsl]	Schloß, Burg
cat [kæt]	Katze
catalogue ['kætəlɒg]	Katalog
to catch* [kætʃ]	fangen
to catch fire	Feuer fangen
to catch a train	einen Zug nehmen
(cathedral) [kəˈθiːdrəl]	Dom
cattle ['kætl]	Vieh
(cattle drive) ['kætl ˌdraɪv]	Viehtrieb
cause [kɔːz]	Ursache
to cause	verursachen
CB radio ['siːˈbiː]	CB-Funk *(Privatfunk)*
cello ['tʃeləʊ]	Cello
cent (¢) [sent]	Cent
(centilitre (cl))	Zentiliter
central ['sentrəl]	Zentral-, Mittel-
central heating ['hiːtɪŋ]	Zentralheizung
centre ['sentə]	Zentrum, (Stadt-)Mitte
century ['sentʃərɪ]	Jahrhundert
certain ['sɜːtn]	sicher
certainly	sicherlich, gewiß
chair [tʃeə]	Stuhl
chance [tʃɑːns]	Chance, Möglichkeit
to take a chance	etwas riskieren
to change [tʃeɪndʒ]	(sich) ändern; umsteigen
change	(Ver-)Änderung
the Channel ['tʃænl]	der Ärmelkanal
(to chant) [tʃɑːnt]	singen
to be in charge of [tʃɑːdʒ]	die Verantwortung haben
chase [tʃeɪs]	Jagd
to chase	jagen
cheap [tʃiːp]	billig
[to cheat] [tʃiːt]	schummeln, mogeln
to check [tʃek]	(über)prüfen
check-list	Kontrolliste
check-up	Überprüfung; (ärztl.) Untersuchung
by check (AE)	mit Scheck
three cheers [tʃɪəz]	ein dreifaches Hoch
cheese [tʃiːz]	Käse
(cheeseburger)	Cheeseburger
cheetah ['tʃiːtə]	Gepard
(chemical) ['kemɪkl]	chemisch
chemist ['kemɪst]	Apotheker(in)
chemist's	Apotheke
chemistry ['kemɪstrɪ]	Chemie
by cheque [tʃek]	mit Scheck
chess [tʃes]	Schach
chest [tʃest]	Brust
(to chew) [tʃuː]	kauen
(chick) [tʃɪk]	Küken
(chicken) ['tʃɪkn]	Hähnchen, Hühnchen
chief [tʃiːf]	Häuptling
child, children [tʃaɪld, 'tʃɪldrən]	Kind, Kinder
chili con carne [ˌtʃɪlɪ kɒn 'kɑːnɪ]	*mexikanisches Gericht*
chimney ['tʃɪmnɪ]	Kamin
chin [tʃɪn]	Kinn
Chinese [ˌtʃaɪˈniːz]	chinesisch; Chinese, Chinesin
chips [tʃɪps]	Pommes frites
chip shop ['tʃɪp ˌʃɒp]	Imbißstube
chocolate ['tʃɒklət]	Schokolade
choir [kwaɪə]	Chor
cholera ['kɒlərə]	Cholera
to choose* [tʃuːz]	(aus)wählen
(chorus) ['kɔːrəs]	Refrain
Christmas ['krɪsməs]	Weihnachten
Christmas Day	1. Weihnachtsfeiertag
Christmas Eve [iːv]	Heiligabend
chrome [krəʊm]	Chrom
church [tʃɜːtʃ]	Kirche
cinema ['sɪnəmə]	Kino
circle ['sɜːkl]	Kreis
circus ['sɜːkəs]	Zirkus
[citizen] ['sɪtɪzn]	Bürger(in)
city ['sɪtɪ]	Stadt, Großstadt
[civilization] [ˌsɪvɪlaɪˈzeɪʃn]	Zivilisation
(to clap) [klæp]	klatschen
class [klɑːs]	Klasse
classmate ['klɑːsmeɪt]	Klassenkamerad(in)
classroom	Klassenzimmer
clean [kliːn]	sauber
to clean (up)	putzen, reinigen
cleaner	Putzfrau, Reiniger(in)
vacuum cleaner ['vækjʊəm ˌkliːnə]	Staubsauger
clear [klɪə]	klar
to clear	auf-, abräumen; freimachen
clever ['klevə]	klug
climate ['klaɪmɪt]	Klima
to climb [klaɪm]	klettern
to climb the mountains ['maʊntɪnz]	bergsteigen
climber ['klaɪmə]	Kletterer(in), Bergsteiger(in)
cloak [kləʊk]	Umhang
clock [klɒk]	Uhr
alarm clock	Wecker
to close [kləʊz]	schließen
closing-time	Ladenschlußzeit
close to [kləʊs]	nahe bei
cloth [klɒθ]	Stoff, Tuch
piece of cloth	Lappen
clothes [kləʊðz]	Kleider, Kleidung
[clothing] ['kləʊðɪŋ]	Kleidung
cloud [klaʊd]	Wolke
cloudy ['klaʊdɪ]	wolkig
club [klʌb]	Klub, Verein
coach [kəʊtʃ]	(Reise-)Bus
to coach	(jdn) trainieren
coal-mine ['kəʊlmaɪn]	Kohlebergwerk
coast [kəʊst]	Küste
coastguard ['kəʊstgɑːd]	Küstenwache
coat [kəʊt]	Mantel
(cockles) ['kɒklz]	Muscheln
cocktail stick ['kɒkteɪl ˌstɪk]	Spieß
coffee ['kɒfɪ]	Kaffee
coin [kɔɪn]	Münze
cold [kəʊld]	kalt; Kälte
blue with cold	blau vor Kälte
to have a cold	eine Erkältung haben
to get cold	kalt werden
(collage) ['kɒlɑːʒ]	Collage
to collapse [kəˈlæps]	zusammenbrechen
to collect [kəˈlekt]	abholen; sammeln
[colonist] ['kɒlənɪst]	Siedler(in)
colour ['kʌlə]	Farbe
school colours	Farben von Schuluniform etc.
What colour is ...	Welche Farbe hat ...
coloured ['kʌləd]	farbig
(colt) [kəʊlt]	Colt *(Revolver)*
comb [kəʊm]	Kamm
to come* [kʌm]	kommen
to come down	herunterkommen
to come in	sich melden *(Funksprache)*
Come on!	Los! Komm schon!
to come open	aufgehen
to come loose [luːs]	sich lösen
to come out	herauskommen
(to come right about)	wieder funktionieren
to come round	vorbeikommen, hereinschauen
to come up to s.o.	auf jdn zukommen
to come upstairs	nach oben kommen
comeback ['--]	Comeback
comfortable ['kʌmfətəbl]	bequem
comic ['kɒmɪk]	Comic-Heft
comment ['kɒment]	Kommentar
community [kəˈmjuːnətɪ]	Gemeinschaft
commuter [kəˈmjuːtə]	Pendler(in)
(to commute)	pendeln
company ['kʌmpənɪ]	Unternehmen, Firma
to compare [kəmˈpeə]	vergleichen
competition [ˌkɒmpəˈtɪʃn]	Wettbewerb
to complain [kəmˈpleɪn]	sich beschweren
to complete [kəmˈpliːt]	vervollständigen
completely [kəmˈpliːtlɪ]	vollständig
[compound] ['kɒmpaʊnd]	zusammengesetztes Wort
comprehension [ˌkɒmprɪˈhenʃn]	Textverständnis
comprehensive school [ˌkɒmprɪˈhensɪv]	Gesamtschule
computer [kəmˈpjuːtə]	Computer
computer company ['kʌmpənɪ]	Computergesellschaft
personal computer	PC, Personalcomputer
con [kɒn]	*(Argument)* dagegen
concert ['kɒnsət]	Konzert
[living conditions] [kənˈdɪʃnz]	Lebensbedingungen
congratulations! [kənˌgrætjʊˈleɪʃnz]	Wir gratulieren!
to conquer ['kɒŋkə]	erobern
continued on page ... [kənˈtɪnjuːd]	Fortsetzung auf Seite ...
contrast ['kɒntrɑːst]	Gegensatz, Kontrast
to control [kənˈtrəʊl]	kontrollieren, steuern
under control	unter Kontrolle
(conversation) [ˌkɒnvəˈseɪʃn]	Unterhaltung
to cook [kʊk]	kochen
cook	Koch, Köchin
cool [kuːl]	kühl
cop (sl.) [kɒp]	Polizist(in)
to copy ['kɒpɪ]	kopieren, nachmachen
copy	Exemplar
(corn) [kɔːn]	Mais
corner ['kɔːnə]	Ecke
cornflakes ['kɔːnfleɪks]	Cornflakes
(corral) [kɔːˈrɑːl]	Korral; Pferch für Tiere
to correct [kəˈrekt]	korrigieren
correct	richtig
to cost* [kɒst]	kosten
costs	Kosten
cottage ['kɒtɪdʒ]	Häuschen
could [kʊd]	könnte; könnte
it could have	es hätte können
to count [kaʊnt]	zählen
counter ['kaʊntə]	Schalter, Ladentisch; Spielmarke
country ['kʌntrɪ]	Land
country (music)	Countrymusik
countryside ['kʌntrɪsaɪd]	Landschaft
county ['kaʊntɪ]	Grafschaft *(GB)*, Bezirk *(USA)*
county inspector	Bezirksschulrat (-rätin)
couple ['kʌpl]	Paar
courage ['kʌrɪdʒ]	Mut
of course [ɒv ˈkɔːs]	natürlich, sicher

Alphabetical word list

cousin ['kʌzn]	Vetter, Kusine	
cover ['kʌvə]	Hülle	
cow [kaʊ]	Kuh	
cowboy ['kaʊbɔɪ]	Cowboy	
craft [krɑːft]	Handwerk, Kunstgewerbe	
⟨cranberry sauce⟩ ['krænbərɪ ˌsɔːs]	Preiselbeersauce	
crash [kræʃ]	Unfall, Zusammenstoß, Absturz	
to crash	zusammenstoßen, abstürzen	
crazy ['kreɪzɪ]	verrückt	
crazy about	verrückt nach	
⟨cream⟩ [kriːm]	Sahne	
credit card	Kreditkarte	
to pay by credit card	mit Kreditkarte bezahlen	
cricket ['krɪkɪt]	Kricket	
crime [kraɪm]	Kriminalität, Verbrechen	
crisps [krɪsps]	Chips	
crops [krɒps]	Feldfrüchte, Ernte	
to cross [krɒs]	überqueren	
to do a crossword ['krɒswɜːd]	ein Kreuzworträtsel machen	
crossing ['krɒsɪŋ]	Überfahrt	
cross-country skiing ['krɒs ˌkʌntrɪ ˌskiːɪŋ]	Skilanglauf	
⟨crow⟩ [krəʊ]	Krähe	
crowd [kraʊd]	(Menschen-)Menge	
cruel [krʊəl]	grausam	
to cry [kraɪ]	weinen, schreien	
⟨cuckoo⟩ ['kʊkuː]	Kuckuck	
cup [kʌp]	Tasse	
a cup of tea	eine Tasse Tee	
cupboard ['kʌbəd]	Schrank	
current ['kʌrənt]	Strömung	
customs ['kʌstəmz]	Zoll	
customs officer	Zollbeamter, -beamtin	
to cut* [kʌt]	schneiden	
to cut down	verringern, senken	
short cut	Abkürzung	
to cycle ['saɪkl]	radfahren	
⟨cycleroute⟩ ['saɪklruːt]	Fahrradweg	
⟨cycle shop⟩ ['saɪkl ʃɒp]	Fahrradladen	
⟨cycle test⟩ ['saɪkl test]	Fahrradprüfung	

D

dad [dæd]	Vati, Papa
daily ['deɪlɪ]	täglich
to damage ['dæmɪdʒ]	beschädigen
damn! [dæm]	verdammt!
dance [dɑːns]	Tanz
to dance	tanzen
dancer	Tänzer(in)
[danger] ['deɪndʒə]	Gefahr
dangerous ['deɪndʒərəs]	gefährlich
Danish ['deɪnɪʃ]	dänisch
dark [dɑːk]	dunkel; Dunkel(heit)
date [deɪt]	Datum
daughter ['dɔːtə]	Tochter
day [deɪ]	Tag
all day	den ganzen Tag
the day after tomorrow	übermorgen
the day before yesterday	vorgestern
⟨to daydream⟩ ['deɪdriːm]	mit offenen Augen träumen
⟨dead⟩ [ded]	tot
dear [dɪə]	Schatz; liebe(r, -s) *(Anrede)*
Oh dear!	O je! Ach du meine Güte!
⟨dearly⟩	von ganzem Herzen
December [dɪ'sembə]	Dezember
to decide [dɪ'saɪd]	entscheiden
deck [dek]	Deck
deck-chair	Liegestuhl
to declare [dɪ'kleə]	deklarieren, verzollen; erklären
[declaration] [ˌdekləˈreɪʃn]	Erklärung
to decorate ['dekəreɪt]	schmücken
decorations [ˌdekəˈreɪʃnz]	Dekoration, (Weihnachts-)Schmuck
deep [diːp]	tief
deer [dɪə]	Hirsch(e), Reh(e); Rotwild
degree [dɪ'griː]	Grad
delicious [dɪ'lɪʃəs]	lecker
to deliver [dɪ'lɪvə]	liefern, austragen
dentist ['dentɪst]	Zahnarzt,-ärztin
department [dɪ'pɑːtmənt]	Abteilung
department store [stɔː]	Kaufhaus
to depend on [dɪ'pend]	abhängen von
depot ['depəʊ]	Zentrale, Depot
⟨depressed⟩ [dɪ'prest]	deprimiert, niedergeschlagen
[derivative] [dɪ'rɪvətɪv]	Ableitung
[to describe] [dɪ'skraɪb]	beschreiben
⟨description⟩ [dɪ'skrɪpʃn]	Beschreibung
desert ['dezət]	Wüste
design [dɪ'zaɪn]	Entwurf, Muster, Design
desk [desk]	Schreibtisch; Schalter
⟨detached house⟩ [dɪ'tætʃt]	Einzelhaus
to develop [dɪ'veləp]	(sich) entwickeln
development [dɪ'veləpmənt]	Entwicklung
⟨dew(fall)⟩ [djuː(fɔːl)]	Tau
diagram ['daɪəgræm]	Diagramm, graphische Darstellung
to dial [daɪəl]	wählen *(Telefon)*
dialogue ['daɪəlɒg]	Dialog
⟨diamond⟩ ['daɪəmənd]	Diamant
diary ['daɪərɪ]	Tagebuch
dice [daɪs]	Würfel
dictionary ['dɪkʃənrɪ]	Wörterbuch
to die [daɪ]	sterben
different ['dɪfrənt]	verschieden
difference ['dɪfrəns]	Unterschied
⟨not a dime's worth of difference⟩ ['daɪmz wɜːθ]	kein Unterschied
difficult ['dɪfɪkəlt]	schwierig, schwer
⟨to dine⟩ [daɪn]	speisen
⟨diner⟩ [daɪnə]	Gast, Speisende(r)
dining-room ['daɪnɪŋruːm]	Eßzimmer
dinner ['dɪnə]	Mittag-, Abendessen
direction [dɪ'rekʃn]	Richtung
director [dɪ'rektə]	Regisseur(in), Direktor(in)
dirty ['dɜːtɪ]	schmutzig
⟨dirt⟩ [dɜːt]	Schmutz
to disagree [ˌdɪsəˈgriː]	nicht übereinstimmen
disappointed [ˌdɪsəˈpɔɪntɪd]	enttäuscht
to disbelieve [ˌdɪsbɪˈliːv]	nicht glauben
disc jockey ['dɪsk dʒɒkɪ]	Diskjockey
disco ['dɪskəʊ]	Disko
discussion [dɪ'skʌʃn]	Diskussion
[disease] [dɪ'ziːz]	Krankheit
dishes ['dɪʃɪz]	Geschirr
dish-washer ['dɪʃˌwɒʃə]	Geschirrspüler
dishonest [dɪs'ɒnɪst]	unehrlich
to dislike [dɪs'laɪk]	nicht mögen
displeased [dɪs'pliːzd]	verärgert
to disqualify [dɪs'kwɒlɪfaɪ]	disqualifizieren
to divide [dɪ'vaɪd]	(auf)teilen
divorced [dɪ'vɔːst]	geschieden
to do [duː]	machen, tun
to do a crossword	ein Kreuzworträtsel machen
to do a paper route	Zeitungen austragen
to do my homework	meine Hausaufgaben machen
to do the shopping	einkaufen
⟨done brought⟩ (sl.) [dʌn 'brɔːt] = brought	brachte
docker ['dɒkə]	Hafenarbeiter
doctor ['dɒktə]	Arzt, Ärztin
doctor's set	Arztköfferchen
dog [dɒg]	Hund
doggy ['dɒgɪ]	Hündchen
⟨doll⟩ (sl.) [dɒl]	Puppe, Mädchen
dollar ['dɒlə]	Dollar
door [dɔː]	Tür
back door	Hintertür
front door	Haustür
next door	nebenan
doorbell	Türklingel
doorstep	Stufe vor der Tür
double ['dʌbl]	doppelt, Doppel-
double oh	null null
[to double]	verdoppeln
down [daʊn]	her-, hinunter
to break down	kaputtgehen
to come down	herunterkommen
to fall down	herunterfallen, hinfallen
to get down	heruntersteigen
to knock down	anfahren, umstoßen
to put down	aufschreiben
to sit down	sich hinsetzen
to tear down	abreißen
downstairs [ˌdaʊnˈsteəz]	unten, nach unten
drama ['drɑːmə]	Drama, Schauspiel
to draw* [drɔː]	zeichnen
drawing	Zeichnung
dream [driːm]	Traum
to dream*	träumen
dress [dres]	Kleid
to dribble ['drɪbl]	dribbeln
electric drill [drɪl]	Bohrmaschine
drink [drɪŋk]	Getränk
to drink*	trinken
to drive* [draɪv]	fahren; (ver)treiben
taxi driver	Taxifahrer(in)
driver's license (AE) ['laɪsəns]	Führerschein
⟨drive-in store⟩ (AE) ['draɪvɪn ˌstɔː]	Laden, in dem man vom Auto aus einkaufen kann
to drop [drɒp]	fallen lassen
the penny dropped	der Groschen ist gefallen
⟨drum⟩ [drʌm]	Trommel
oil-drum ['ɔɪldrʌm]	Öltrommel
dry [draɪ]	trocken
to dry	(ab)trocknen
duck [dʌk]	Ente
⟨Duke⟩	Herzog
during ['djʊərɪŋ]	während
⟨dust⟩ [dʌst]	Staub
⟨Dutchman⟩ ['dʌtʃmən]	Holländer
duty ['djuːtɪ]	Zoll; Pflicht, Aufgabe
duty-free	zollfrei

E

each [iːtʃ]	jede, -r, -s
each other [iːtʃ 'ʌðə]	sich (gegenseitig), einander
eagle ['iːgl]	Adler
ear [ɪə]	Ohr
ear-plugs [plʌgz]	Ohrpfropfen
early ['ɜːlɪ]	früh
to earn [ɜːn]	verdienen
earth [ɜːθ]	Erde
earthquake ['ɜːθkweɪk]	Erdbeben
East [iːst]	Osten
easy ['iːzɪ]	leicht
to eat* [iːt]	essen
⟨eater⟩	Esser
education [ˌedjuːˈkeɪʃn]	Bildung
⟨educated⟩ ['edjuːkeɪtɪd]	gebildet, erzogen
effect [ɪ'fekt]	Wirkung
effort ['efət]	Anstrengung, Mühe
e.g. [ˌiːˈdʒiː]	zum Beispiel

Alphabetical word list

egg [eg]	Ei	**F**		to keep fit [fɪt]	fit bleiben
(egg nog) [nɒg]	amerik. Getränk			**five** [faɪv]	fünf
(egg yolk) [jəʊk]	Eigelb	**face** [feɪs]	Gesicht	to **fix** [fɪks]	befestigen, reparieren
eight [eɪt]	acht	**fact** [fækt]	Tatsache	**flag** [flæg]	Fahne
eighteen [ˌeɪˈtiːn]	achtzehn	in fact	tatsächlich	**flare** [fleə]	Leuchtsignal
eighth [eɪtθ]	achte(r,s)	**factory** [ˈfæktərɪ]	Fabrik	**flash** [flæʃ]	Blitz
(not)... **either** [ˈaɪðə]	auch (nicht)	**fair** [feə]	Markt, Jahrmarkt	to flash	aufblinken
(either...or)	entweder...oder	**fair** [feə]	gerecht, fair	to flash by	vorbeisausen
electric [ɪˈlektrɪk]	elektrisch	(fair) [feə]	schön	**flat** [flæt]	Wohnung; flach
electric drill [drɪl]	Bohrmaschine	**fall** (AE) [fɔːl]	Herbst	**flight** [flaɪt]	Flug
electric saw [sɔː]	Elektrosäge	to fall [fɔːl]	fallen	**floor** [flɔː]	Fußboden
electrician	Elektriker	to fall down	herunterfallen	**flour** [ˈflaʊə]	Mehl
[ˌɪlekˈtrɪʃən]		to fall behind	zurückbleiben	(to flow) [fləʊ]	fließen, strömen
electronics	Elektronik	**family** [ˈfæmɪlɪ]	Familie	**flu** [fluː]	Grippe
[ˌɪlekˈtrɒnɪks]		**famous** [ˈfeɪməs]	berühmt	to **fly** [flaɪ]	fliegen
electronically	elektronisch	**fan** [fæn]	Fan, Anhänger(in)	**fog** [fɒg]	Nebel
elephant [ˈelɪfənt]	Elefant	**fantastic** [fænˈtæstɪk]	phantastisch	foggy	neblig
eleven [ɪˈlevn]	elf	**far** [fɑː]	weit	(to fold) [fəʊld]	falten
else [els]	sonst noch	**farm** [fɑːm]	Bauernhof, Farm	**folk hero**	Volksheld
anything else?	sonst noch etwas?	farmer [ˈfɑːmə]	Bauer, Landwirt	[ˈfəʊk ˌhɪərəʊ]	
emergency	Notfall, Not-	farm house	Bauernhaus	to **follow** [ˈfɒləʊ]	folgen
[ɪˈmɜːdʒənsɪ]		**fast** [fɑːst]	schnell	**food** [fuːd]	Essen
to **emigrate**	auswandern	to **fasten** [ˈfɑːsn]	befestigen, festmachen	**fool** [fuːl]	Narr, Idiot
[ˈemɪgreɪt]		**fat** [fæt]	dick	**foot, feet** [fʊt, fiːt]	Fuß, Füße
emphasis [ˈemfəsɪs]	Betonung	**father** [ˈfɑːðə]	Vater	foot	Längenmaß
empty [ˈemptɪ]	leer	(Father Christmas)	Weihnachtsmann		(= 30,4 cm)
to empty	(aus)leeren	(Father)	Anrede für einen	20 feet high	20 Fuß hoch
end [end]	Ende		Priester	football	Fußball
to end	enden	**fault** [fɔːlt]	Schuld, Fehler	on foot	zu Fuß
ending	Ende, Schluß	**favourite** [ˈfeɪvrɪt]	Lieblings-	(footstep)	Schritt, Fußstapfen
(endless) [ˈendlɪs]	endlos	(fear) [fɪə]	(Ehr-)Furcht	**for** [fɔː]	für
enemy [ˈenəmɪ]	Feind	**February** [ˈfebruərɪ]	Februar	for a minute	einen Augenblick,
energy [ˈenədʒɪ]	Energie	**Federal Republic of**	Bundesrepublik		eine Minute lang
engine [ˈendʒɪn]	Motor, Maschine	**Germany** [ˈfedərəl]	Deutschland	for an answer	als Antwort
English [ˈɪŋglɪʃ]	englisch	to **feed*** [fiːd]	füttern	for breakfast	zum Frühstück
to **enjoy** [ɪnˈdʒɔɪ]	genießen	to **feel*** [fiːl]	(sich) fühlen	for example	zum Beispiel
enough [ɪˈnʌf]	genug	to feel well	sich wohl fühlen	for hours	stundenlang
entrance [ˈentrəns]	Eingang	I feel sick	mir ist übel	for miles and miles	meilenweit
equipment	Ausrüstung	feeling	Gefühl	to ask for	bitten um
[ɪˈkwɪpmənt]		**felt pen** [ˌfelt ˈpen]	Filzstift	to be sorry for s.o.	Mitleid mit jdm haben
to **escape** [ɪˈskeɪp]	entkommen	**fence** [fens]	Zaun	to look for	suchen
Eskimo [ˈeskɪməʊ]	Eskimo	**ferry** [ˈferɪ]	Fähre	to take s.o. for a ride	jdn spazierenfahren
especially	besonders	to **fetch** [fetʃ]	holen	to wait for	warten auf
[ɪˈspeʃəlɪ]		**fete** [feɪt]	Fest	**foreign** [ˈfɒrɪn]	Fremd-, ausländisch
(eternal) [iːˈtɜːnl]	ewig	(fever) [ˈfiːvə]	Fieber	foreign language	Fremdsprache
European	europäisch;	a **few** [fjuː]	ein paar	**forest** [ˈfɒrɪst]	Wald
[ˌjʊərəˈpiːən]	Europäer(in)	fewer	weniger	(forever)	(für) immer
even [ˈiːvn]	sogar	**science fiction**	Science Fiction	to **forget*** [fəˈget]	vergessen
not even	nicht einmal	[ˈfɪkʃən]		**fork** [fɔːk]	Gabel
evening [ˈiːvnɪŋ]	Abend	**field** [fiːld]	Feld, Weide	**form** [fɔːm]	Form
ever [ˈevə]	jemals, irgendwann	**fifteen** [ˌfɪfˈtiːn]	fünfzehn	**form master**	Klassenlehrer
every [ˈevrɪ]	jeder, jede, jedes	**fifth** [fɪfθ]	fünfte(r, s)	[ˈfɔːm ˌmɑːstə]	
every two minutes	alle zwei Minuten	(figgy pudding)	Feigenpudding	**forward** [ˈfɔːwəd]	vorwärts, nach vorne
everybody [- ˌbɒdɪ]	jeder	[ˌfɪgɪ ˈpʊdɪŋ]		to look **forward** to	sich auf etw. freuen
everyone [- wʌn]	jeder	to **fight*** [faɪt]	kämpfen	s.th.	
everything [- θɪŋ]	alles	[to fight off]	abwehren, ankämpfen	[to **found**] [faʊnd]	gründen
everywhere	überall		gegen	**four** [fɔː]	vier
[- weə]		(fighting)	Kampf	**fourteen** [ˌfɔːˈtiːn]	vierzehn
[everyday]	alltäglich	**figure** [ˈfɪgə]	Gestalt; Zahl, Ziffer	**fourth** [fɔːθ]	vierte(r, s)
exact [ɪgˈzækt]	genau	to **fill** [fɪl]	füllen	(fox) [fɒks]	Fuchs
exam [ɪgˈzæm]	Prüfung	to fill out	ausfüllen	**frame** [freɪm]	Rahmen
to **examine**	untersuchen	**film** [fɪlm]	Film	**free** [friː]	frei
[ɪgˈzæmɪn]		a film is on	ein Film läuft	[freedom] [ˈfriːdəm]	Freiheit
example [ɪgˈzɑːmpl]	Beispiel	to film	filmen	(to freeze)* [friːz]	frieren
for example	zum Beispiel	film star	Filmstar	**freezer** [ˈfriːzə]	Tiefkühltruhe
except [ɪkˈsept]	außer	to **filter** [ˈfɪltə]	filtern	**French** [frentʃ]	französisch
exchange	Austausch	**finals** [ˈfaɪnlz]	Endspiel	(French fries) (AE)	Pommes frites
[ɪksˈtʃeɪndʒ]		finally [ˈfaɪnəlɪ]	endlich	[fraɪz]	
exchange student	Austauschschüler(in)	to **find*** [faɪnd]	finden	**fresh** [freʃ]	frisch
to exchange	austauschen, wech-	to find out	herausfinden	**Friday** [ˈfraɪdɪ]	Freitag
	seln	**fine** [faɪn]	gut, in Ordnung	**friend** [frend]	Freund(in)
excited [ɪkˈsaɪtɪd]	aufgeregt	**finger** [ˈfɪŋgə]	Finger	to make friends	Freundschaften
exciting	aufregend	fish fingers	Fischstäbchen		schließen
excursion	Ausflug	to **finish** [ˈfɪnɪʃ]	(be)enden	friendly	freundlich
[ɪkˈskɜːʃn]		**fire** [ˈfaɪə]	Feuer	to **frighten** [ˈfraɪtn]	erschrecken
Excuse me!	Entschuldigung!	fireman	Feuerwehrmann	to be frightened	Angst haben
[ɪkˈskjuːz]		fireplace	Kamin	(frog) [frɒg]	Frosch
exercise [ˈeksəsaɪz]	Übung	fire-brigade	Feuerwehr	**from** [frɒm, frəm]	von, aus
exercise book	Heft	[brɪˈgeɪd]		**front** [frʌnt]	Vorderseite, Vorder-
to **expect** [ɪkˈspekt]	erwarten	(to fire)	(ab)feuern, schießen	in front of	vor
expensive	teuer	**firm** [fɜːm]	Firma	front door	Haustür
[ɪkˈspensɪv]		**first** [fɜːst]	zuerst, zunächst	front wheel	Vorderrad
expert [ˈekspɜːt]	Expert(in)	**fish** [fɪʃ]	Fisch(e)	[**frontier**] [ˈfrʌntɪə]	Grenze
to **explain**	erklären	(fish bones)	Gräten	(frosty) [ˈfrɒstɪ]	frostig, eisig
[ɪkˈspleɪn]		fish fingers	Fischstäbchen	**fruit** [fruːt]	Obst
(expression)	Ausdruck	(fishmonger)	Fischverkäufer(in)	**full** [fʊl]	voll, satt
[ɪksˈpreʃn]		[ˈfɪʃˌmʌŋgə]		full up	belegt
extra [ˈekstrə]	zusätzlich	fisherman	Fischer	**fun** [fʌn]	Spaß
(extract) [ˈekstrækt]	Auszug, Extrakt	[ˈfɪʃəmən]		to make fun of	auslachen, sich lustig
eye [aɪ]	Auge	(to fit) [fɪt]	passen		machen über

141

Alphabetical word list

funny	witzig, komisch	to go surfing	wellenreiten/surfen gehen	hamburger ['hæmbɜːgə]	Hamburger (Frikadelle im Brötchen)
further ['fɜːðə]	weiter	to go swimming	schwimmen gehen	hammer ['hæmə]	Hammer
fuse [fjuːz]	Sicherung	to go to bed	ins Bett gehen	hamster ['hæmstə]	Hamster
fuse-box ['fjuːzbɒks]	Sicherungskasten	to go to school	in die Schule gehen	hand [hænd]	Hand
in future ['fjuːtʃə]	in Zukunft, künftig	to go on to	zu etw. übergehen	Hands up!	Hände hoch!
		to go well	gutgehen	handle ['hændl]	Griff, Klinke
G		I'm going to go-kart	ich werde Go-Kart	handlebars ['--ˌbɑː]	Lenkstange
gallows ['gæləʊz]	Galgen	⟨to go⟩	zum Mitnehmen	to hang (up)* [hæŋ]	(auf)hängen
game [geɪm]	Spiel	goal [gəʊl]	Tor	hangman ['hæŋmən]	Henker
games (building)	Sport(halle)	God [gɒd]	Gott	to happen ['hæpən]	geschehen
gang [gæŋ]	Bande	God bless you!	Gott segne dich!	to happen to	passieren mit
garage ['gærɑːʒ]	Garage, Werkstatt	gold [gəʊld]	Gold	happy ['hæpɪ]	glücklich
garbage can (AE) ['gɑːbɪdʒˌkæn]	Mülleimer	golden ['gəʊldn]	golden, Gold-	⟨Happy birthday to you.⟩	Herzlichen Glückwunsch zum Geburtstag!
garden ['gɑːdn]	Garten	golden eagle	Steinadler	harbour ['hɑːbə]	Hafen
back garden	Garten (hinter dem Haus)	gold rush [rʌʃ]	Goldrausch	hard [hɑːd]	schwierig, hart
gas [gæs]	Benzin, Gas	goldfish ['gəʊldfɪʃ]	Goldfisch	hardship ['hɑːdʃɪp]	Not, Elend
gas station	Tankstelle	gone [gɒn]	weg	hardly ['hɑːdlɪ]	kaum
gate [geɪt]	Tor	good [gʊd]	gut	hat [hæt]	Hut
⟨gay⟩ [geɪ]	fröhlich, lustig	to be good at s.th.	gut sein in etwas, etwas gut können	to hatch [hætʃ]	(aus)schlüpfen
gear [gɪə]	Gang	goodbye [gʊd'baɪ]	auf Wiedersehen	to hate [heɪt]	hassen
gee! (AE) [dʒiː]	(Ausdruck des Erstaunens) Mensch!	goods [gʊdz]	Waren, Güter	to have* [hæv]	haben
⟨general view⟩	Gesamtansicht	⟨goose, geese⟩ [guːs, giːs]	Gans, Gänse	have got	haben
[ˌdʒenrəl 'vjuː]		gosh! [gɒʃ]	(Ausdruck des Erstaunens) Mensch!	haven't got	nicht haben
geography [dʒɪ'ɒgrəfɪ]	Erdkunde	gospel (music) ['gɒspəl]	Gospel	to have got on	tragen, anhaben
German ['dʒɜːmən]	deutsch	to have got [gɒt]	haben, besitzen	to have (got) to	müssen
to get* [get]	bekommen, holen	to have got on	tragen, anhaben	had to	mußte
to get back (into)	zurückgehen, -kommen (in)	government ['gʌvənmənt]	Regierung	didn't have to	mußte nicht
to get better	gesund werden	grade (AE) [greɪd]	Klasse	Have a good time!	Viel Spaß!
to get cold	kalt werden	⟨grand⟩ [grænd]	großartig	Have a piece of cake!	nimm ein Stück Kuchen!
to get down	heruntersteigen	grandchildren ['græntʃɪldrən]	Enkel	Haven't you?	Nicht wahr?
to get home	nach Hause kommen	grandfather ['grænˌfɑːðə]	Großvater	⟨I've got it⟩	Verstanden.
to get in	einsteigen	grandma ['grænˌmɑː]	Oma	to have a bath	baden
⟨to get into trouble⟩	Ärger bekommen	grandmother ['grænˌmʌðə]	Großmutter	to have a cold	erkältet sein
to get late	spät werden	grandpa ['grænˌpɑː]	Opa	to have a look at	(kurz) anschauen
to get lost	verlorengehen, sich verlaufen	grandparents ['grænˌpeərənts]	Großeltern	to have breakfast	frühstücken
to get off	aussteigen (aus einem Bus/Zug)	grass [grɑːs]	Gras	to have for breakfast	zum Frühstück essen
to get on (with)	weitermachen, vorankommen	great [greɪt]	prima; sehr groß	to have tea	Abendbrot essen
to get out	herauskommen, fahren	the Great Spirit ['spɪrɪt]	der Große Geist	to have (got) on	tragen, anhaben
to get out of	aussteigen	Greek [griːk]	griechisch	⟨to have the blues⟩	niedergeschlagen sein, einen „Moralischen" haben
to get s.th. out	etw. herausholen	green [griːn]	grün	hay [heɪ]	Heu
to get ready	sich bereitmachen	greengrocer's ['griːnˌgrəʊsəz]	Gemüseladen	⟨hayseed⟩ (AE, sl.) ['heɪsiːd]	tölpelhaft, naiv
to get o.s. ready	sich fertigmachen	⟨greeting⟩ ['griːtɪŋ]	Gruß	he [hiː]	er
to get to school	die Schule erreichen	⟨greeter⟩	Grußkarte	he's [hiːz] = he is	er ist
to get up	aufstehen	grey [greɪ]	grau	head [hed]	Kopf
⟨to get to know s.o.⟩	jdn kennenlernen	ground [graʊnd]	(Erd)boden	headache ['hedeɪk]	Kopfweh
Get well soon!	Gute Besserung!	grounds [graʊndz]	Gelände	headphones ['hedfəʊnz]	Kopfhörer
ghost [gəʊst]	Geist, Gespenst	sports ground	Sportplatz	⟨to head for⟩	in Richtung ... fahren
giant ['dʒaɪənt]	Riese	group [gruːp]	Gruppe	heading ['hedɪŋ]	Überschrift
giant redwood	Mammutbaum	to grow* [grəʊ]	wachsen	headmaster [ˌhed'mɑːstə]	Schulleiter, (Di-)Rektor
⟨gift⟩ [gɪft]	Geschenk	to grow s.th.	etw. anbauen	[headword] ['hedwɜːd]	Stichwort
⟨gimme = give me⟩ (sl.) ['gɪmɪ]	gib mir	⟨grown-up⟩ ['grəʊnʌp]	Erwachsene(er), erwachsen	to hear* [hɪə]	hören
girl [gɜːl]	Mädchen	to guess [ges]	raten; vermuten	heart [hɑːt]	Herz
girlfriend ['gɜːlfrend]	(feste) Freundin	I guess (AE)	ich meine, ich denke	⟨heart beat⟩	Herzschlag
to give* [gɪv]	geben	guest [gest]	Gast	heating ['hiːtɪŋ]	Heizung
to give up	aufgeben	guide [gaɪd]	Führer(in)	central heating	Zentralheizung
glad [glæd]	froh	⟨guide dog⟩	Blindenhund	⟨heater⟩ ['hiːtə]	Heizgerät
glass [glɑːs]	Glas	['gaɪd ˌdɒg]		⟨heaven⟩ ['hevn]	Himmel
⟨glitter⟩ ['glɪtə]	Glitzersterne, -material	guitar [gɪ'tɑː]	Gitarre	heavy ['hevɪ]	schwer
to go* [gəʊ]	gehen	gun [gʌn]	Schußwaffe, Gewehr	height [haɪt]	Höhe
to go for a walk	spazierengehen	guy (AE) [gaɪ]	Typ, Kerl	helicopter ['helɪkɒptə]	Hubschrauber
to go home	nach Hause gehen			hello [hə'ləʊ]	hallo, guten Tag
⟨to go back home⟩	nach Hause zurückkehren	**H**		help [help]	Hilfe
to go in	hineingehen	hacker ['hækə]	‚Hacker', Computerfan	to help	helfen
to go mad	verrückt werden			⟨to help s.o. out⟩	jdm helfen
to go near	sich nähern	⟨haggis⟩ ['hægɪs]	schottisches Gericht	hen [hen]	Huhn, Henne
to go off with s.o.	mit jdm weggehen	hair [heə]	Haar(e)	her [hɜː]	ihr; sie
to go on	weitermachen	half [hɑːf]	halb	her name	ihr Name
what's going on?	was ist los?	half past seven	halb acht	hers [hɜːz]	ihre(r, s)
to go out	weggehen	half-time	Halbzeit	herself [hɜː'self]	sich, (sie) selbst
to go past	vorbeigehen	⟨half way⟩	auf halbem Wege	[herd] [hɜːd]	Herde
to go red	erröten	hall [hɔːl]	Diele, Flur; Halle	here [hɪə]	hier, hierher
to go round to see	besuchen	⟨ham⟩ [hæm]	Schinken	here you are	bitte schön
to go shopping	einkaufen gehen			hero ['hɪərəʊ]	Held
				folk hero	Volksheld
				hey! [heɪ]	he (du)
				hi! [haɪ]	hallo, guten Tag, he (du)

Alphabetical word list

to **hide*** [haɪd]	(sich) verstecken	
high [haɪ]	hoch	
high school	weiterführende Schule in den USA	
highway	autobahnähnliche Landstraße	
hill [hɪl]	Hügel	
him [hɪm]	ihn, ihm	
himself [hɪm'self]	sich, (er) selbst	
[hip, hip hurray] [ˌhɪpˌhɪp hʊ'reɪ]	hipp, hipp, hurra	
his [hɪz]	sein(e)	
Hispanic [hɪ'spænɪk]	(hi)spanisch; jmd aus einem spanischsprachigen Land	
history ['hɪstərɪ]	Geschichte	
to **hit*** [hɪt]	schlagen, treffen	
hobby ['hɒbɪ]	Hobby, Steckenpferd	
⟨hobo⟩ (AE) ['həʊbəʊ]	Landstreicher, Wanderarbeiter	
hockey ['hɒkɪ]	Hockey	
hockey stick ['hɒkɪˌstɪk]	Hockeyschläger	
to **hold*** [həʊld]	halten	
to hold on to	festhalten an	
hole [həʊl]	Loch	
holiday ['hɒlɪdeɪ]	Ferien, Urlaub	
holly ['hɒlɪ]	Stechpalme	
home [həʊm]	Haus, Heim	
at home	zu Hause	
to get home	nach Hause kommen	
to go home	nach Hause gehen	
⟨to go back home⟩	nach Hause zurückkehren	
to take home	nach Hause bringen	
⟨homeless⟩ ['həʊmlɪs]	obdachlos	
Home Economics [ˌhəʊm iːkə'nɒmɪks]	Hauswirtschaftslehre	
homework ['həʊmwɜːk]	Hausaufgaben	
to do my homework	meine Hausaufgaben machen	
honest ['ɒnɪst]	ehrlich	
honey ['hʌnɪ]	Honig; Schätzchen	
hoof, hooves [huːf, huːvz]	Huf, Hufe	
hooray [hʊ'reɪ]	hurra	
hope [həʊp]	Hoffnung	
to hope	hoffen	
hopscotch ['hɒpskɒtʃ]	Huckekasten, Himmel und Hölle (Hüpfspiel)	
⟨horn⟩ [hɔːn]	Hupe	
horse [hɔːs]	Pferd	
⟨horse drawn carriage⟩ [ˌhɔːs drɔːn 'kærɪdʒ]	Pferdekutsche	
on horseback ['hɔːsbæk]	zu Pferd	
hose [həʊz]	Schlauch	
hospital ['hɒspɪtl]	Krankenhaus	
youth **hostel** ['hɒstəl]	Jugendherberge	
hot [hɒt]	heiß	
hot dog [ˌhɒt 'dɒg]	Hot Dog (Würstchen im Brötchen)	
hotel [həʊ'tel]	Hotel	
hour ['aʊə]	Stunde	
for hours	stundenlang	
house [haʊs]	Haus	
how [haʊ]	wie	
How are you?	Wie geht's?	
⟨How do you do⟩	Guten Tag (förmlicher Gruß)	
how many	wie viele	
how much	wieviel	
how old	wie alt	
huge [hjuːdʒ]	riesig	
a **hundred** ['hʌndrəd]	hundert	
hunger ['hʌŋgə]	Hunger	
hungry ['hʌŋgrɪ]	hungrig	
to be hungry	hungrig sein	
to **hunt** [hʌnt]	jagen	
[hunting grounds] ['hʌntɪŋ graʊndz]	Jagdgebiete	
to **hurry (up)** ['hʌrɪ]	sich beeilen	
⟨in a hurry⟩	in Eile	
hurt [hɜːt]	verletzt	
to hurt* [hɜːt]	verletzen	
husband ['hʌzbənd]	(Ehe-)Mann	
hut [hʌt]	Hütte	

I

I [aɪ]	ich	
I'm [aɪm] = I am	ich bin	
⟨ice⟩ [aɪs]	Eis	
ice-cream [ˌaɪs'kriːm]	Eis(krem)	
ice-hockey	Eishockey	
[ice-show] ['aɪsʃəʊ]	Show auf dem Eis	
ice-skating	Schlittschuhlaufen	
icy ['aɪsɪ]	eisig	
idea [aɪ'dɪə]	Idee	
no idea	keine Ahnung	
idiot ['ɪdɪət]	Idiot	
if [ɪf]	wenn, falls; ob	
if I were you ...	(Ich) an deiner Stelle ...	
ill [ɪl]	krank	
to **imagine** [ɪ'mædʒɪn]	sich etwas vorstellen	
immediately [ɪ'miːdjətlɪ]	sofort	
⟨immigrant⟩ ['ɪmɪgrənt]	Einwanderer	
imperfect [ɪm'pɜːfɪkt]	unvollkommen	
important [ɪm'pɔːtənt]	wichtig	
impossible [ɪm'pɒsəbl]	unmöglich	
improbable [ɪm'prɒbəbl]	unwahrscheinlich	
in [ɪn]	in	
in a mess	in Unordnung	
in English	auf englisch	
in front of	vor	
in the morning	morgens, vormittags	
in time	rechtzeitig	
to come in	sich melden (Funksprache)	
in fact	tatsächlich	
to get in	einsteigen	
to go in	hineingehen	
Is he in?	Ist er zu Hause?	
to look in	hineinschauen	
⟨to include⟩ [ɪn'kluːd]	einschließen	
incorrect [ˌɪnkə'rekt]	falsch	
[independence] [ˌɪndɪ'pendəns]	Unabhängigkeit	
Indian ['ɪndɪən]	Indianer(in); Inder(in), indisch	
indoor swimming-pool [ˌɪndɔː 'swɪmɪŋ puːl]	Hallenbad	
industrial [ɪn'dʌstrɪəl]	Industrie-, industriell	
industry ['ɪndəstrɪ]	Industrie	
inexpensive [ˌɪnɪk'spensɪv]	preiswert	
influence ['ɪnflʊəns]	Einfluß	
information [ˌɪnfə'meɪʃn]	Information	
injection [ɪn'dʒekʃn]	Spritze, Injektion	
injured ['ɪndʒəd]	verletzt	
inside [ɪn'saɪd]	innen, drinnen, hinein	
the inside	das Innere, Innenraum	
county **inspector** [ɪn'spektə]	Bezirksschulrat(-rätin)	
instruction [ɪn'strʌkʃn]	Anweisung	
instrument ['ɪnstrəmənt]	(Musik-)Instrument	
interest ['ɪntrɪst]	Interesse	
to be interested in ['ɪntrɪstɪd]	sich für etwas interessieren	
interesting ['ɪntrɪstɪŋ]	interessant	
international [ˌɪntə'næʃnəl]	international	
interview ['ɪntəvjuː]	Interview	
to interview	interviewen	
interviewer	Interviewer(in)	
into ['ɪntə]	in (hinein)	
to **invent** [ɪn'vent]	erfinden	
invitation [ˌɪnvɪ'teɪʃn]	Einladung	
to invite [ɪn'vaɪt]	einladen	
Irish ['aɪrɪʃ]	irisch	
Irish coffee [ˌaɪrɪʃ 'kɒfɪ]	Irish Coffee (Kaffee mit Whisky und Schlagsahne)	
Irish stew	irisches Eintopfgericht	
⟨Irishman⟩	Ire	
iron ['aɪən]	Eisen	
Iron Age	Eisenzeit	
irregular [ɪ'regjʊlə]	unregelmäßig	
is [ɪz]	ist	
isn't ['ɪznt] = is not	ist nicht	
island ['aɪlənd]	Insel	
British **Isles** [aɪlz]	Britische Inseln	
it [ɪt]	es	
it's [ɪts] = it is	es ist	
itself	sich, selbst	
its [ɪts]	sein(e), ihr(e)	
Italian [ɪ'tæljən]	Italiener(in), italienisch	

J

jacket ['dʒækɪt]	Jacke	
jail [dʒeɪl]	Gefängnis	
Jamaican [dʒə'meɪkən]	jamaikanisch; Jamaikaner(in)	
January ['dʒænjʊərɪ]	Januar	
Japanese [ˌdʒæpə'niːz]	Japaner(in), japanisch	
jeans [dʒiːnz]	Jeans	
⟨Jesus⟩ ['dʒiːzəs]	Jesus	
⟨jet⟩ [dʒet]	Jet, Düsenflugzeug	
jetty ['dʒetɪ]	Landungssteg	
⟨Jew⟩ [dʒuː]	Jude, Jüdin	
job [dʒɒb]	Arbeit, Job; „Ding" (Straftat)	
to **jog** [dʒɒg]	joggen	
to **join** [dʒɔɪn]	sich anschließen, Mitglied werden	
joke [dʒəʊk]	Witz, Scherz	
journey ['dʒɜːnɪ]	Reise	
⟨Judgement Day⟩ ['dʒʌdʒmənt ˌdeɪ]	das Jüngste Gericht	
⟨judo⟩ ['dʒuːdəʊ]	Judo	
juice [dʒuːs]	Saft	
⟨juke box⟩ ['dʒuːkbɒks]	Musikbox	
July [dʒʊ'laɪ]	Juli	
jumble sale ['dʒʌmbl seɪl]	Flohmarkt (für Wohltätigkeitszwecke)	
⟨jumbo⟩ ['dʒʌmbəʊ]	Riesen-, riesig	
to **jump** [dʒʌmp]	springen	
to jump about	herumspringen	
June [dʒuːn]	Juni	
⟨jungle⟩ ['dʒʌŋgl]	Urwald	
just [dʒʌst]	nur, gerade, eben	
just a minute	einen Augenblick	
just now	gerade eben	
Just sit down here.	Setz dich/Setzen Sie sich einfach hierher.	
just when...	jetzt, wo ...	
not just	nicht nur	

K

to **keep*** [kiːp]	behalten, (ein Tier) halten	
to keep to	bleiben auf/bei	
to keep s.th. under control	etwas unter Kontrolle halten	
to keep fit	sich fit halten	
(tomato) **ketchup** ['ketʃəp]	(Tomaten-)Ketchup	
key [kiː]	Schlüssel	
to **kick** [kɪk]	treten (gegen)	
kid	Kind, jünger Mensch	
to **kill** [kɪl]	töten	
kilo ['kiːləʊ]	Kilo	
kilometre ['kɪləʊˌmiːtə]	Kilometer	
⟨kin⟩ [kɪn]	Verwandtschaft	
kind [kaɪnd]	Art, Sorte	

Alphabetical word list

king [kɪŋ]	König
⟨to kiss⟩ [kɪs]	küssen
kitchen ['kɪtʃɪn]	Küche
kite [kaɪt]	Drachen
⟨kitten⟩ ['kɪtn]	Kätzchen
knife [naɪf]	Messer
to **knit** [nɪt]	stricken
knitwear ['nɪtweə]	Strickwaren
to **knock down** [nɒk]	anfahren, umstoßen
⟨to knock⟩	klopfen
to **know*** [nəʊ]	wissen, kennen
to know one's way around	sich auskennen (örtlich)

L

language lab [læb]	Sprachlabor
ladder ['lædə]	Leiter
lady ['leɪdɪ]	Dame
lake [leɪk]	(ein) See
lamp [læmp]	Lampe
land [lænd]	Land
to land	landen
landscape ['lænskeɪp]	Landschaft
lane [leɪn]	(Feld-)Weg, Gasse
language ['læŋgwɪdʒ]	Sprache
language lab [læb]	Sprachlabor
foreign language	Fremdsprache
large [lɑːdʒ]	groß
⟨lassie⟩ ['læsɪ]	Mädchen
last [lɑːst]	letzte(r, -s)
last year	letztes Jahr
last week	letzte Woche
at last	endlich, schließlich
⟨to last⟩ [lɑːst]	dauern
late [leɪt]	spät
to be late	zu spät kommen
later	später
to **laugh** [lɑːf]	lachen
to laugh at	auslachen
law [lɔː]	Gesetz
lawn [lɔːn]	Rasen
to **lead*** [liːd]	führen
leaf [liːf]	Blatt
leaflet ['liːflɪt]	Merkblatt
to **learn*** [lɜːn]	lernen
learner ['lɜːnə]	Lernende(r)
at **least** [ət 'liːst]	wenigstens
leather ['leðə]	Leder
to **leave*** [liːv]	verlassen, (weg)gehen; zurücklassen
left [left]	übrig
left [left]	links
on the left	links, auf der linken Seite
to turn left	links abbiegen
leg [leg]	Bein
lemonade [ˌleməˈneɪd]	Limonade
to **lend*** [lend]	leihen
lesson ['lesn]	(Unterrichts-)Stunde
to **let*** [let]	lassen
let me see	laß mich mal sehen
let's [lets] = let us	laß(t) uns
letter ['letə]	Brief; Buchstabe
library ['laɪbrərɪ]	Bücherei
driver's **license** (AE) ['laɪsnz]	Führerschein
lid [lɪd]	Deckel
to **lie*** [laɪ]	liegen
lying	liegend
to **lie** [laɪ]	lügen
⟨lie⟩ [laɪ]	Lüge
life [laɪf]	Leben
lifeboat	Rettungsboot
lifejacket	Schwimmweste
lift [lɪft]	Lift, Fahrstuhl
⟨to lift⟩	(auf)heben; (Nebel) sich lichten
light [laɪt]	Licht
traffic lights	Ampel
lightning ['laɪtnɪŋ]	Blitz
to **like** [laɪk]	mögen, lieben
Would you like …	Hättest du/Hätten Sie gerne …
like [laɪk]	wie
like this	so, folgendermaßen
to feel like	Lust haben zu/auf
to look like	aussehen wie
What was it like?	Wie war es?
⟨limerick⟩ ['lɪmərɪk]	Limerick
⟨limp⟩ [lɪmp]	schlaff, kraftlos
line [laɪn]	Linie, Zeile
to stand in line (AE)	Schlange stehen
to **link** [lɪŋk]	verbinden
⟨liquid⟩ ['lɪkwɪd]	flüssig
list [lɪst]	Liste
to list	auflisten
to **listen** ['lɪsn]	zuhören
listener ['lɪsnə]	Zuhörer(in)
litre ['liːtə]	Liter
litter ['lɪtə]	Abfälle
little ['lɪtl]	klein
little time	wenig Zeit
⟨little bitty⟩	klitzeklein
a little	ein bißchen
to **live** [lɪv]	leben, wohnen
[living conditions]	Lebensbedingungen
local ['ləʊkl]	örtlich, lokal
to **lock** [lɒk]	abschließen
lonely ['ləʊnlɪ]	einsam
long [lɒŋ]	lang
⟨to long for⟩ [lɒŋ]	sich sehnen nach
to **look** [lʊk]	sehen, aussehen, schauen
to look after s.o.	auf jdn aufpassen
to look and sound sorry	so aussehen und so klingen, als ob es einem leid täte
to look at	ansehen
to look for	suchen
to look forward to	sich freuen auf
to look in	hineinschauen
to look like	aussehen wie
to look out for	Ausschau halten nach
to look up	aufblicken
to look up (a word)	nachschlagen
to look unhappy	unglücklich aussehen
to have a look at	(kurz) anschauen
loose [luːs]	lose, locker
⟨loosely⟩	locker (Adverb)
to come loose [luːs]	sich lösen
⟨Lord⟩ [lɔːd]	Herr, Gott
lorry ['lɒrɪ]	Lastwagen
to **lose*** [luːz]	verlieren
to ge lost	verloren gehen, sich verlaufen
⟨loser⟩ ['luːzə]	Verlierer(in), Versager(in), „Niete"
a **lot** [lɒt]	viel
a lot of	viel(e)
lots of	viel(e)
loud [laʊd]	laut
lounge [laʊndʒ]	Wohnzimmer, Aufenthaltsraum
love [lʌv]	Liebe
⟨love (from)⟩	viele Grüße (von)
to love	lieben
lovely ['lʌvlɪ]	schön, herrlich
low [ləʊ]	niedrig
luck [lʌk]	Glück
bad luck	Pech
good luck!	alles Gute!
lucky ['lʌkɪ]	glücklich
you're lucky	du hast Glück
lunch [lʌntʃ]	Mittagessen
lunch hour	Mittagspause

M

machine [məˈʃiːn]	Maschine
mad [mæd]	verrückt
to go mad	verrückt werden
madam ['mædəm]	gnädige Frau
magazine [ˌmæɡəˈziːn]	Zeitschrift
magic ['mædʒɪk]	Zauberei
magic trick	Zauberkunststück
magician [məˈdʒɪʃn]	Zauberer
mailman (AE) ['meɪlmən]	Briefträger
main [meɪn]	Haupt-, hauptsächlich
to **make*** [meɪk]	machen, bilden
⟨to make s.o. do s.th.⟩	jdn etwas machen lassen
to make sure	sichergehen, versichern
to make money	Geld verdienen
to make new friends	neue Freundschaften schließen
to make fun of s.o.	sich über jdn lustig machen
⟨make-up⟩ ['meɪkʌp]	Make-up, Schminke
man, men [mæn, men]	Mann, Männer
[Man]	der Mensch
mankind ['mænkaɪnd]	Menschheit
to **manage** ['mænɪdʒ]	es schaffen, zurechtkommen
manager	Geschäftsführer(in)
how **many** ['menɪ]	wie viele
map [mæp]	(Land-)Karte
March [mɑːtʃ]	März
⟨to march⟩ [mɑːtʃ]	marschieren
mark [mɑːk]	(Schul-)Note
to mark	korrigieren, benoten
market (square) ['mɑːkɪt ˌskweə]	Markt(platz)
marmalade ['mɑːməleɪd]	(Orangen-)Marmelade
to **marry** ['mærɪ]	heiraten
mashed potatoes [mæʃt]	Kartoffelbrei
⟨mass⟩ [mæs]	Messe
[**massacre**] ['mæsəkə]	Massaker
match [mætʃ]	Spiel
maths [mæθs]	Mathe(matik)
to **matter** ['mætə]	von Bedeutung sein
What's the matter?	Was ist los?
⟨mattress⟩ ['mætrɪs]	Matratze
May [meɪ]	Mai
may [meɪ]	dürfen; können
maybe ['meɪbiː]	vielleicht
me [miː]	mir, mich; ich
it's me	ich bin's
meal [miːl]	Mahlzeit, Essen
to **mean*** [miːn]	bedeuten, meinen
you mean …	Sie meinen also …
meaning ['miːnɪŋ]	Bedeutung
measles ['miːzlz]	Masern
meat [miːt]	Fleisch
mechanic [mɪˈkænɪk]	Mechaniker(in)
mechanical [mɪˈkænɪkl]	mechanisch
medicine ['medɪsɪn]	Arznei, Medizin
to **meet*** [miːt]	(sich) treffen
meeting ['miːtɪŋ]	Treffen
PTA meeting	Elternabend
member ['membə]	Mitglied
menu ['menjuː]	Speisekarte, Menü
merry ['merɪ]	fröhlich
mess [mes]	Unordnung, Durcheinander
in a mess	in Unordnung
message ['mesɪdʒ]	Botschaft, Nachricht
to give s.o. a message	jdm etwas ausrichten
messenger ['mesɪndʒə]	Bote, Botin
method ['meθəd]	Methode
metre ['miːtə]	Meter
Mexican ['meksɪkən]	mexikanisch, Mexikaner(in)
mouse, mice [maʊs, maɪs]	Maus, Mäuse
in the **middle** ['mɪdl]	in der Mitte
midnight ['mɪdnaɪt]	Mitternacht
might (even) [maɪt]	könnte (sogar)
⟨mighty⟩ ['maɪtɪ]	mächtig
mile [maɪl]	Meile
for miles and miles	meilenweit
miles per hour	Meilen pro Stunde
milk [mɪlk]	Milch
⟨milkman⟩ ['mɪlkmən]	Milchmann
⟨milk shake⟩	Milchshake, Milchmixgetränk
a **million** ['mɪljən]	Million
millionth	millionste
to **mind** [maɪnd]	etwas dagegen haben
I don't mind	ich habe nichts dagegen
never mind	macht nichts

Alphabetical word list

⟨to have s.th. on one's mind⟩ [maɪnd]	sich mit etw gedanklich beschäftigen	name [neɪm]	Name	⟨to number⟩	numerieren
mine [maɪn]	meine(r, -s)	to name	nennen	nurse [nɜːs]	Krankenschwester
⟨miner⟩ ['maɪnə]	Bergmann	⟨narrow⟩ ['næɾəʊ]	eng	nylon ['naɪlɒn]	Nylon
minute ['mɪnɪt]	Minute	national ['næʃnəl]	Landes-, National-		
just a minute	einen Augenblick	nature ['neɪtʃə]	Natur	**O**	
Wait a minute.	Augenblick mal.	⟨natural⟩ ['nætʃərəl]	natürlich		
mirage ['mɪrɑːʒ]	Luftspiegelung	near [nɪə]	nahe, in der Nähe von	⟨oak⟩ [əʊk]	Eiche
mirror ['mɪrə]	Spiegel	to go near	sich nähern	ocean ['əʊʃn]	Ozean
Miss [mɪs]	Fräulein	⟨nearly⟩ ['nɪəlɪ]	beinahe	o'clock [ə'klɒk]	Uhr (Uhrzeit)
to miss [mɪs]	verpassen, vermissen	⟨neck⟩ [nek]	Hals	October [ɒk'təʊbə]	Oktober
to miss a turn	eine Runde aussetzen	⟨necklace⟩ ['nekləs]	Halskette	of [ɒv, əv]	von
missing	fehlend	to need [niːd]	brauchen	of course	natürlich, sicher
mistake [mɪ'steɪk]	Fehler	I needn't pay	ich brauche nicht zu zahlen	a lot of	viel(e)
to mix [mɪks]	mischen	neighbour ['neɪbə]	Nachbar(in)	a packet of biscuits	eine Packung Kekse
⟨mixture⟩ ['mɪkstʃə]	Mischung	neighbourhood ['neɪbəhʊd]	Nachbarschaft	to be afraid of	Angst haben vor
mobile home [ˌməʊbaɪl'həʊm]	Wohnmobil	⟨neither ... nor⟩ ['naɪðə ... 'nɔː]	weder ... noch	in front of	vor
model ['mɒdl]	Modell	nephew ['nevjuː]	Neffe	off [ɒf]	von, weg, ab
modern ['mɒdən]	modern	nervous ['nɜːvəs]	nervös	to get off	aussteigen
modest ['mɒdɪst]	bescheiden	nervous breakdown	Nervenzusammenbruch	to go off	abgehen, losgehen
mom (AE) [mɒm]	Mutti, Mama			to set off	losgehen, aufbrechen
moment ['məʊmənt]	Augenblick	nest [nest]	Nest	to take off	ausziehen; starten
at that moment	in diesem Augenblick	nest-robber ['nestˌrɒbə]	Nesträuber	to turn off	ausschalten, ausmachen
Monday ['mʌndeɪ]	Montag	never ['nevə]	nie, niemals	to be off one's route	nicht auf jds Weg liegen
money ['mʌnɪ]	Geld	never mind	macht nichts		
monkey ['mʌŋkɪ]	Affe	new [njuː]	neu	to offer ['ɒfə]	anbieten
monster ['mɒnstə]	Ungeheuer, Monster	news [njuːz]	Nachrichten, Neuigkeiten	office ['ɒfɪs]	Büro
month [mʌnθ]	Monat			post office	Postamt
mood [muːd]	Laune, Stimmung	newsagent ['njuːzˌeɪdʒənt]	Zeitungshändler	customs officer ['ɒfɪsə]	Zollbeamter, -beamtin
to be in a bad mood	schlechter Laune sein	⟨newsboy⟩ ['njuːzbɔɪ]	Zeitungsjunge	Road Safety Officer ['seɪftɪ]	Verkehrssicherheitsbeamter
⟨moon⟩ [muːn]	Mond	newsletter ['njuːzˌletə]	Mitteilungsblatt	often ['ɒfn]	oft, häufig
moor(s) [mʊə, -z]	Moor	newspaper ['njuːsˌpeɪpə]	Zeitung	oh [əʊ]	oh; null
more [mɔː]	mehr, noch etwas	newsreader ['njuːzˌriːdə]	Nachrichtensprecher(in)	Oh dear!	O je! Ach du meine Güte!
more terrible	schrecklicher (Komparativ)	next [nekst]	danach, als nächstes	oil [ɔɪl]	Öl
not ... any more	nicht mehr	next door	nebenan	oil-drum	Öltrommel
morning ['mɔːnɪŋ]	Morgen	the next day	am nächsten Tag	oil rig	Bohrinsel
in the morning	morgens, vormittags	next to	direkt neben	OK [əʊ'keɪ]	ist gut
on Saturday morning	am Samstagvormittag	nice [naɪs]	nett	old [əʊld]	alt
⟨this morning⟩	heute morgen	niece [niːs]	Nichte	ten-year-old	zehnjährig, Zehnjährige(r)
most [məʊst]	meist	night [naɪt]	Nacht	⟨old-fashioned⟩ [ˌəʊld'fæʃnd]	altmodisch
the most modern	der/die/das modernste, am modernsten	at night	nachts	⟨oldie⟩ ['əʊldɪ]	Oldie (alter Schlager)
most of them	die meisten von ihnen	⟨nil⟩ [nɪl]	null	⟨omelette⟩ ['ɒmlɪt]	Omelette
motel [məʊ'tel]	Motel	nine [naɪn]	neun	on [ɒn]	auf
mother ['mʌðə]	Mutter	nineteen [naɪn'tiːn]	neunzehn	⟨on his own⟩	allein
⟨motorbike⟩ ['məʊtəbaɪk]	Motorrad	ninth [naɪnθ]	neunte(r, -s)	to be on	laufen (Film)
motorboat ['məʊtəbəʊt]	Motorboot	no [nəʊ]	nein; kein(e)	Come on.	Los! Gehen wir!
mountain ['maʊntɪn]	Berg	no idea	keine Ahnung	you're on	du bist dran
mouse, mice [maʊs, maɪs]	Maus, Mäuse	⟨no one⟩ ['nəʊwʌn]	niemand	to be on holiday	Ferien/Urlaub machen
mouth [maʊθ]	Mund	nobody	niemand	to go on	weitermachen
to move [muːv]	(sich) bewegen; umziehen	to nod [nɒd]	nicken	to have got on	tragen, anhaben
to move closer	näherrücken	noise [nɔɪz]	Geräusch, Lärm	on Saturday	am Samstag
movie (AE) ['muːvɪ]	Film	noisy ['nɔɪzɪ]	laut, lärmend	on the left/right	links/rechts
movies (AE)	Kino	none [nʌn]	keine(r, -s)	on time	pünktlich
movie theater (AE)	Kino	Norman ['nɔːmən]	normannisch; Normanne, Normannin	on your own	allein
Mr ['mɪstə]	Herr			on foot	zu Fuß
Mrs ['mɪsɪz]	Frau	north [nɔːθ]	(nach) Norden, Nord-, nördlich	on horseback	zu Pferd
much [mʌtʃ]	viel			to play a trick on s.o.	jdm einen Streich spielen
how much	wieviel	northern ['nɔːðən]	Nord-, nördlich	to put on	anziehen
mud [mʌd]	Schlamm, Matsch	nose [nəʊz]	Nase	to put on s.th.	etw. dranmachen, befestigen
mudguard ['mʌdgɑːd]	Schutzblech	not [nɒt]	nicht	straight on	geradeaus
multi-storey ['mʌltɪˌstɔːrɪ]	mehrgeschossig	not ... any longer	nicht mehr	to turn on	anschalten, anmachen
mum [mʌm]	Mutti, Mama	not ... any more	nicht mehr	once [wʌns]	einmal, einst
museum [mjuː'zɪəm]	Museum	not ... at all	überhaupt nicht	at once	sofort
music ['mjuːzɪk]	Musik	not even	nicht einmal	one [wʌn]	eins, ein(e)
⟨music man⟩	Musikant	not just	nicht nur	⟨one by one⟩	einer nach dem anderen
⟨mussels⟩ ['mʌslz]	Muscheln	not really	eigentlich nicht	the only one/ones	der, die, das einzige/die einzigen
must [mʌst]	muß, müssen	not ... yet	noch nicht	this one	diese(r, -s)
mustn't ['mʌsnt]	darf nicht	note [nəʊt]	Notiz, Anmerkung	onion ['ʌnjən]	Zwiebel
my [maɪ]	mein(e)	⟨note⟩ [nəʊt]	(Geld-)Note, Schein; Nachricht	only ['əʊnlɪ]	nur
my!	(Ausdruck des Erstaunens) meine Güte!	nothing ['nʌθɪŋ]	nichts	the only one/ones	der, die, das einzige/die einzigen
myself	mir/mich, (ich) selbst	notice ['nəʊtɪs]	Schild, Hinweis	only just	gerade, eben
		notice-board	Schwarzes Brett	onto ['ɒntʊ]	auf
N		to notice	bemerken	to open ['əʊpən]	öffnen, aufmachen
		noun [naʊn]	Nomen	[to open up]	öffnen, erschließen
nail [neɪl]	(Finger-)Nagel	November [nəʊ'vembə]	November	open	offen, auf
nailbrush ['neɪlbrʌʃ]	Nagelbürste	now [naʊ]	jetzt	tin opener	Dosenöffner
		number ['nʌmbə]	Nummer, Zahl	opera ['ɒpərə]	Oper
		box number ['bɒksˌnʌmbə]	Postfach, Chiffre		

145

Alphabetical word list

⟨operation⟩ [ˌɒpəˈreɪʃn]	Operation	⟨to take a part⟩ ⟨to part⟩ [pɑːt] [part of speech]	eine Rolle spielen (sich) trennen Wortart
operator [ˈɒpəreɪtə]	Telefonvermittlung	**partition** [pɑːˈtɪʃn]	Trennwand, Teilung
⟨**opportunity**⟩ [ˌɒpəˈtjuːnəti]	Chance, Gelegenheit	**partner** [ˈpɑːtnə]	Partner(in)
opposite [ˈɒpəzɪt]	Gegenteil, gegenüber (liegend)	**party** [ˈpɑːti] **to pass** [pɑːs]	Party, Fête vergehen
⟨**optimist**⟩ [ˈɒptɪmɪst]	Optimist(in)	⟨to pass s.th.⟩	an etwas vorbeigehen, -fahren
or [ɔː]	oder	to pass a test	eine Prüfung bestehen
orange [ˈɒrɪndʒ]	Apfelsine; Orange (Farbe)	to pass s.th. to s.o. to pass the ball to s.o.	jdm etwas reichen jdm den Ball zuspielen
orchestra [ˈɔːkəstrə]	Orchester	**passage** [ˈpæsɪdʒ]	Gang
to **order** [ˈɔːdə]	bestellen	**passenger** [ˈpæsɪndʒə]	Passagier
word **order** [ˈɔːdə]	Wortstellung	**passive** [ˈpæsɪv]	passiv, Passiv
other [ˈʌðə]	andere(r, -s)	**passport** [ˈpɑːspɔːt]	Paß
the others	die anderen	**past** [pɑːst]	nach; vorbei
our [ˈaʊə]	unser(e)	half past seven	halb acht
ours	unsere(r, -s)	to go past	vorbeigehen, -fahren
ourselves	uns, (wir) selbst	past form	Vergangenheitsform
out [aʊt]	draußen, nicht zu Hause	**path(s)** [pɑːθ, ˈpɑːðz] ⟨**patient**⟩ [ˈpeɪʃnt]	Pfad(e), Weg(e) Patient(in)
to come out	herauskommen	⟨**pavement**⟩ [ˈpeɪvmənt]	Bürgersteig
to fly out	hinfliegen, abfliegen	**paw** [pɔː]	Pfote
to get out	herauskommen, herausnehmen	to **pay*** [peɪ] payment [ˈpeɪmənt]	bezahlen Bezahlung
to get out of	aussteigen	to refund a payment	eine Zahlung zurückerstatten
to go out	ausgehen	**pea** [piː]	Erbse
to take out	herausnehmen	**[peace]** [piːs]	Frieden
⟨out of breath⟩	außer Atem	⟨peace of mind⟩ [ˌpiːs əv ˈmaɪnd]	innere Ruhe, Seelenfrieden
out of work	arbeitslos	peaceful [ˈpiːsfʊl]	friedlich, friedliebend
out of school	nicht mehr in der Schule	**peach** [piːtʃ] it's a peach	Pfirsich es ist prima
out of money	ohne Geld	**pedal** [ˈpedl]	Pedal
over and out	Ende der Durchsage (Funk)	**pen** [pen] pen-friend	Füller, Füllfederhalter Brieffreund(in)
⟨out in the country⟩	auf dem Lande	⟨pen pal⟩ [ˈpen ˌpæl]	Brieffreund(in)
outdoor [ˈaʊtdɔː]	Freiluft-, im Freien	**pencil** [ˈpensl]	Bleistift
outdoor centre	Freizeit- und Ferienzentrum	pencil case **penny** [ˈpeni]	Federmäppchen, Etui britische Münze
outdoor swimming-pool	Freibad	pence the penny dropped	Plural von penny der Groschen ist gefallen
outlaw [ˈaʊtlɔː]	Geächteter	**pension** [ˈpenʃn]	Pension
⟨to outnumber⟩ [ˌaʊtˈnʌmbə]	mehr sein als, zahlenmäßig überlegen sein	**people** [ˈpiːpl] a people miles **per hour**	Leute, Menschen ein Volk Meilen pro Stunde
outside [aʊtˈsaɪd]	draußen; außerhalb; vor	[pər ˈaʊə] per cent [pəˈsent]	Prozent
oven [ˈʌvn]	(Back-)Ofen	**perfect** [ˈpɜːfɪkt]	perfekt
over [ˈəʊvə]	über	⟨performance⟩ [pəˈfɔːməns]	Aufführung
over and out	Ende der Durchsage (Funk)	**perhaps** [pəˈhæps]	vielleicht
over there	dort drüben	**person** [ˈpɜːsn]	Person
over to you	du bist dran	personal	persönlich
to be over	vorbei sein	personal computer	PC, Personal Computer
to take over	übernehmen	⟨pessimist⟩ [ˈpesɪmɪst]	Pessimist(in)
own [əʊn]	eigen	⟨pessimistic⟩ [ˌpesɪˈmɪstɪk]	pessimistisch
owner [ˈəʊnə]	Besitzer(in)	**pet** [pet]	Haustier, Liebling
ox, oxen [ɒks, ˈɒksn]	Ochse(n)	pet shop	Tierhandlung
		petrol [ˈpetrəl]	Benzin
P		to **phone** [fəʊn]	anrufen, telefonieren
p [piː] = penny/pence	kleinste britische Münzeinheit	phone phone-in [ˈfəʊnɪn]	Telefon Rundfunksendung, an der sich Zuhörer telefonisch beteiligen können
to **pack** [pæk]	packen, einpacken	**photo(graph)** [ˈfəʊtəʊ(grɑːf)]	Foto
packet [ˈpækɪt]	Packung, Schachtel	to photograph	fotografieren
paddle [ˈpædl]	Paddel	to take a photo-(graph)	fotografieren
page [peɪdʒ]	Seite	photography [fəˈtɒgrəfi]	Fotografie
pain [peɪn]	Schmerz	**phrase** [freɪz]	Redewendung, Phrase
to **paint** [peɪnt]	(be)malen	**Physical Education** [ˌfɪzɪkl ˌedjuːˈkeɪʃn]	Leibesübungen, Sport
paintbrush [ˈpeɪntbrʌʃ]	Pinsel	to **pick up** [ˌpɪk ˈʌp] ⟨to pick⟩	aufheben; lernen auswählen
pair [peə]	Paar	**picnic** [ˈpɪknɪk]	Picknick
⟨in pairs⟩	zu zweit, in Zweiergruppen	⟨picnic-site⟩ **picture** [ˈpɪktʃə]	Picknickplatz Bild
paper [ˈpeɪpə]	Papier		
⟨to do a paper route [ruːt]⟩	Zeitungen austragen		
paragraph [ˈpærəgrɑːf]	Absatz, Abschnitt		
⟨parcel⟩ [ˈpɑːsl]	Paket		
pardon? [ˈpɑːdn]	Wie bitte?		
parents [ˈpeərənts]	Eltern		
park [pɑːk]	Park		
to park	parken		
car park	Parkplatz		
parking-space [speɪs]	Parklücke		
part (of) [pɑːt]	Teil; Rolle		
to take part (in s.th.)	(an etwas) teilnehmen		

picture-book	Bilderbuch
piece [piːs]	Stück, Teil
piece of cloth	Lappen
⟨pieman⟩ [ˈpaɪmən]	Pastetenverkäufer
pig [pɪg]	Schwein
⟨pill⟩ [pɪl]	Pille, Tablette
pilot [ˈpaɪlət]	Pilot(in)
pineapple [ˈpaɪnˌæpl]	Ananas
pine tar [ˈpaɪnˌtɑː]	Kienteer
⟨pink⟩ [pɪŋk]	rosa
[pioneer] [ˌpaɪəˈnɪə]	Pionier(in)
⟨pipes⟩ [paɪps]	Dudelsack
pitch-black [ˌpɪtʃˈblæk]	pechschwarz
place [pleɪs]	Ort, Stelle
in their place	an ihre(r) Stelle
plan [plæn]	Plan
to plan	planen
plane [pleɪn]	Flugzeug
⟨to plant⟩ [plɑːnt]	pflanzen
plastic [ˈplæstɪk]	Plastik
plate [pleɪt]	Teller
platform [ˈplætfɔːm]	Bahnsteig
play [pleɪ]	Spiel; Theaterstück
to play	spielen
to play a trick on s.o.	jdm einen Streich spielen
role play	Rollenspiel
player	Spieler(in)
playground [ˈpleɪgraʊnd]	Spielplatz
playtime [ˈpleɪtaɪm]	Pause
plaza (AE) [ˈplɑːzə]	Einkaufszentrum
pleasant [ˈpleznt]	angenehm
please [pliːz]	bitte
⟨to please s.o.⟩	jdn zufriedenstellen
to be pleased	erfreut sein
⟨pleasure boat⟩ [ˈpleʒə]	Vergnügungsboot
plug [plʌg]	Zündkerze; Stecker
plum pudding [ˌplʌmˈpʊdɪŋ]	Plumpudding (kuchenartiger Pudding mit Rosinen etc.)
plural [ˈplʊərəl]	Mehrzahl, Plural
5 pm [piːˈem]	5 Uhr nachmittags
pocket [ˈpɒkɪt]	Tasche
⟨poem⟩ [ˈpəʊɪm]	Gedicht
point [pɔɪnt]	Spitze
to point to	zeigen auf
poisoned [ˈpɔɪznd]	vergiftet
⟨pole⟩ [pəʊl]	Stange, Mast
police [pəˈliːs]	Polizei
police car	Polizeiwagen
policeman	Polizist
police station	Polizeirevier
policewoman	Polizistin
to **polish** [ˈpɒlɪʃ]	polieren
polite [pəˈlaɪt]	höflich
politician [ˌpɒlɪˈtɪʃn]	Politiker(in)
pollution [pəˈluːʃn]	(Umwelt-)Verschmutzung
pony [ˈpəʊni]	Pony
indoor swimming-pool	Hallenbad
outdoor swimming-pool	Freibad
poor [pʊə]	arm
pop group [ˈpɒp gruːp]	Popgruppe
popular [ˈpɒpjʊlə]	beliebt
population [ˌpɒpjʊˈleɪʃn]	Bevölkerung
port [pɔːt]	Hafen
position [pəˈzɪʃn]	Platz, Stelle, Position, Lage
possible [ˈpɒsɪbl]	möglich
post [pəʊst]	Pfosten
post office [ˈpəʊst ˌɒfɪs]	Postamt
postcard [ˈpəʊstkɑːd]	Postkarte
postman [ˈpəʊstmən]	Briefträger
poster [ˈpəʊstə]	Poster
pot [pɒt]	Topf, Kanne
potty	Töpfchen
potato [pəˈteɪtəʊ]	Kartoffel
mashed potatoes	Kartoffelbrei
roast potatoes	Röst-, Bratkartoffeln

Alphabetical word list

pound [paʊnd]	Pfund
a pound of strawberries	ein Pfund Erdbeeren
⟨to pour⟩ [pɔː]	gießen
poverty ['pɒvətɪ]	Armut
powerful ['paʊəfʊl]	mächtig
powerless ['paʊəlɪs]	machtlos
practice ['præktɪs]	Übung, Stunde, Training
a doctor's practice	Arztpraxis
to practise	üben
prairie ['preərɪ]	Prärie
⟨praise⟩ [preɪz]	Lob
pram [præm]	Kinderwagen
prayer [preə]	Gebet
prefix ['priːfɪks]	Vorsilbe
⟨pregnant⟩ ['pregnənt]	schwanger
to prepare [prɪ'peə]	vorbereiten
preposition [ˌprepə'zɪʃn]	Präposition
prescription [prɪ'skrɪpʃn]	Rezept
present ['preznt]	Geschenk
president ['prezɪdənt]	Präsident(in)
⟨to press⟩ [pres]	drücken
pretty ['prɪtɪ]	hübsch
⟨pretzel⟩ ['pretsl]	Brezel
⟨prickly pear⟩ ['prɪklɪ peə]	Feigenkaktus
pride [praɪd]	Stolz
primitive ['prɪmɪtɪv]	primitiv
prince [prɪns]	Prinz
princess [prɪn'ses]	Prinzessin
to print [prɪnt]	drucken
prison ['prɪzn]	Gefängnis
prisoner	Gefangene(r)
private ['praɪvɪt]	privat
prize [praɪz]	Preis
pro [prəʊ]	(Argument) für
probably ['prɒbəblɪ]	wahrscheinlich
problem ['prɒbləm]	Problem
to produce [prə'djuːs]	produzieren, erzeugen
producer [prə'djuːsə]	Produzent(in)
production [prə'dʌkʃn]	Produktion, Erzeugung
programme ['prəʊgræm]	Programm
to programme	programmieren
progress ['prəʊgres]	Fortschritt
to promise ['prɒmɪs]	versprechen
to pronounce [prə'naʊns]	aussprechen
pronunciation [prəˌnʌnsɪ'eɪʃn]	Aussprache
properly ['prɒpəlɪ]	richtig
proud [praʊd]	stolz
to prove [pruːv]	beweisen
⟨to provide⟩ [prə'vaɪd]	geben, bereitstellen
PTA meeting [ˌpiːtiː'eɪ ˌmiːtɪŋ]	Elternabend
pub [pʌb]	Kneipe, Lokal
public ['pʌblɪk]	öffentlich
public baths [bɑːθs]	Hallenbad
⟨published by⟩ ['pʌblɪʃt]	veröffentlicht von
pudding ['pʊdɪŋ]	Pudding, Nachspeise
to pull [pʊl]	ziehen
to pull down	niederreißen
to pull off	herunterziehen
pullover ['pʊlˌəʊvə]	Pulli
to pump [pʌmp]	pumpen
bicycle pump	Fahrradpumpe
water pump	Wasserpumpe
pupil ['pjuːpl]	Schüler(in)
⟨purple⟩ ['pɜːpl]	violett
purse [pɜːs]	Geldbeutel
to push [pʊʃ]	drücken, schieben
to put* [pʊt]	stellen, legen, setzen
to put on	anziehen
to put together	zusammensetzen
to put up	aufstellen, aufhängen
to put down	aufschreiben
to put one's name down	sich eintragen
to put out a fire	Feuer löschen
to put s.o. through	jdn verbinden
puzzle ['pʌzl]	Puzzle, Rätsel
pyjamas [pə'dʒɑːməz]	Pyjama, Schlafanzug

Q

to qualify ['kwɒlɪfaɪ]	sich qualifizieren
quarter ['kwɔːtə]	viertel; ein Viertel
quarter to nine	viertel vor neun
⟨quarter⟩	25 Cent
⟨quarter pounder⟩ ['kwɔːtə ˌpaʊndə]	Viertelpfünder
⟨queen⟩ [kwiːn]	Königin
question ['kwestʃən]	Frage
to question	(be)fragen
questionnaire [ˌkwestʃə'neə]	Fragebogen
quick [kwɪk]	schnell
quiet ['kwaɪət]	ruhig
quite [kwaɪt]	ganz, ziemlich
quite a ...	ein(e) ziemliche (-r, -s) ...
quiz [kwɪz]	Quiz

R

rabbit ['ræbɪt]	Kaninchen
rabies ['reɪbiːz]	Tollwut
race [reɪs]	Rasse
⟨race⟩	Rennen
radio ['reɪdɪəʊ]	Radio, Rundfunkgerät, Funk
radio station	Sender, Rundfunkstation
by radio	per Funk
CB radio	CB-Funk (Privatfunk)
raft [rɑːft]	Floß
⟨rags⟩ [rægz]	Lumpen
[railroad] (AE) ['reɪlrəʊd]	Eisenbahn
railway ['reɪlweɪ]	Eisenbahn
rain [reɪn]	Regen
to rain	regnen
rainy	regnerisch
⟨rainbow⟩ ['reɪnbəʊ]	Regenbogen
⟨to raise⟩ [reɪz]	(er)heben, aufziehen
⟨to ramble⟩ ['ræmbl]	wandern, umherziehen
ranch [rɑːntʃ]	Ranch, Viehfarm
[rancher] ['rɑːntʃə]	Rancher, Viehzüchter
rat [ræt]	Ratte
suicide rate ['sjuːɪsaɪd ˌreɪt]	Selbstmordrate
⟨rather⟩ ['rɑːðə]	ziemlich
to reach [riːtʃ]	erreichen
to read* (out) [riːd]	lesen
ready ['redɪ]	fertig
real ['rɪəl]	echt, wirklich
really	wirklich (Adverb)
not really	eigentlich nicht
realistic [ˌrɪə'lɪstɪk]	realistisch
reason ['riːzn]	Grund
receptionist [rɪ'sepʃənɪst]	Empfangschef(in)
⟨reception hall⟩	Eingangshalle, Abflughalle
⟨to recognize⟩ ['rekəgnaɪz]	erkennen
record ['rekɔːd]	Schallplatte; Rekord
record-player	Plattenspieler
to record [rɪ'kɔːd]	aufnehmen
recording [rɪ'kɔːdɪŋ]	Aufnahme
red [red]	rot
reduced in size [rɪˌdjuːst ɪn ˌsaɪz]	verkleinert
giant redwood ['redwʊd]	Mammutbaum
refrigerator [rɪ'frɪdʒəˌreɪtə]	Kühlschrank
⟨refugee⟩ [ˌrefjʊ'dʒiː]	Flüchtling
to refund [rɪ'fʌnd]	zurückzahlen
to refund a payment	eine Zahlung zurückerstatten
register ['redʒɪstə]	Klassenbuch
°registration [ˌredʒɪ'streɪʃn]	Anmeldung
⟨regular⟩ ['regjʊlə]	regelmäßig
⟨reign⟩ [reɪn]	Herrschaft
reindeer ['reɪndɪə]	Rentier(e)
relation [rɪ'leɪʃn]	Verwandte(r), Verwandtschaftsbeziehung
Religious Education [rɪˌlɪdʒəs ˌedjʊ'keɪʃn]	Religionsunterricht
to remember [rɪ'membə]	sich erinnern
to remind s.o. of s.th. [rɪ'maɪnd]	jdn an etwas erinnern
to repair [rɪ'peə]	reparieren
repeatedly [rɪ'piːtɪdlɪ]	wiederholt
⟨to replace⟩ [rɪ'pleɪs]	ersetzen
report [rɪ'pɔːt]	Bericht
to report	berichten
reporter	Reporter(in)
republic [rɪ'pʌblɪk]	Republik
request [rɪ'kwest]	(Platten-)Wunsch, Bitte
rescue ['reskjuː]	Rettung
to rescue	retten, befreien
reservation [ˌrezə'veɪʃn]	Reservat
reserve [rɪ'zɜːv]	Ersatzspieler(in)
respect [rɪ'spekt]	Respekt
⟨the rest⟩ [rest]	die anderen, der restliche Teil, Rest
rest [rest]	Rast, Erholungspause
to take a rest	sich ausruhen
[restless] ['restlɪs]	rastlos
restaurant ['restərɒnt]	Restaurant
result [rɪ'zʌlt]	Ergebnis, Resultat
⟨to return⟩ [rɪ'tɜːn]	zurückkehren
⟨to return s.th.⟩	etwas zurückgeben
⟨reunion⟩ [ˌriː'juːnjən]	Versammlung, Treffen
[revenge] [rɪ'vendʒ]	Rache
revue [rɪ'vjuː]	Revue, Musikshow
rhyme [raɪm]	Reim, Gedicht
rhythm ['rɪðəm]	Rhythmus
⟨ribbon⟩ ['rɪbən]	Band, Schleife
rich [rɪtʃ]	reich
⟨riddle⟩ ['rɪdl]	Rätsel
ride [raɪd]	Ritt, Fahrt
to take s.o. for a ride	jdn spazierenfahren
to ride*	reiten, fahren
to ride away	wegreiten, -fahren
rider	Reiter(in); Fahrer(in)
oil rig [rɪg]	Bohrinsel
right [raɪt]	Recht; richtig; rechts; gerade, sofort, genau
to be right	recht haben
⟨to come right about⟩	wieder funktionieren
on the right	rechts, auf der rechten Seite
to turn right	rechts abbiegen
right where ...	gerade da, wo ...
⟨rim⟩ [rɪm]	Rand (einer Tasse)
to ring* [rɪŋ]	klingeln
to ring up	anrufen
river ['rɪvə]	Fluß
[riverboat]	Flußdampfer
road [rəʊd]	Straße
Road Safety Officer	Verkehrssicherheitsbeamter
⟨to roam⟩ [rəʊm]	wandern
⟨roast potatoes⟩ [rəʊst]	Röst-, Bratkartoffeln
to rob [rɒb]	rauben, berauben, ausrauben
nest-robber	Nesträuber
robbery	Raub
robot ['rəʊbɒt]	Roboter
rock [rɒk]	Fels, Felsen
rock (music) [rɒk]	Rock(musik)
rodeo ['rəʊdɪəʊ]	Rodeo
role play ['rəʊl ˌpleɪ]	Rollenspiel
roll [rəʊl]	Brötchen
to roll [rəʊl]	rollen, schlingern, gehen
⟨rolling hills⟩ ['rəʊlɪŋ]	sanft ansteigende Hügel

Alphabetical word list

rollerskate ['rəʊləskeɪt]	Rollschuh	scrapbook ['skræpbʊk]	Sammelalbum	to do the shopping	einkaufen
(romantic) [rəʊ'mæntɪk]	romantisch	scratch [skrætʃ]	Kratzer	to go shopping	einkaufen gehen
roof [ru:f]	Dach	scratched [skrætʃt]	zerkratzt	shopping centre	Einkaufszentrum
room [ru:m]	Zimmer	to scream [skri:m]	schreien	shop-lifter ['lɪftə]	Ladendieb(in)
there's room	es gibt (genug) Platz	screen [skri:n]	Bildschirm, Leinwand	short [ʃɔ:t]	kurz
root [ru:t]	Wurzel	screw [skru:]	Schranke	short cut	Abkürzung
rope [rəʊp]	Seil	to screw	schranken	shorts [ʃɔ:ts]	Shorts, kurze Hosen
rose [rəʊz]	Rose	screwdriver ['skru:,draɪvə]	Schraubenzieher	(shotgun) ['ʃɒtɡʌn]	Schrotflinte
round [raʊnd]	Runde	sculpture ['skʌlptʃə]	Skulptur, Plastik	(should) [ʃʊd]	sollte
round the house	um das Haus herum	sea [si:]	Meer	shoulder ['ʃəʊldə]	Schulter
to round up	zusammentreiben	seaman ['si:mən]	Seemann	shout [ʃaʊt]	Ruf, Schrei
route [ru:t]	Route	sea-level ['si:‚levl]	Meeresspiegel	shouter ['ʃaʊtə]	Schreier(in)
to be off one's route	nicht auf jds Weg liegen	to go to the seaside ['si:saɪd]	ans Meer fahren	to show*	zeigen
royal ['rɔɪəl]	königlich	(season) ['si:zn]	Jahreszeit	to show s.o. around	jdn herumführen
rubber ['rʌbə]	Radiergummi	(Season's Greetings)	Fröhliche Weihnachten, etc.	show	Schau, Vorstellung
rubbish ['rʌbɪʃ]	Quatsch, Blödsinn	seat [si:t]	Sitz(platz)	shower ['ʃaʊə]	Dusche; (Regen-) Schauer
rucksack ['rʌksæk]	Rucksack	seat-belt ['si:tbelt]	Sicherheitsgurt	to shrink* [ʃrɪŋk]	schrumpfen, einlaufen
rugby ['rʌɡbɪ]	Rugby	second ['sekənd]	Sekunde	to shut* [ʃʌt]	schließen
rule [ru:l]	Regel	second-hand [‚sekənd 'hænd]	gebraucht, Gebraucht-	shut [ʃʌt]	geschlossen, zu
ruler ['ru:lə]	Lineal	secret ['si:krɪt]	geheim, Geheim-	I feel sick [sɪk]	mir ist übel
to run* [rʌn]	laufen, rennen	secretary ['sekrətrɪ]	Sekretär(in)	sick	krank
to run away	weglaufen	sector ['sektə]	Sektor	side [saɪd]	Seite
to run up to ...	auf ... zurennen	to see* [si:]	sehen	sidewalk (AE) ['saɪdwɔ:k]	Gehweg, Bürgersteig
to run s.th.	etwas führen, leiten	I see	ich verstehe, ach so	(side order) ['saɪd‚ɔ:də]	Beilage
runner ['rʌnə]	Läufer(in)	You see, ...	Wissen Sie, ...	sigh [saɪ]	Seufzer
to rush [rʌʃ]	stürzen, rennen, eilen	See you	Tschüß, bis dann	sights [saɪts]	Sehenswürdigkeiten
to rush after	hinterherrennen	bird seed ['bɜ:d si:d]	Vogelfutter	sign [saɪn]	Hinweis(schild), Zeichen
rush hour	Hauptverkehrszeit	to seem [si:m]	(er)scheinen	signal ['sɪɡnəl]	Zeichen
gold rush	Goldrausch	to sell* [sel]	verkaufen	silent ['saɪlənt]	stumm, still
		(semi) ['semɪ]	Sattelschlepper	silly ['sɪlɪ]	doof, albern, dumm
S		(semi-detached house) [‚semɪdɪ'tætʃt]	Doppelhaushälfte	simple ['sɪmpl]	einfach; beschränkt
sad [sæd]	traurig	to send* [send]	schicken	since [sɪns]	seit
saddle ['sædl]	Sattel	sensible ['sensəbl]	vernünftig	to sing* [sɪŋ]	singen
safe [seɪf]	sicher, in Sicherheit	sentence ['sentəns]	Satz	singer	Sänger(in)
safety ['seɪftɪ]	Sicherheit	separately ['seprətlɪ]	getrennt	singular ['sɪŋɡjʊlə]	Einzahl, Singular
road safety	Verkehrssicherheit	(to separate) ['sepəreɪt]	trennen	to sink* [sɪŋk]	sinken
to sail [seɪl]	segeln	September [sep'tembə]	September	sir [sɜ:]	mein Herr *(respektvolle Anrede)*
sailboat	Segelboot	series ['sɪərɪ:z]	Serie, Sendereihe	sister ['sɪstə]	Schwester
sailor ['seɪlə]	Seemann, Segler(in)	serious ['sɪərɪəs]	schwerwiegend, ernst	to sit* [sɪt]	sitzen
salad ['sæləd]	Salat	service ['sɜ:vɪs]	Dienst(stelle)	to sit down	sich hinsetzen, Platz nehmen
salesman ['seɪlzmən]	Verkäufer, Vertreter	(serves four) [‚sɜ:vz 'fɔ:]	ergibt 4 Portionen	to sit up	sich aufrichten
salt [sɔ:lt]	Salz	set	Satz; Gerät	sitting-room	Wohnzimmer
the same [seɪm]	der-, die-, dasselbe, gleiche	doctor's set [set]	Arztausrüstung *(als Spielzeug)*	situation [‚sɪtjʊ'eɪʃn]	Situation, Lage
sand [sænd]	Sand	to set*	setzen, stellen, legen, einstellen *(Zeit, Temperatur)*	six [sɪks]	sechs
sands [sændz]	Sandstrand			sixteen [‚sɪks'ti:n]	sechzehn
sandwich ['sænwɪdʒ]	Sandwich, Butterbrot	to set the alarm [ə'lɑ:m]	den Wecker stellen	sixth [sɪkθ]	sechste(r, -s)
Saturday ['sætədeɪ]	Samstag	to set the table	den Tisch decken	size [saɪz]	Größe
saucer ['sɔ:sə]	Untertasse	(to set one's eyes on)	erblicken	skateboard ['skeɪtbɔ:d]	Skateboard
sausage ['sɒsɪdʒ]	Wurst, Würstchen	to set off	losgehen, aufbrechen	(skates)	Rollschuhe
to save [seɪv]	retten; sparen	the setting sun	die untergehende Sonne	to ski [ski:]	skifahren
electric saw [ɪ'lektrɪk sɔ:]	Elektrosäge			skin [skɪn]	Haut
Saxon ['sæksən]	sächsisch; Sachse, Sächsin	to settle ['setl]	siedeln	skirt [skɜ:t]	Rock
saxophone ['sæksəfəʊn]	Saxophon	(settler) ['setlə]	Siedler(in)	sky [skaɪ]	Himmel
to say* [seɪ]	sagen	(settlement) ['setlmənt]	Siedlung	(skyline) ['skaɪlaɪn]	Horizont; Silhouette
scarf [skɑ:f]	Schal, Halstuch	seven ['sevn]	sieben	skyscraper ['skaɪ‚skreɪpə]	Wolkenkratzer
scene [si:n]	Szene	seventeen [‚sevn'ti:n]	siebzehn	(skyway) ['skaɪweɪ]	Himmel
school [sku:l]	Schule	seventh ['sevnθ]	siebte(r, -s)	to slam into [slæm]	knallen (gegen)
school children	Schulkinder	shadow ['ʃædəʊ]	Schatten	slaughterhouse ['slɔ:təhaʊs]	Schlachthof
school colours	Farben von Schuluniformen, -abzeichen usw.	(to shake)* [ʃeɪk]	schütteln; zittern	slave [sleɪv]	Sklave, Sklavin
school uniform	Schuluniform	shall I ...? [ʃæl]	soll ich ...?	to sleep* [sli:p]	schlafen
schoolyard [jɑ:d]	Schulhof	shampoo [ʃæm'pu:]	Shampoo	sleeping-bag	Schlafsack
at school	in der Schule	to share [ʃeə]	teilen, aufteilen	(sleep)	Schlaf
to get to school	die Schule erreichen	she [ʃi:]	sie	to slip [slɪp]	(aus)rutschen
to go to school	in die/zur Schule gehen	she's = she is [ʃi:z]	sie ist	slot [slɒt]	Schlitz
comprehensive school	Gesamtschule	shed [ʃed]	Schuppen	slow [sləʊ]	langsam
high school	*weiterführende Schule in USA*	sheep [ʃi:p]	Schaf(e)	small [smɔ:l]	klein
school-bag	Schultasche	sheepskin ['ʃi:pskɪn]	Schaffell	smart [smɑ:t]	gescheit, gewitzt
science fiction [‚saɪəns 'fɪkʃn]	Science Fiction	sheriff ['ʃerɪf]	Sheriff	smell [smel]	Geruch
(scissors) ['sɪzəz]	Schere	shield [ʃi:ld]	(Schutz-)Schild	to smell* [smel]	riechen
score [skɔ:]	Spielstand	to shine* [ʃaɪn]	scheinen	(smile) [smaɪl]	Lächeln
What's the score?	Wie steht's?	ship [ʃɪp]	Schiff	to smile	lächeln
to score	ein Tor schießen	shirt [ʃɜ:t]	Hemd	smoke [sməʊk]	Rauch
Scottish ['skɒtɪʃ]	schottisch	shock [ʃɒk]	Schock, Schreck	snack bar ['snæk ‚bɑ:]	Imbißstube
		shoe [ʃu:]	Schuh	(to snap) [snæp]	schnippen
		to shoot* [ʃu:t]	(er)schießen	snow [snəʊ]	Schnee
		shop [ʃɒp]	Geschäft, Laden	[to snow]	schneien
		shop-assistant	Verkäufer(in)	snowy ['snəʊɪ]	schneereich, verschneit
				so [səʊ]	so; also; deshalb
				so clever	so klug

Alphabetical word list

I don't think so.	Das glaub' ich nicht.	
so that	so daß	
So long.	Tschüß.	
soap [səʊp]	Seife	
sock [sɒk]	Socke, Kniestrumpf	
[sofa] ['səʊfə]	Sofa	
soldier ['səʊldʒə]	Soldat	
(sole) [səʊl]	Sohle	
some [sʌm]	einige; etwas	
somebody ['-bɒdɪ]	(irgend)jemand	
someone ['-wʌn]	(irgend)jemand	
something ['-θɪŋ]	(irgend)etwas	
sometimes ['-taɪmz]	manchmal	
somewhere ['-weə]	irgendwo	
son [sʌn]	Sohn	
song [sɒŋ]	Lied	
soon [su:n]	bald	
sorry ['sɒrɪ]	Entschuldigung, tut mir leid	
he is very sorry	es tut ihm sehr leid	
to be sorry for s.o.	Mitleid mit jdm haben	
soul (music) ['səʊl]	Soulmusik	
to sound [saʊnd]	klingen	
(sound)	Klang	
(soup) [su:p]	Suppe	
south [saʊθ]	südlich, Süd-; Süden	
souvenir [ˌsu:vəˈnɪə]	Andenken	
spaceship ['speɪsʃɪp]	Raumschiff	
Spanish ['spænɪʃ]	Spanier(in), spanisch	
(to sparkle) ['spɑ:kl]	glitzern	
to speak* [spi:k]	sprechen	
speaker	Sprecher(in)	
special ['speʃl]	besondere(r, -s), Sondersendung	
speciality [ˌspeʃɪˈælɪtɪ]	Spezialität	
speed [spi:d]	Geschwindigkeit	
(to speed)	(zu) schnell fahren, rasen	
speed limit ['spi:d lɪmɪt]	Geschwindigkeitsbegrenzung	
speedway bike ['spi:dweɪ]	Motorrad *(für Aschenbahn)*	
to spell* [spel]	buchstabieren	
to spend* [spend]	ausgeben; *(Zeit)* verbringen	
the Great Spirit ['spɪrɪt]	der Große Geist	
Splash! [splæʃ]	flatsch!	
sponge [spʌndʒ]	Schwamm	
spoon [spu:n]	Löffel	
sport [spɔ:t]	Sport, Sportart	
sports ground	Sportplatz	
(spouse) [spaʊz]	Gemahl(in)	
spring [sprɪŋ]	Frühling	
(spring cleaning)	Frühjahrsputz	
(spring) [sprɪŋ]	Quelle	
(to spring)* [sprɪŋ]	springen	
sprinkler ['sprɪŋklə]	Sprinkler, Rasensprenger	
square [skweə]	Platz	
square kilometre	Quadratkilometer	
Ssh [ʃ]	Sch(t), Psst	
staff room ['stɑ:f rʊm]	Lehrerzimmer	
stained glass ['steɪnd glɑ:s]	Buntglas	
stairs [steəz]	Treppe	
(to stamp) [stæmp]	stampfen (mit)	
stamp [stæmp]	Briefmarke	
stand [stænd]	Stand	
to stand* [stænd]	stehen	
to stand up	aufstehen	
to stand in line (AE)	Schlange stehen	
I can't stand ...	ich kann ... nicht ausstehen	
star [stɑ:]	Stern; (Pop-)Star	
to stare at [steə]	(an)starren	
start [stɑ:t]	Anfang	
to start	anfangen, losfahren	
state [steɪt]	(Bundes-)Staat	
station ['steɪʃn]	Bahnhof	
bus station	Busbahnhof	
gas station (AE)	Tankstelle	
police station	Polizeirevier	
radio station	Sender, Radiostation	
statistics [stəˈtɪstɪks]	Statistik	
statue ['stætju:]	Statue, Denkmal	
to stay [steɪ]	bleiben, übernachten	
(steady) ['stedɪ]	ruhig, fest	
(steak) [steɪk]	Steak	
to steal* [sti:l]	stehlen	
steam [sti:m]	Dampf	
steel [sti:l]	Stahl	
steelworks ['sti:lwɜ:ks]	Stahlwerk(e)	
steep [sti:p]	steil	
(to steer) [stɪə]	lenken, steuern	
step [step]	Schritt, Stufe	
to step on s.th. [step]	(auf etw.) treten	
stew [stju:]	Eintopfgericht	
stewardess ['stjʊəˈdes]	Stewardeß	
stick [stɪk]	Stock	
cocktail stick	Spieß	
hockey stick	Hockeyschläger	
sticker ['stɪkə]	Aufkleber	
still [stɪl]	(immer) noch	
(to stir) [stɜ:]	(um)rühren	
stocking ['stɒkɪŋ]	Strumpf	
stolen ['stəʊlən]	gestohlen	
stone [stəʊn]	Stein	
to stop [stɒp]	aufhören, anhalten	
bus stop	Haltestelle	
truck stop	Raststätte	
stopover ['stɒpəʊvə]	Zwischenlandung	
to store [stɔ:]	lagern, speichern	
department store	Kaufhaus	
(store) (AE)	Laden	
storm [stɔ:m]	Sturm	
stormy	stürmisch	
story ['stɔ:rɪ]	Geschichte	
storyteller	Geschichtenerzähler(in)	
stove [stəʊv]	Herd	
straight [streɪt]	gerade(wegs)	
straight on	geradeaus	
strange [streɪndʒ]	fremd, seltsam	
[stranger]	Fremde(r)	
strawberry ['strɔ:brɪ]	Erdbeere	
street [stri:t]	Straße	
(to stretch) [stretʃ]	(sich er)strecken	
string [strɪŋ]	Schnur, Kordel	
(to stroll) [strəʊl]	schlendern	
strong [strɒŋ]	stark	
to struggle ['strʌgl]	kämpfen	
stuck [stʌk]	eingeklemmt	
the door is stuck	die Tür klemmt	
(student) ['stju:dnt]	Student(in), Schüler(in)	
studio ['stju:dɪəʊ]	Studio	
stupid ['stju:pɪd]	dumm, blöd	
subject ['sʌbdʒɪkt]	Fach	
suburb ['sʌbɜ:b]	Vorort	
(subway) (AE) ['sʌbweɪ]	U-Bahn	
such a ['sʌtʃə]	so, so ein(e)	
suddenly ['sʌdnlɪ]	plötzlich	
[to suffer] ['sʌfə]	(er)leiden	
sugar ['ʃʊgə]	Zucker	
suggestion [səˈdʒestʃən]	Vorschlag	
suicide ['sjʊɪsaɪd]	Selbstmord	
suicide rate	Selbstmordrate	
suitcase ['su:tkeɪs]	Koffer	
summary ['sʌmərɪ]	Zusammenfassung	
summer ['sʌmə]	Sommer	
sun [sʌn]	Sonne	
sun hat	Sonnenhut	
(sunlit) ['sʌnlɪt]	sonnenbeschienen	
sunny	sonnig	
Sunday ['sʌndeɪ]	Sonntag	
supermarket ['su:pəˌmɑ:kɪt]	Supermarkt	
supper (time) ['sʌpə]	Abendbrot(zeit)	
supporter [səˈpɔ:tə]	Anhänger(in), Fan	
to suppose [səˈpəʊz]	annehmen, denken	
sure [ʃʊə, ʃɔ:]	sicher	
Sure!	*Ausdruck der Zustimmung*	
to make sure	sichergehen	
surely	sicher *(Adverb)*	
to go surfing ['sɜ:fɪŋ]	wellenreiten, surfen	
surgery ['sɜ:dʒərɪ]	Praxis	
surprise [səˈpraɪz]	Überraschung	
surprised [səˈpraɪzd]	überrascht	
[to surrender] [səˈrendə]	sich ergeben; aufgeben	
(to survive) [səˈvaɪv]	überleben, am Leben bleiben	
(to swallow) ['swɒləʊ]	schlucken	
Swedish ['swi:dɪʃ]	Schwede, Schwedin; schwedisch	
sweet [swi:t]	süß	
sweets [swi:ts]	Süßigkeiten, Bonbons	
sweet shop	Süßwarenladen	
to swim* [swɪm]	schwimmen	
to go swimming	schwimmen gehen	
indoor swimming-pool	Hallenbad	
outdoor swimming-pool	Freibad	
swimmer	Schwimmer(in)	
to switch [swɪtʃ]	vertauschen	
to switch s.th. off	ausschalten	
swollen ['swəʊlən]	geschwollen	
sword [sɔ:d]	Schwert	
[symphony] ['sɪmfənɪ]	Symphonie	
system ['sɪstəm]	System, Anlage	

T

table ['teɪbl]	Tisch	
to set the table	den Tisch decken	
(table-spoon) ['teɪblspu:n]	Eßlöffel	
table-tennis ['teɪbl tenɪs]	Tischtennis	
tablet ['tæblɪt]	Tablette	
tail [teɪl]	Schwanz	
to take* [teɪk]	nehmen; bringen; dauern	
to take a photo(graph)/a picture	fotografieren	
to take s.o.'s temperature	Fieber messen	
to take for a walk	spazierenführen	
to take home	nach Hause bringen	
to take off	ausziehen; starten	
(take-off)	Absprung, Start *(Flugzeug)*	
to take out	herausnehmen, herausholen	
to take to bed	mit ins Bett nehmen	
to take turns	sich abwechseln	
to take a chance	etwas riskieren	
to take over	übernehmen	
to take part in	teilnehmen an	
(to take a part)	eine Rolle spielen	
to take to pieces	auseinandernehmen	
to take a rest	sich ausruhen	
to take a test	eine Prüfung machen	
Take care.	Paß auf dich auf!	
to talk (to) [tɔ:k]	sprechen (mit)	
talk	Gespräch, Unterhaltung	
tall [tɔ:l]	groß, hochgewachsen	
to taste [teɪst]	schmecken, probieren	
tax [tæks]	Steuer, Abgabe	
taxi ['tæksɪ]	Taxi	
taxi driver	Taxifahrer(in)	
tea [ti:]	Tee, Abendessen	
teapot ['ti:pɒt]	Teekanne	
teaspoon ['ti:spu:n]	Teelöffel	
to teach* [ti:tʃ]	unterrichten, lehren, beibringen	
teacher	Lehrer(in)	
team [ti:m]	Mannschaft	
tear [tɪə]	Träne	
(to tear down)* [teə]	abreißen	
teddy	Teddy(bär)	
teenager ['ti:nˌeɪdʒə]	Teenager, Jugendliche(r)	
tooth, teeth [tu:θ, ti:θ]	Zahn, Zähne	
telephone ['telɪfəʊn]	Telefon	
to telephone	anrufen, telefonieren (mit)	
telephone box	Telefonzelle	
telephoto lens [ˌtelɪfəʊtəʊ 'lenz]	Teleobjektiv	
telex ['teleks]	Telex(gerät), Fernschreiben	
to tell* [tel]	erzählen, berichten	
temblor ['temblə]	leichtes Erdbeben	

Alphabetical word list

temperature ['temprətʃə]	Temperatur, Fieber	Have a good time!	Viel Spaß!	⟨to tremble⟩ ['trembl]	zittern
to take s.o.'s temperature	Fieber messen	at a time	auf einmal	**tremor** ['tremə]	Beben, Zittern
ten [ten]	zehn	in time	rechtzeitig	**[tribe]** [traıb]	Stamm
tennis ['tenıs]	Tennis	⟨in time⟩	im Takt	**trick** [trık]	Kunststück, Trick, Streich
tense [tens]	Zeitform, Tempus	on time	pünktlich	**tricycle** ['traısıkl]	Dreirad
tent [tent]	Zelt	this time	diesmal	**trip** [trıp]	Fahrt, Reise
tepee ['ti:pi:]	(Indianer-)Zelt	five times	fünfmal	**trouble** ['trʌbl]	Ärger, Schwierigkeiten
term [tɜ:m]	Trimester	What time is it?	Wie spät ist es?	to be in trouble	Ärger haben
⟨terminal⟩ ['tɜ:mınəl]	Terminal, Abfertigungsgebäude	by the time	bis	⟨to get into trouble⟩	Ärger bekommen
⟨terraced house⟩ ['terəst]	Reihenhaus	timetable ['taım,teıbl]	Fahrplan, Stundenplan	**trousers** ['trauzəz]	Hose
terrible ['terəbl]	schrecklich	**tin** [tın]	Dose, Büchse	**truck** (AE) [trʌk]	Lastwagen
territory ['terıtərı]	Gebiet	tin-opener	Dosenöffner	**trucker** ['trʌkə]	LKW-Fahrer(in)
test [test]	Prüfung, Klassenarbeit	**tired** ['taıəd]	müde	truck plaza ['plɑ:zə]	große Raststätte mit Läden etc.
to pass a test	eine Prüfung machen	**to** [tu:, tə]	zu	truck stop ['trʌk stɒp]	Raststätte
to take a test	eine Prüfung bestehen	to belong to s.o.	jdm gehören	**true** [tru:]	wahr
to test	prüfen, abfragen	to talk to s.o.	mit jdm sprechen	truth [tru:θ]	Wahrheit
text [tekst]	Text	over to you	du bist dran	⟨to trust⟩ [trʌst]	vertrauen
textbook ['tekstbʊk]	Lehrbuch	quarter to nine	viertel vor neun	to **try** [traı]	versuchen, (aus)probieren
than [ðæn, ðən]	als *(beim Komparativ)*	to school	zur/in die Schule	**T-shirt** ['ti:.ʃɜ:t]	T-Shirt
to **thank** [θæŋk]	(sich be-)danken	**toast** [təʊst]	Toast	⟨tube⟩ [tju:b]	Röhre
thank you	danke (schön)	**toaster** ['təʊstə]	Toaster	**Tuesday** ['tju:zdeı]	Dienstag
thanks [θæŋks]	danke	**today** [tə'deı]	heute	channel **tunnel** ['tʃænl 'tʌnl]	Kanaltunnel
that [ðæt, ðət]	das; daß; der, die, das *(Rel.pron.)*	**together** [tə'geðə]	zusammen	**turkey** ['tɜ:kı]	Truthahn
that boy	der Junge da	to put together	zusammensetzen	**Turkish** ['tɜ:kıʃ]	Türke, Türkin; türkisch
that good	so gut	**toilet** ['tɔılıt]	Toilette		
that's why	daher, deshalb	**tomato ketchup** [tə,mɑ:təʊ 'ketʃəp]	(Tomaten-)Ketchup	**turn** [tɜ:n]	Runde
the [ðə, ðı]	der, die, das	**tomorrow** [tə'mɒrəʊ]	morgen	it's his turn	er ist an der Reihe
theatre ['θıətə]	Theater	**ton** [tʌn]	Tonne	to miss a turn	eine Runde aussetzen
their [ðeə]	ihr	**tonight** [tə'naıt]	heute abend	to take turns	sich abwechseln
theirs	ihre(s, -r)	**too** [tu:]	auch	to **turn**	abbiegen, (sich) drehen
them [ðem, ðəm]	sie, ihnen	too small [tu:]	zu klein	to turn s.o. back	jdn abwehren, zurückweisen
themselves	sich, sie selbst	**tool** [tu:l]	Werkzeug	to turn off	abdrehen, ausschalten
then [ðen]	dann, danach	**tooth, teeth** [tu:θ, ti:θ]	Zahn, Zähne	to turn on	andrehen, einschalten
there [ðeə]	da, dort(hin)	toothbrush ['tu:θbrʌʃ]	Zahnbürste	**TV** [ti:'vi:]	Fernseher, Fernsehen
there are	es gibt, es sind	toothpaste ['tu:θpeıst]	Zahnpasta	TV announcer [ə'naʊnsə]	Fernsehansager(in)
there is	es gibt, es ist; da ist	**top** [tɒp]	Spitze	TV dinner	Fertiggericht
⟨there'd be⟩	es wären	at the top of	oben auf	TV set	Fernseher, Fernsehgerät
over there	dort drüben	to **touch** [tʌtʃ]	berühren	to watch TV	fernsehen
up there	dort oben	⟨to touch down⟩	landen	⟨'twas = it was⟩ [twɒz]	es war
these [ði:z]	diese (hier)	**tour** [tʊə]	Rundfahrt; Konzertreise, Tournee	**twelfth** [twelfθ]	zwölfte(r, -s)
they [ðeı]	sie; man	to tour	eine Rundfahrt machen	**twelve** [twelv]	zwölf
they're = they are [ðeə]	sie sind	⟨tourist⟩ ['tʊərıst]	Tourist(in)	**twentieth** ['twentıəθ]	zwanzigste(r, -s)
thief, thieves [θi:f, θi:vz]	Dieb(e)	tourist industry	Fremdenverkehr	**twenty** ['twentı]	zwanzig
thin [θın]	dünn	**towards** [tə'wɔ:dz]	auf ... zu	**twice** [twaıs]	zweimal
thing [θıŋ]	Sache, Ding	**towel** ['taʊəl]	Handtuch	⟨twin town⟩ [twın]	Partnerstadt
to **think** [θıŋk]	denken, meinen	**tower** ['taʊə]	Turm	⟨twinkling⟩ ['twıŋklıŋ]	Glitzern, Funkeln
to think of	denken an	**town** [taʊn]	Stadt	to **twist s.th. around** [twıst]	(her)umdrehen, verdrehen
I don't think so.	Ich glaube nicht.	⟨townspeople⟩	Stadtbewohner	**twit** [twıt]	Dummkopf
third [θɜ:d]	der, die, das dritte	⟨town hall⟩	Rathaus	**two** [tu:]	zwei
thirsty ['θɜ:stı]	durstig	⟨town plan⟩	Stadtplan	**typical** ['tıpıkl]	typisch
to be thirsty	Durst haben	**toy** [tɔı]	Spielzeug	**tyre** ['taıə]	Reifen
thirteen [,θɜ:'ti:n]	dreizehn	toy car	Spielzeugauto		
this [ðıs]	dies(e, -er, -es), das	toyshop ['tɔıʃɒp]	Spielwarenladen	**U**	
this one	diese(r, -s)	**tractor** ['træktə]	Traktor		
⟨this-a-way⟩	so, auf diese Weise	[to trade] [treıd]	handeln	**ugh!** [ɜ:h]	I! Igitt!
those [ðəʊz]	diese dort	**tradition** [trə'dıʃən]	Tradition	**ugly** ['ʌglı]	häßlich
⟨though⟩ [ðəʊ]	jedoch, obwohl	⟨traditional⟩ [trə'dıʃənl]	volkstümlich, traditionell	**Uhhh?** [ɜ:]	Was? Wie?
⟨thoughtful⟩ ['θɔ:tfʊl]	nachdenklich	**traffic** ['træfık]	Straßenverkehr	**umbrella** [ʌm'brelə]	Regenschirm
a **thousand** ['θaʊznd]	Tausend, tausend	traffic light	Ampel	**unable** [ʌn'eıbl]	unfähig
three [θri:]	drei	traffic warden	Verkehrspolizist, Politesse	**uncle** ['ʌŋkl]	Onkel
through [θru:]	durch, hindurch	**trail** [treıl]	Pfad, Weg	**uncomfortable** [ʌn'kʌmfətəbl]	unbequem
to **throw** [θrəʊ]	werfen	**train** [treın]	Zug	**under** ['ʌndə]	unter
to throw away	wegwerfen	by train	mit dem Zug	**underground** ['ʌndəgraʊnd]	unterirdisch
to throw about	herumwerfen	wagon train ['wægən ,treın]	Planwagenkolonne, Treck	the Underground	U-Bahn
thunder ['θʌndə]	Donner	⟨trainer⟩ ['treınə]	Ausbilder(in), Trainer(in)	to **understand** [,ʌndə'stænd]	verstehen
thunderstorm	Gewitter	⟨training⟩	Ausbildung, Training	**underwear** ['ʌndəweə]	Unterwäsche
Thursday ['θɜ:zdeı]	Donnerstag	[to **translate**] [træns'leıt]	übersetzen	**unemployed** [,ʌnım'plɔıd]	arbeitslos
ticket ['tıkıt]	(Eintritts-)Karte, Flugschein	**transport** ['trænspɔ:t]	Transport, Beförderung	unemployment [,ʌnım'plɔımənt]	Arbeitslosigkeit
⟨tidings⟩ ['taıdıŋz]	Botschaft, Kunde	[trapper] ['træpə]	Fallensteller, Trapper		
tidy ['taıdı]	ordentlich, aufgeräumt	to **travel** ['trævl]	reisen		
to tidy	aufräumen	**traveller** ['trævlə]	Reisende(r)		
to **tie** [taı]	binden	traveller's cheque	Reisescheck		
⟨tiger⟩ ['taıgə]	Tiger	**treasure** ['treʒə]	Schatz		
to **tighten** ['taıtn]	festziehen, straffen	[to **treat**] [tri:t]	behandeln		
tights [taıts]	Strumpfhose	[**treaty**] ['tri:tı]	Abkommen, Vertrag		
time [taım]	Zeit, Uhrzeit	**tree** [tri:]	Baum		

Alphabetical word list

unfortunately [ʌnˈfɔːtʃnətli]	leider	to **wake up*** [ˌweɪk ˈʌp]	aufwachen	what colour is ...?	welche Farbe hat ...?
unfriendly [ˌʌnˈfrendli]	unfreundlich	to wake s.o. up	jdn wecken	What for?	Wofür?
unhappy [ʌnˈhæpi]	unglücklich	**walk** [wɔːk]	Spaziergang	What's for lunch?	Was gibt es zu Mittag?
uniform [ˈjuːnɪfɔːm]	Uniform	to go for a walk	spazierengehen	What's the matter?	Was ist (los)?
unimportant [ˌʌnɪmˈpɔːtənt]	unwichtig	to take for a walk	spazierenführen	What's the weather like?	Wie ist das Wetter?
uninteresting [ˌʌnˈɪntrɪstɪŋ]	uninteressant	to walk	gehen	What time is it?	Wie spät ist es?
unit [ˈjuːnɪt]	Einheit; Lektion	walkman	Walkman	**wheat** [wiːt]	Weizen
to **unlock** [ʌnˈlɒk]	aufschließen	walkway	Fußweg	**wheel** [wiːl]	Rad
unlucky [ʌnˈlʌki]	unglücklich, ohne Glück	**wall** [wɔːl]	Mauer, Wand	to wheel [wiːl]	schieben, fahren
unpopular [ʌnˈpɒpjʊlə]	unbeliebt	garden wall	Gartenmauer	Big Wheel (wheelbarrow) [ˈwiːlˌbærəʊ]	Riesenrad Schubkarren
unsure [ʌnˈʃʊə]	unsicher	⟨to wander⟩ [ˈwɒndə]	umherwandern, schlendern	**when** [wen]	als; wann; wenn
untidy [ʌnˈtaɪdi]	unordentlich	⟨wanderer⟩	Wandervogel	**where** [weə]	wo, wohin
to **untie** [ʌnˈtaɪ]	losbinden	to **want** [wɒnt]	wollen, möchten	⟨wherever⟩ [ˌweərˈevə]	wo(hin) auch immer
until [ʌnˈtɪl]	bis	[**war**] [wɔː]	Krieg	**whether** [ˈweðə]	ob
⟨unto⟩ [ˈʌntʊ]	zu	⟨warrior⟩ [ˈwɒrɪə]	Krieger	**which** [wɪtʃ]	welche(r, -s), der, die, das *(Rel.pron.)*
⟨unwanted⟩ [ˌʌnˈwɒntɪd]	unwillkommen, unerwünscht	**warden** [ˈwɔːdn]	Herbergsvater, -mutter	a **while**	eine Weile
up [ʌp]	hinauf	traffic warden	Verkehrspolizist, Polizesse	**while** [waɪl]	während
upstairs	(nach) oben	***warehouse** [ˈweəhaʊs]	Lager(haus)	⟨to whip⟩ [wɪp]	schlagen
up there	dort oben	⟨ware⟩ [weə]	Ware	⟨whipping cream⟩ [ˈwɪpɪŋ kriːm]	Schlagsahne
to come up to s.o.	auf jdn zukommen	**warm** [wɔːm]	warm	**whisk(e)y** [ˈwɪski]	Whisky
to get up	aufstehen	to **wash** [wɒʃ]	waschen	to **whisper** [ˈwɪspə]	flüstern
Hands up!	Hände hoch!	to wash up	spülen, abwaschen	**whistle** [ˈwɪsl]	Pfeife; Pfiff, Abpfiff
to look up	aufblicken	washing-machine	Waschmaschine	**white** [waɪt]	weiß
to pick up	aufheben; lernen	**waste** [weɪst]	Verschwendung	**who** [huː]	wer; der, dem, den, die *(Rel.pron.)*
to put up	aufstellen, aufhängen	**watch** [wɒtʃ]	(Armband-)Uhr	⟨who cares?⟩	was soll's?
to ring up	anrufen	to **watch** [wɒtʃ]	zuschauen	**whole** [həʊl]	ganze(r, -s)
to run up to	zurennen auf	to watch out	aufpassen	**whose** [huːz]	wessen; dessen, deren
to sit up	sich aufrichten	to watch the world go by	alles um sich herum beobachten	**why** [waɪ]	warum
to wake s.o. up	jdn aufwecken	to watch TV	fernsehen	that's why	deshalb
to wash up	spülen, abwaschen	watchman [ˈwɒtʃmən]	Wächter	**wife** [waɪf]	(Ehe-)Frau
⟨upon⟩ [əˈpɒn]	auf	**water** [ˈwɔːtə]	Wasser	**wild** [waɪld]	wild
us [ʌs]	uns	waterproof [ˈ-ˌpruːf]	wasserdicht	wilderness [ˈwɪldənɪs]	Wildnis
to **use** [juːz]	benutzen	watermelon [ˈ-ˌmelən]	Wassermelone	**will** [wɪl]	wird, werde(n)
to be used to	gewohnt sein	water-pistol [ˈ-ˌpɪstl]	Wasserpistole	won't [wəʊnt] = will not	wird nicht
useful [ˈjuːsfəl]	nützlich	to **wave** [weɪv]	schwenken, winken	to **win*** [wɪn]	gewinnen
useless [ˈjuːslɪs]	nutzlos	⟨to wave s.th. about⟩	umherschwenken	winner	Sieger(in)
usually [ˈjuːʒʊəli]	normalerweise	**waxworks** [ˈwæksˌwɜːks]	Wachsfiguren	**wind** [wɪnd]	Wind
		way [weɪ]	Weg; Art und Weise	windy	windig
V		the wrong way	(in) die falsche Richtung	windmill [ˈ-mɪl]	Windmühle
vacancy [ˈveɪkənsi]	freies Zimmer, freie Stelle	way of life	Lebensstil	**window** [ˈwɪndəʊ]	Fenster
to **vacuum** [ˈvækjʊəm]	staubsaugen	to know one's way around	sich auskennen	**windscreen wiper** [ˈwɪndskriːn ˌwaɪpə]	Scheibenwischer
vacuum cleaner	Staubsauger	in some ways	in mancher Hinsicht	**wing** [wɪŋ]	Flügel
valley [ˈvæli]	Tal	**we** [wiː]	wir	**winter** [ˈwɪntə]	Winter
van [væn]	Lieferwagen	we're [wɪə] = we are	wir sind	**wire** [waɪə]	Draht
vanilla [vəˈnɪlə]	Vanille	[**weakness**] [ˈwiːknɪs]	Schwäche	⟨wisdom⟩ [ˈwɪzdəm]	Weisheit
vegetable [ˈvedʒətəbl]	Gemüse	to **wear*** [weə]	tragen, anhaben	⟨to wish⟩ [wɪʃ]	wünschen
verb [vɜːb]	Verb	**weasel** [ˈwiːzəl]	Wiesel	⟨I wish to God⟩	ich wünsche bloß
very [ˈveri]	sehr	**weather** [ˈweðə]	Wetter	**with** [wɪð]	mit
vet [vet]	Tierarzt, -ärztin	weatherman [ˈ-mæn]	Meteorologe *(TV)*	without [wɪˈðaʊt]	ohne
[**victory**] [ˈvɪktəri]	Sieg	**Wednesday** [ˈwenzdeɪ]	Mittwoch	**woman, women** [ˈwʊmən, ˈwɪmɪn]	Frau, Frauen
video [ˈvɪdɪəʊ]	Video	**week** [wiːk]	Woche	**wonder** [ˈwʌndə]	Wunder
video-games	Videospiele	weekend [ˈ-end]	Wochenende	⟨to wonder⟩	sich wundern
video recorder	Videorekorder	to **weigh** [weɪ]	wiegen	⟨no wonder⟩	kein Wunder
view [vjuː]	Aussicht	**welcome** [ˈwelkəm]	willkommen	**wonderful** [ˈwʌndəfəl]	wunderbar
⟨general view⟩	Gesamtansicht	you're welcome	aber gerne; gern geschehen	**wood** [wʊd]	Holz
⟨TV-viewer⟩	Fernsehzuschauer(in)	**well** [wel]	Brunnen	wooden	Holz-, hölzern
⟨villa⟩ [ˈvɪlə]	Villa	**well** [wel]	also; gut	**word** [wɜːd]	Wort
village [ˈvɪlɪdʒ]	Dorf	to feel well	sich wohl fühlen	word order	Wortstellung
visit [ˈvɪzɪt]	Besuch	well done	gut gemacht	**work** [wɜːk]	Arbeit
to visit	besuchen	**Welsh** [welʃ]	walisisch	to work	arbeiten, funktionieren
visiting hours	Besuchszeiten	**west** [west]	Westen; West-, westlich	(to work out)	Problem, Frage lösen
visitor's centre	Besucherzentrum	West Indian [ˌwest ˈɪndɪən]	westindisch	worker	Arbeiter(in)
vocabulary [vəʊˈkæbjʊləri]	Vokabular; Wortschatz	Western [ˈwestən]	Western	workshop [ˈwɜːkʃɒp]	Werkstatt
voice [vɔɪs]	Stimme	westward [ˈwestwəd]	westwärts	**world** [wɜːld]	Welt
		wet [wet]	naß	⟨worn out⟩ [ˌwɔːn ˈaʊt]	abgetragen
W		wet through	durchnäßt	to **worry** [ˈwʌri]	sich Sorgen machen
wagon [ˈwægən]	(Plan-)Wagen, Waggon	**what** [wɒt]	was	don't worry	mach dir keine Sorgen
wagon train [treɪn]	Planwagenkolonne, Treck	So what.	Na und!	worried	besorgt, beunruhigt
to **wait** [weɪt]	warten	what a ...!	was für ein ...!	**worse, worst** [wɜːs, wɜːst]	schlechter/am schlechtesten
to wait for	warten auf	what about ...?	was ist mit ...?	**would** [wʊd]	würde(n)
Wait a minute.	Augenblick mal!			Would you like ...?	Möchtest du ...?/ Möchten Sie ...?
⟨waiter⟩ [ˈweɪtə]	Kellner			**Wow!** [waʊ]	Toll! *(Ausruf)*
⟨waitress⟩ [ˈweɪtrɪs]	Kellnerin			to **write*** [raɪt]	schreiben

Alphabetical word list / List of names

°writer Schriftsteller(in)
wrong [rɒŋ] falsch
  that's wrong das stimmt nicht
  the wrong way (in) die falsche Richtung

Y

⟨yard⟩ [jɑːd] Längenmaß (= 91,4 cm)
year [jɪə] Jahr
yellow [ˈjeləʊ] gelb
yes [jes] ja; doch
yesterday [ˈjestədeɪ] gestern

yet [jet] (immer) noch, schon, doch, bis jetzt
  not ... yet noch nicht
  ⟨yolk⟩ [jəʊk] Eigelb
you [juː] du, dir, dich; ihr, euch; Sie, Ihnen
  you're [jʊə] = you are du bist, Ihr seid, Sie sind
  over to you du bist dran
young [jʌŋ] jung
your [jɔː] dein(e), euer, eure, Ihr(e)
  yours deine/eure/Ihre(s, -r)
  Yours sincerely [sɪnˈsɪəlɪ] Mit freundlichen Grüßen

Yours faithfully [ˈfeɪθfʊlɪ] Mit freundlichen Grüßen
yourself, -ves dich, dir, euch, sich (selbst)
[Youth Club] [ˈjuːθ ˌklʌb] Jugendhaus
youth hostel [ˈjuːθ ˌhɒstl] Jugendherberge

Z

zip [zɪp] Reißverschluß
⟨zoo⟩ [zuː] Zoo

List of names

Surnames:

Bell [bel]
Cabot [ˈkæbət]
Casey [ˈkeɪsɪ]
Christiansen [ˈkrɪstjənsn]
Clarke [klɑːk]
⟨Conti [ˈkɒntɪ]⟩
Díaz [dɪas]

Donahue [ˈdɒnəjuː]
Ehrhardt [ˈerhɑːt]
Ellis [ˈelɪs]
Fernandez [fəˈnændez]
Ferranti [fəˈræntɪ]
⟨Fitzgerald [fɪtsˈdʒerəld]⟩
García [gɑːˈsɪa]

Gregson [ˈgregsn]
Hernandez [hɜːˈnændəz]
Jarell [dʒəˈrel]
⟨Lowe [ləʊ]⟩
O'Reilly [əʊˈraɪlɪ]
Philpott [ˈfɪlpɒt]
Robinson [ˈrɒbɪnsn]

Rosenbaum [ˈrəʊzənbaʊm]
Schulz [ʃʊlts]
⟨Spouse [spaʊz]⟩
Stubbs [stʌbz]
Wagner [ˈwægnə]

Boys' names:

Al [æl]
Barnaby [ˈbɑːnəbɪ]
Barney [ˈbɑːnɪ]
Bernie [ˈbɜːnɪ]
Bret [bret]
Bryan [ˈbraɪən]
⟨Ed [ed]⟩

Frank [fræŋk]
Garth [gɑːθ]
⟨Gary [ˈgærɪ]⟩
Greg [greg]
Herbie [ˈhɜːbɪ]
⟨Jack [dʒæk]⟩
Joel [dʒəʊəl]

LeRoy [ˈliːrɔɪ]
Lincoln [ˈlɪŋkən]
Marc(o) [mɑːk(əʊ)]
Marvin [ˈmɑːvɪn]
Moose [muːs]
Phil [fɪl]
Roberto [rəˈbɜːtəʊ]

⟨Sam [sæm]⟩
Stan [stæn]
Steve [stiːv]
Ted [ted]
Wayne [weɪn]
Wes [wes]

Girls' names:

Anne-Marie [ˌænməˈriː]
⟨Angie [ˈændʒɪ]⟩
⟨Bernadette [ˌbɜːnəˈdet]⟩
Carmen [ˈkɑːmən]
Donna [ˈdɒnə]
Janey [ˈdʒeɪnɪ]

Jolene [dʒəˈliːn]
Julie [ˈdʒuːlɪ]
Mary [ˈmeərɪ]
Margie [ˈmɑːdʒɪ]
⟨Odetta [əʊˈdetə]⟩
Ramona [rəˈməʊnə]

Ruth [ruːθ]
Sal [sæl]
Sandy [ˈsændɪ]
Sheena [ˈʃiːnə]
⟨Tammy [ˈtæmɪ]⟩
Tessie [ˈtesɪ]

Tracey [ˈtreɪsɪ]
Victoria [vɪkˈtɔːrɪə]
⟨Zara [ˈzærə]⟩

Geographical names:

Alaska [əˈlæskə]
Albany [ˈɔːlbənɪ]
[the Appalachians [ˌæpəˈleɪtʃənz]]
Arizona [ˌærɪˈzəʊnə]
Atlanta [ətˈlæntə]
Bilbao [bɪlˈbɑːəʊ]
Baltimore [ˈbɔːltɪmɔː]
Black Forest [ˌblæk ˈfɒrɪst]
Bluff City [ˌblʌf ˈsɪtɪ]
Boston [ˈbɒstən]
Broadway [ˈbrɔːdweɪ]
⟨the Bronx [brɒŋks]⟩
Brooklyn [ˈbrʊklɪn]
⟨Calico Ghost Town [ˈkælɪkəʊ]⟩
California [ˌkælɪˈfɔːnjə]
Central Park [ˌsentrəl ˈpɑːk]
Cheyenne [ʃaɪˈæn]
Colorado [ˌkɒləˈrɑːdəʊ]
Coney Island [ˌkəʊnɪ ˈaɪlənd]
Cuba [ˈkjuːbə]
Death Valley [ˌdeθ ˈvælɪ]
Denver [ˈdenvə]
Detroit [dɪˈtrɔɪt]
Doswell [ˈdɒswel]
⟨Dublin [ˈdʌblɪn]⟩
El Mercado [el merˈkɑːdəʊ]
⟨El Paso [el ˈpæsəʊ]⟩
European Community [ˌjʊərəˌpiːən kəˈmjuːnətɪ]
Federal Republic of Germany [ˌfedərəl rɪˌpʌblɪk əv ˈdʒɜːmənɪ]

⟨Fifth Avenue [fɪfθ ˈævənjuː]⟩
Florida [ˈflɒrɪdə]
Frisco [ˈfrɪskəʊ] = San Francisco
Georgia [ˈdʒɔːdʒə]
Golden Gate Bridge [ˌgəʊldən ˈgeɪt]
Greenwich Village [ˌgrɪnɪdʒ ˈvɪlɪdʒ]
Harlem [ˈhɑːləm]
Hollywood [ˈhɒlɪwʊd]
Kansas City [ˌkænzəs ˈsɪtɪ]
Lake Winnebago [ˌwɪnəˈbeɪgəʊ]
Laramie [ˈlærəmɪ]
Las Vegas [ˌlæs ˈveɪgəs]
La Villita [lɑː vɪˈliːtə]
[Little Big Horn [ˌlɪtl ˈbɪg ˈhɔːn]]
⟨L.A. [elˈeɪ] = Los Angeles⟩
Los Angeles [lɒs ˈændʒɪliːz]
⟨Louisiana [luːˌiːzɪˈænə]⟩
Macon [ˈmeɪkən]
Manhattan [mænˈhætn]
Memphis [ˈmemfɪs]
Mexico [ˈmeksɪkəʊ]
Miami [maɪˈæmɪ]
⟨Missouri [mɪˈzʊərɪ]⟩
Mount Whitney [ˌmaʊnt ˈwɪtnɪ]
Mojave River [məʊˈhɑːvɪ]
Nashville [ˈnæʃvɪl]
[New Mexico [ˌnjuː ˈmeksɪkəʊ]]
Nutbush [ˈnʌtbʊʃ]
Oshkosh [ˈɒʃkɒʃ]
[the Pacific [pəˈsɪfɪk]]
[Panama [ˌpænəˈmɑː]]

Pennsylvania [ˌpensɪlˈveɪnjə]
⟨Philadelphia [fɪləˈdelfjə]⟩
Pittsburgh [ˈpɪtsbɜːg]
Puerto Rico [ˌpwɜːtəʊ ˈriːkəʊ]
⟨Queens [kwiːnz]⟩
Salt Lake City [ˌsɔːlt leɪk ˈsɪtɪ]
San Antonio [ˌsæn_ænˈtəʊnɪəʊ]
San Francisco [ˌsæn frənˈsɪskəʊ]
San Juan [ˌsæn ˈhwɑːn]
Seattle [sɪˈætl]
Smoky Mountains [ˌsməʊkɪ ˈmaʊntɪnz]
South Dakota [dəˈkəʊtə]
St. Louis [snt ˈluːɪs]
⟨Staten Island [ˌsteɪtn ˈaɪlənd]⟩
Switzerland [ˈswɪtsələnd]
⟨Tel Aviv [ˌtelə viːv]⟩
Tennessee [ˌtenəˈsiː]
Texas [ˈteksəs]
Times Square [ˌtaɪmz ˈskweə]
Utah [ˈjuːtɔː]
⟨Vietnam [ˌvjetˈnæm]⟩
Virginia [vəˈdʒɪnjə]
⟨Wall Street [ˈwɔːl striːt]⟩
⟨Washington, D.C. [ˌwɒʃɪŋtən diːˈsiː]⟩
Washington Square [ˌwɒʃɪŋtən ˈskweə]
Wisconsin [wɪsˈkɒnsɪn]
[Wounded Knee [ˌwuːndɪd ˈniː]]
Wyoming [waɪˈəʊmɪŋ]

Other names:

the Alamo [ˈæləməʊ]
Anna "Tina" Mae Bullock [meɪ ˈbʊlək]
⟨Apache (Indians) [əˈpætʃi]⟩
Aretha Franklin [əˈriːθə ˈfræŋklɪn]
the Astrodome [ˈæstrəʊdəʊm]
AstroTV [ˈæstrəʊ]
the Beatles [ˈbiːtlz]
Big Boggles [ˈbɪg ˈbɒglz]
⟨Bob Dylan [bɒb ˈdɪlən]⟩
Buick [ˈbjuːɪk]
the Chapman Family [ˈtʃæpmən]
Cherokee (Indians) [ˈtʃerəkiː]
[Cheyenne (Indians) [ʃaɪˈæn]]
Chinatown [ˈtʃaɪnətaʊn]
Chuck Berry [tʃʌk ˈberi]
⟨Cochise [kəʊˈtʃiːz]⟩
[Columbus [kəˈlʌmbəs]]
Dave Dudley [deɪv ˈdʌdli]
Davy Crockett [ˈdeɪvi ˈkrɒkɪt]
Debbie Preston [ˈdebi ˈprestən]
[Delaware (Indians) [ˈdeləweə]]
Denver Dreamers [ˈdriːməz]
⟨Disneyland [ˈdɪzniˌlænd]⟩
⟨Doc Pepper [dɒk ˈpepə]⟩
⟨Dorsey [ˈdɔːsi]⟩
Elvis Presley [ˈelvɪs ˈpresli]
⟨Empire State Building
 [ˈempaɪə steɪt ˈbɪldɪŋ]⟩
⟨Eve Merriam [iːv ˈmeriəm]⟩
Fats Domino [fæts ˈdɒmɪnəʊ]
Frankenstein [ˈfræŋkənstaɪn]
[General Custer [ˈdʒenərəl ˈkʌstə]]

⟨Geronimo [dʒəˈrɒnɪməʊ]⟩
⟨the Governor's Palace [ˈgʌvənəz ˈpælɪs]⟩
⟨Grand Central Station [grænd ˈsentrəl ˈsteɪʃn]⟩
⟨Greyhound [ˈgreɪhaʊnd]⟩
⟨Gulf Stream [gʌlf striːm]⟩
Hemisfair [ˈhemɪsfeə]
the Hertzberg Collection [hɜːtsbɜːg kəˈlekʃn]
Horizon Holidays [həˈraɪzn ˈhɒlɪdeɪz]
Ike Turner [aɪk ˈtɜːnə]
the Institute of Texan Cultures
 [ˈɪnstɪtjuːt əv ˈteksn ˈkʌltʃəz]
Irish Coffee [ˈaɪərɪʃ ˈkɒfi]
Isaac Asimov [ˌaɪzək ˈæzɪmɒv]
James Brown [dʒeɪmz braʊn]
⟨Jesus [ˈdʒiːzəs]⟩
⟨John Cougar Mellencamp
 [dʒɒn ˈkuːgə ˈmelənkæmp]⟩
John Trimble [dʒɒn ˈtrɪmbl]
Little Italy [ˌlɪtl ˈɪtəli]
Little Richard [ˌlɪtl ˈrɪtʃəd]
⟨Louis L'Amour [ˈluːɪs lə ˈmʊə]⟩
Louis Nusbaumer [ˈluːɪs ˈnʊsbaʊmə]
[Louisiana Purchase [luːˌiːziˈænə ˈpɜːtʃəs]]
Macy's [ˈmeɪsiːz]
⟨Madison Square Garden
 [ˈmædɪsn skweə ˈgɑːdn]⟩
Martin Luther King [ˌmɑːtɪn ˈluːθə kɪŋ]
⟨Martyn Wiley [ˈmɑːtɪn ˈwaɪli]⟩
Mc Duck's [mək ˈdʌks]
Mercy Medical Center Hospital
 [ˈmɜːsi ˈmedɪkl ˈsentə ˈhɒspɪtl]
⟨the Mission Concepción [ˈmɪʃn kɒnsepˈsjɒn]⟩

Muddy Waters [ˈmʌdi ˈwɔːtəz]
Navajo (Indians) [ˈnævəhəʊz]
⟨New York Times [taɪmz]⟩
Park Plaza Shopping Center
 [ˌpɑːk ˈplɑːzə ˈʃɒpɪŋ ˈsentə]
⟨Paseo del Rio [pæˈseɪəʊ del ˈriːəʊ]⟩
⟨Peter Minuit [ˈmɪnjʊɪt]⟩
⟨Pete Seeger [piːt ˈsiːgə]⟩
Ray Charles [reɪ tʃɑːlz]
Redwood High [ˈredwʊd haɪ]
Robert Johnson [ˈrɒbət ˈdʒɒnsən]
⟨Rockefeller Center [ˈrɒkəfelə ˈsentə]⟩
the Rolling Stones [ˈrəʊlɪŋ stəʊnz]
⟨San Francisco Zephyr
 [ˌsæn frənˈsɪskəʊ ˈzefə]⟩
Santa Claus [ˌsæntə ˈklɔːz]
Sequoya [sɪˈkwɔɪə]
Sesame Street [ˈsesəmi striːt]
Shane West [ʃeɪn west]
Shea Stadium [ˌʃeɪ ˈsteɪdjəm]
[Sioux (Indians) [suː] pl. [suː]]
Statue of Liberty [ˈstætʃuː əv ˈlɪbəti]
Tina Turner [ˈtiːnə ˈtɜːnə]
UN [juː en] = United Nations [ˌjuːnaɪtɪd ˈneɪʃnz]
UniTV [ˈjuːni]
Walt Disney [wɔːlt ˈdɪzni]
⟨Walter Knott [ˈwɔːltə nɒt]⟩
[William Penn [ˈwɪljəm pen]]
Winchester [ˈwɪntʃestə]
⟨Woody Guthrie [ˈwʊdi ˈgʌθri]⟩
⟨World Trade Center [wɜːld treɪd ˈsentə]⟩
YMCA [waɪəm si eɪ]

⟨Useful phrases in class⟩

What you can say to your friends or to the teacher

- What's this in English/German?
  What does ... mean?

Was heißt dies auf englisch/deutsch?
Was bedeutet ...?

- Can I ask a question, please?
  How do you do this exercise?
  Can/Could you help me, please?
  I don't understand this word/sentence.
  Pardon?
  Could you write it on the board, please?
  What must we do for homework?

Kann ich bitte eine Frage stellen?
Wie macht man/geht diese Übung?
Können Sie/Kannst du mir bitte helfen?
Ich verstehe dieses Wort/diesen Satz nicht.
Wie bitte?
Können Sie es an die Tafel schreiben?
Was haben wir als Hausaufgabe auf?

What you can say when you talk about stories, poems, songs etc.

- This story is good/great/
  interesting/exciting/terrific/sad/
  awful/funny.
  I think it's terrible/boring/good/
  fantastic.
  I find it ...
  I like it./I enjoyed it.
  Why didn't you like it?

Diese Geschichte ist gut/großartig/
interessant/spannend/toll/traurig/
schrecklich/komisch.
Ich meine, sie ist schecklich/langweilig/gut/
fantastisch.
Ich halte sie für ...
Mir gefällt sie./Sie hat mir Spaß gemacht.
Warum hat sie dir nicht gefallen?

- It's OK but I have read better ones.

  I didn't like it much.

Sie ist ganz nett, aber ich habe schon bessere
gelesen.
Mir hat sie nicht so gut gefallen.

- The text/song is divided into ... parts.

Der Text/das Lied ist in ... Abschnitte unter-
teilt.

⟨Useful phrases in class⟩

The first part is about …   Der erste Abschnitt handelt von …
I'd suggest the following headings for each part.   Ich würde für die Abschnitte folgende Überschriften vorschlagen.

- There are some details in the text which show that …   Im Text sind einige Details, die zeigen, daß …
  The main points are …   Die Hauptgesichtspunkte sind …
  I think that …   Ich meine, daß …
  In line … it says …   In Zeile … heißt es …

- The story reminds me of …   Die Geschichte erinnert mich an …
  I feel … when I read/hear …   Ich fühle mich … , wenn ich (über) … lese/höre.

- The main/minor characters are … .   Die Haupt-/Nebenfiguren sind … .
  The characters in the story (don't) change.   Die Charaktere in der Geschichte ändern sich (nicht).
  At first … Later …   Zuerst … Später …

What you can say when you discuss things

- What do you think?   Was ist deine Meinung?
  How do you feel about it?   Was hältst du davon?
  I'm not sure.   Ich bin nicht sicher.
  In my opinion …   Meiner Meinung nach …
  I find all this stupid/very interesting.   Ich halte dies alles für blöd/sehr interessant.

- I think she/he is right/wrong.   Ich denke, sie/er hat recht/unrecht.
  That's wrong, I'm afraid.   Das stimmt nicht, fürchte ich.
  I think she/he has got it all wrong.   Ich glaube, sie/er hat es ganz falsch verstanden.
  No, I don't believe that.   Nein, das glaube ich nicht.
  That's not the same at all.   Das ist überhaupt nicht das gleiche.
  How do you know?   Woher weißt du das?
  What makes you think that?   Wie kommst du darauf?
  You can't be sure. I suppose …   Man kann sich nicht sicher sein. Vermutlich …

- I wonder why …   Ich frage mich, warum …
  I suppose …   Ich vermute/Vermutlich …
  It's surprising to hear that …   Es ist erstaunlich zu hören, daß …
  I didn't know that …   Ich habe nicht gewußt, daß …
  I find it hard to believe that …   Für mich ist es schwer zu glauben, daß …
  I hadn't imagined that …   Ich hatte mir nicht vorgestellt, daß …

- I don't agree with you.   Ich stimme dir nicht zu.
  I'm for/against it.   Ich bin dafür/dagegen.
  I think we should find out the facts first.   Ich meine, wir sollten erst einmal die Tatsachen herausfinden.

  Yes, that's a much better idea.   Ja, das ist eine viel bessere Idee.
  On the one/other hand …   Einerseits/andererseits …

- I don't understand.   Ich verstehe nicht.
  Could you explain that again?   Vielleicht kannst du dies nochmal erklären.
  Oh, I see. How stupid of me.   Aha, ich verstehe. Wie dumm von mir.
  But unfortunately/luckily …   Aber unglücklicherweise/glücklicherweise …

- I'd like to make a suggestion: Ich möchte gern einen Vorschlag machen:
  Why don't we …?   Warum … wir nicht …?
  We have to be careful, I suppose.   Wir müssen wohl vorsichtig sein.
  That's why it's so important to …   Deshalb ist es wichtig zu …

List of irregular verbs

Infinitiv Infinitive	Präteritum Preterite (Past Tense)	Partizip Perfekt Past Participle	deutsch
be (am/are/is)	was (were)	been	sein
⟨beat	beat	beaten	schlagen⟩
become	became	become	werden
begin	began	begun	beginnen, anfangen
bet	bet	bet	wetten
bite	bit	bitten	beißen
blow	blew	blown	pfeifen
break	broke	broken	(zer)brechen
bring	brought	brought	(her)bringen
build	built	built	bauen
burn	burnt	burnt	(ver)brennen
burst	burst	burst	platzen
buy	bought	bought	kaufen
catch	caught	caught	fangen
choose	chose	chosen	(aus)wählen, sich aussuchen
come	came	come	kommen
cost	cost	cost	kosten
cut	cut	cut	schneiden
do	did	done	tun
draw	drew	drawn	zeichnen
dream	dreamed, dreamt	dreamed, dreamt	träumen
drink	drank	drunk	trinken
drive	drove	driven	fahren
eat	ate	eaten	essen
fall	fell	fallen	fallen
feed	fed	fed	füttern
feel	felt	felt	(sich) fühlen
fight	fought	fought	(be)kämpfen
find	found	found	finden
fly	flew	flown	fliegen
forget	forgot	forgotten	vergessen
⟨freeze	froze	frozen	(ge)frieren⟩
get	got	got	bekommen
give	gave	given	geben
go	went	gone	gehen
grow	grew	grown	wachsen
hang	hung hanged	hung hanged	(auf)hängen; (er)hängen
have	had	had	haben
hear	heard	heard	hören
hide	hid	hidden	verstecken
hit	hit	hit	treffen, schlagen
hold	held	held	halten
⟨hurt	hurt	hurt	verletzen⟩
keep	kept	kept	behalten
know	knew	known	wissen
lead	led	led	führen
learn	learnt, learned	learnt, learned	lernen

List of irregular verbs

Infinitiv Infinitive	Präteritum Preterite (Past Tense)	Partizip Perfekt Past Participle	deutsch
leave	left	left	lassen, verlassen, zurücklassen
lend	lent	lent	jdm. etwas leihen
let	let	let	lassen
lie	lay	lain	liegen
lose	lost	lost	verlieren
make	made	made	machen
mean	meant	meant	meinen, bedeuten
meet	met	met	(sich) treffen, begegnen
pay	paid	paid	bezahlen
put	put	put	setzen, stellen, legen
read	read	read	lesen
ride	rode	ridden	reiten
ring	rang	rung	läuten
run	ran	run	laufen, rennen
say	said	said	sagen
see	saw	seen	sehen
sell	sold	sold	verkaufen
send	sent	sent	senden, schicken
set	set	set	setzen, stellen, legen
⟨shake	shook	shaken	schütteln⟩
shine	shone	shone	scheinen
shoot	shot	shot	schießen
show	showed	shown	zeigen
shrink	shrank	shrunk	schrumpfen, einlaufen
shut	shut	shut	schließen
sing	sang	sung	singen
sink	sank	sunk	(ver)sinken, untergehen
sit	sat	sat	sitzen, sich setzen
sleep	slept	slept	schlafen
speak	spoke	spoken	sprechen
spell	spelt	spelt	buchstabieren
spend	spent	spent	*(Zeit)* verbringen; *(Geld)* ausgeben
⟨spring	sprang	sprung	springen⟩
stand	stood	stood	stehen
steal	stole	stolen	stehlen
swim	swam	swum	schwimmen
take	took	taken	nehmen, (hin)bringen
teach	taught	taught	lehren, unterrichten
⟨tear	tore	torn	(zer)reißen⟩
tell	told	told	erzählen, sagen
think	thought	thought	denken, glauben
throw	threw	thrown	werfen
understand	understood	understood	verstehen
wake	woke	woken	(auf)wecken, (auf)wachen
wear	wore	worn	tragen *(Kleidung)*
win	won	won	gewinnen
write	wrote	written	schreiben